Flow

Flow

Interior, landscape and architecture in the era of liquid modernity

Edited by

Penny Sparke, Pat Brown,
Patricia Lara-Betancourt, Gini Lee,
and Mark Taylor

BLOOMSBURY VISUAL ARTS

LONDON · NEW YORK · OXFORD · NEW DELHI · SYDNEY

BLOOMSBURY VISUAL ARTS

Bloomsbury Publishing Plc

50 Bedford Square, London, WC1B 3DP, UK

BLOOMSBURY, BLOOMSBURY VISUAL ARTS and the Diana logo are trademarks of Bloomsbury Publishing Plc

First published 2018

© Introductions and editorial material, Penny Sparke, Pat Brown, Patricia Lara-Betancourt, Gini Lee, and Mark Taylor

© Individual chapters, their authors

Cover design Louise Dugdale

Cover image © Gini Lee / Royal Adelaide Hospital (2007)

A catalogue record for this book is available from the British Library.

ISBN: HB: 978-1-47256-803-8
        PB: 978-1-47256-799-4
        ePDF: 978-1-47256-801-4
        ePub: 978-1-47256-802-1

Typeset by Lachina

Printed and bound in China

To find out more about our authors and books visit www.bloomsbury.com and sign up for our newsletters.

Table of Contents

Notes on Contributors

Gladys Arana López is an architectural historian and a specialist in the history of domestic architecture in Mérida, Yucatán, for the period 1886–1916. Her research examines the complex links between elite housing and everyday life. She is a Lecturer in the areas of Architectural Theory and History at the School of Architecture at the Universidad Autónoma de Yucatán (UADY). She holds two MA degrees, one from the Universidad de Andalucía, Spain, with a dissertation on sustainability and architectural design in the Yucatán Peninsula (1997), and the second one from the Universidad de Yucatan, where her research focused on imagery and gender in the vernacular house in Yucatán (2005). She completed her PhD at the School of Architecture at the Universidad Michoacana de San Nicolás de Hidalgo (UMSNH). She has published journal articles in the areas of architecture, housing, and gender.

Suzie Attiwill is Associate Dean, Interior Design in the School of Architecture and Design, RMIT University, Melbourne, Australia. Since 1991, she has practiced in the fields of exhibition design, curatorial work, writing and teaching. Creative practice research is conducted through a practice of designing with a curatorial inflection attending to arrangements (and rearrangements) of spatial, temporal and material relations that re-pose questions of interior and interiority in relation to contemporary conditions of living, inhabitation, subjectivity, pedagogy and praxis. Her research has been published as book chapters, journal articles, keynotes and workshops nationally and internationally. Previous roles include Artistic Director, Craft Victoria; Chair, West Space Artist Led Initiative; Chair, IDEA (Interior Design/Interior Architecture Educators Association) and Executive Editor, IDEA Journal.

Elisa Bernardi graduated in Architecture in 2008 and in 2013 received a PhD in Interior Architecture and Design at the Politecnico di Milano, where she has also worked as Teaching Assistant. In 2007–8 she collaborated with the Prada Foundation on the projects "On Otto" by artist Tobias Rehberger, "The Double Club," and "Unveiling the Prada Foundation" by OMA/Rem Koolhaas in Milan. In 2009 she worked as Teaching Assistant for the International Program Workshop: Student Housing in Italy with Professor Silvia Piardi at the Tshingua University of Beijing, China. She also worked with the Department of Architecture of Politecnico di Milano on the project to reclaim the building Marchiondi by Vittoriano Viganò in Baggio, Milano. In 2010 she participated as Teaching Assistant at the Green Life Workshop with Professor Lola Ottolin and Sara Protasoni at the Politecnico di Milano.

Sarah Breen Lovett is an artist, curator, and Postdoctoral Research Fellow at the University of Sydney, School of Architecture Design and Planning. The title of her recently completed PhD is "Expanded Architectural Awareness: Exploring Intersections of Architecture and Expanded Cinema." Sarah has worked on many exhibitions, symposiums, and publications at the interdisciplinary meeting point of art and architecture. Her publications include "Expanded Architecture: Temporal Spatial Practices," about the most recent Expanded Architecture exhibition she founded and is published by AADR as a Bauhaus Edition 47 (2016), as well as a forthcoming chapter (2017) in *Making Visible: Architecture Filmmaking* published by Intellect.

Pat Brown is an Associate Professor, founder, and director of the Landscape Interface Studio at Kingston University, London. She studied at Kings College, the London School of Economics, London University, and Sheffield University. She works in landscape architecture research, education, and practice, leading landscape research and education at Kingston University. Her interdisciplinary research collaboration themes include well-being, heritage, spatial planning, and design in the public realm, particularly coastal and waterway infrastructures. As a practitioner, she has worked in the United States and the United Kingdom, where her Ruthin Craft Centre project with Sergison Bates Architects received a RIBA Award in 2009. Pat has taught nationally and internationally and represents "landscape" in academic and professional contexts. Her papers and exhibitions include *Spatial Planning Port Cities*, Maritime Institute University of Ghent; *Botanic Gardens in the Cities of the Future*, University of Valencia; and *Heritage and Health* with colleagues at St. Georges Hospital. Landscape Interface Studio European project consultancy has included *Waterways Forward*, which aims to impact the delivery of holistic EU waterways strategy and policy. The collaborative project *Limehouse Cut: Linking Place and Creativity*, Landscape Interface Studio with Shared Assets, was selected for presentation at the AHRC Showcase 2014.

Elias Constantopoulos is Professor of the Department of Architecture, University of Patras, Greece. He has directed an architectural practice in Athens since 1986 and was also the director of the award-winning industrial design practice *Sigma Design* (1990–1995). He has authored over one hundred essays on contemporary architecture and design and has published the books *Nicos Valsamakis, 1950–83*, *Fassianos Building*, and *Kyriakos Krokos* (Wasmuth, 2011). He has been coeditor of the journals *9H* and *Ntizain* and consultant editor of the Annual Reviews for *Architecture in Greece*, as well as for *Design + Art in Greece*. Elias was the curator and organizer of *Architecture of the 20th c. Greece* (Deutsches Architektur Museum exhibition, Frankfurt, 1999), *Aegean—A Dispersed Urbanity* (Greek participation, 10th Biennale of Architecture, Venice, 2006), *On the Modern and the Contemporary in European and Japanese Culture* ("EU-Japan" program, Tokyo, 2006), *The Role of Philosophy in Architectural Education* (conference, University of Patras, 2009), and the *6th Biennale of Young Greek Architects* (Athens, 2010).

Dolly Daou is an interior designer with a Doctorate in the fields of: interior architecture, architecture and urban design, specialising in teaching, research, quality assurance, and leadership, in interior architecture and in multi-disciplinary global design projects. She is currently the Director of the Association of Interior Designers in the MENA region, initiating and maintaining alliances with international associations and industry. As Program Director of Interior Architecture and the Master of Interior Design at Swinburne University of Technology, (Australia and Hong Kong) she successfully managed the reaccreditation and rebranding of the Program worldwide, and was a member of the Board of Directors of the Interior Design/Interior Architecture Educators Association (IDEA) for Australasia. Her publications include the coedited volume (with D. J. Huppatz and D. Quoc Phuong) Unbounded: On the Interior and Interiority (Cambridge Scholars Publishing, 2015).

Sing D'Arcy is Senior Lecturer at the University of New South Wales, Sydney, Australia. He studied architecture and received his doctorate in architectural history from the University of Sydney. His thesis, titled "The Organ as Architecture: Reconfiguring the Ecclesiastical Space of the Hispanic Baroque," investigated the role of the pipe organ in the configuration of cathedral space in Spain during the seventeenth and eighteenth centuries. His research interests focus on the relationship between architectural space, ritual, and musical performance practices, in particular the design and integration of pipe organs in ecclesiastical and civic spaces. Sing regularly contributes to industry journals such as *Artichoke* and *Houses*, reviewing new interior design projects in Sydney. In 2013 he was appointed as an Associate Investigator with the ARC Centre for Excellence for the *History of Emotions: Europe 1100– 1800* Performance Program. His recent publications include "Temples of Commerce: Banking and Insurance Chambers," in *Sydney's Martin Place: A Cultural and Design History* (Allen & Unwin, 2016).

Catherine Ettinger is an architect with a doctorate from the UNAM in México City. She is Full Professor in the Faculty of Architecture at the Universidad Michoacana de San Nicolás de Hidalgo (UMSNH) in western México. Her research interests include architectural theory and modern architecture, in particular the flow of ideas between the United States and México. In 2010 she published *La Transformación de la Vivienda Vernácula en Michoacán: Materialidad, Espacio y Representación* (COLMICH/MSNH, 2010) and is editor and coauthor of *De Paseo de San Pedro a Bosque Cuauhtémoc* (Miguel Ángel Porrúa, 2013). She is coauthor of the collective book *The Construction of Climate in Modern Architectural Culture* (Lampreuve, 2015). She is active in DOCOMOMO and ICOMOS as an expert on twentieth-century architecture.

Vicky Falconer is an art and design librarian and visual artist living and working in London. Vicky was artist in residence at Kingston University, London, for the academic year 2010–11. She studied Fine Art and Art History at the University of Edinburgh between 1998 and 2003, and gained her MA in Fine Art from Central Saint Martins College (University of the Arts, London) in 2008. She completed her postgraduate studies in librarianship at University College, London, and worked at the University of the Arts from 2011 to Dec 2017.

Fiona Fisher is a researcher in design history at the Modern Interiors Research Centre, Kingston University, London, where she is curator of the University's Dorich House Museum. Her research interests include the design and decoration of nineteenth- and twentieth-century leisure interiors and the architecture and design of the British postwar home. Her recent publications include *Designing the British Post-War Home: Kenneth Wood, 1948–1968* (Routledge, 2015); *The Routledge Companion to Design Studies* (coedited with Penny Sparke; Routledge, 2016); and *British Design: Tradition and Modernity After 1948* (coedited with Christopher Breward and Ghislaine Wood; Bloomsbury Academic, 2015). She is currently researching a book on the design of the modern public house.

Chris Hay studied at the Royal College of Art and Duncan of Jordanstone College of Art, now the University of Dundee. He works in architectural research and education. He was, until 2014, a Senior Lecturer at Lincoln School of Architecture, where he led the BA/MA Interior Architecture and Design programs. He was a member of the School's Cultural Contexts research group, and his published papers have examined the primitive in the work of the Norwegian architect Sverre Fehn, as well as the relationship between food, land use, and community sustainability in Todmorden, West Yorkshire. He was a founding member of ARC—the Architecture Centre in Hull, which ran a series of interlinked programs that addressed quality in Urban and Architectural Design aimed at schools, pupils and students, decision makers, developers, residents, built environment professionals, and the general public. He also acted as client sponsor for the Centre's award-winning building designed by Niall McLaughlin, which remains the only purpose-built UK architecture center.

Sandy Isenstadt is a professor and Director of the Center for Material Culture Studies at the University of Delaware, specializing in the history of modern architecture. His writings span post–World War II reformulations of Modernism by émigré architects such as Richard Neutra, Josep Lluis Sert, and Henry Klumb, visual polemics in the urban proposals of Leon Krier and Rem Koolhaas, and histories of American refrigerators, picture windows, landscape views, and real estate appraisal. Isenstadt is the author of *The Modern American House: Spaciousness and Middle-Class Identity* (Cambridge University Press, 2006), which describes the visual enhancement of spaciousness in the architectural, interior, and landscape design of American domestic architecture. He is coeditor of *Modernism and the Middle East: Architecture and Politics in the Twentieth Century* (University of Washington Press, 2008) and *Cities of Light: Two Centuries of Urban Illumination*, with Margaret Petty and Dietrich Neumann (Routledge, 2014). His current book project, *The Architecture of Artificial Light*, examines the novel luminous spaces introduced by electric lighting, with chapters on switches, automobile headlights, factory lighting, illuminated signage, and blackouts.

Sarah Jamieson is Director of Catseye Bay, an interior design practice in Sydney, and a PhD candidate in Architecture and Design at RMIT University in Melbourne, Australia.

Robin D. Jones is an independent scholar whose research engages with the material and cultural histories of South Asia from the nineteenth to the mid-twentieth centuries. Up until 2016 he worked as an associate professor at Southampton Solent University, UK. Using the methods of design history, his doctoral research examined key aspects of the material culture of Sri Lanka from 1800 to 1948, including the local and European-influenced built environment, domestic space, and furnishings. His present research investigates the negotiation of modernity and history in South Asia after 1948 through an examination of objects, spaces, and visual representations. His article "Furnished in English Style: Anglicization of Local Elite Domestic Interiors in Ceylon (Sri Lanka), c 1850–1910," was published in M. Taylor (ed.), *Interior Design and Architecture: Critical and Primary Sources* (Berg, 2013). He is the author of *Interiors of Empire: Objects, Space and Identity within the Indian Subcontinent, 1800–1947* (Manchester University Press, 2007).

Pat Kirkham is Professor of Design History at Kingston University and Professor Emerita at Bard Graduate Center, New York. She studied history as an undergraduate at the University of Leeds and received her PhD from the University of London. She taught the history of architecture and design, as well as film and media studies, at De Montfort University before moving to Bard Graduate Center in 1996. Her many publications include *Charles and Ray Eames: Designers of the Twentieth Century* (1995); *Women Designers in the USA, 1900–2000: Diversity and Difference* (ed. and contributing author, 2000); *Saul Bass: A Life in Film and Design* (2011); *The Gendered Object* (ed. and contributing author, 1996); and *History of Design: Decorative Arts and Material Culture, 1400–2000* (coeditor and contributing author, 2013). She is currently completing a book on Charles and Ray Eames and Hollywood.

Patricia Lara-Betancourt is a design historian and research fellow at the Modern Interiors Research Centre, Kingston University, London. Within the field of modern interiors and design history, her research focuses on the themes of modernity, representation, and identity. Recent publications include the coedited volume (with A. Lasc and M. Petty) *Architectures of Display: Department Stores and Modern Retailing* (Routledge, 2017); "The Quest for Modernity: A Global/National Approach to a History of Design in Latin America," in *Designing Worlds: National Design Histories in the Age of Globalization* (Berghahn, 2016); "Contesting the Modernity of Domestic Space: Design Reform and the Middle-Class Home, 1890–1914," in *Space and Place: Exploring Critical Issues* (Inter Disciplinary Press, 2014); and her coauthored chapter, "Latin America 1830–1900," in *History of Design: Decorative Arts and Material Culture, 1400–2000* (Yale University Press, 2013). She is coeditor of *Seductive Discourses: Design Advice for the Home*, an *Interiors* special issue (Vol. 5, Issue 2, July 2014), and of *Performance, Fashion and the Modern Interior: From the Victorians to Today* (Berg, 2011).

Anca I. Lasc is Assistant Professor of History and Theory of Design at Pratt Institute. Her work focuses on the invention and commercialization of the modern French interior and on the development of the profession of interior designer in the nineteenth century. She has published articles in *Interiors: Design, Architecture, Culture* and the *Journal of Design History* and has presented at numerous conferences, including those organized by the College Art Association, the Society of Architectural Historians, and the Society for French Historical Studies. Her coedited books include *Architectures of Display: Department Stores and Modern Retailing*, with P. Lara-Betancourt and M. Petty (Routledge, 2017), and *Designing the French Interior: The Modern Home and Mass Media*, with G. Downey and M. Taylor (Bloomsbury, 2015). She also edited *Visualizing the Nineteenth-Century Home: Modern Art and the Decorative Impulse* (Routledge, 2016). Lasc's monograph, *Interior Decorating in Nineteenth-Century France: The Visual Culture of a New Profession*, is forthcoming (Manchester University Press, 2018).

Gini Lee is a landscape architect, interior designer and pastoralist and is Professor at the University of Melbourne, Australia after acting as the Elisabeth Murdoch Chair of Landscape Architecture since 2011. Her academic focus in research and teaching is on cultural and critical landscape architecture and spatial interior design theory and studio practice, to engage with the curation and postproduction of complex landscapes. Focusing on arid environments, her multidisciplinary research into the water landscapes of remote territories contributes to the scientific, cultural, and Indigenous understanding of and management strategies for fragile landscapes. Her recent landscape curation and installation practice is an experiment with Deep Mapping methods to investigate the cultural and scientific landscapes of remote and rural Australia, Scandinavia, global archipelagos and the arid lands of western USA. Since 2014 she is an invited researcher at SLU Malmo where she collaborates in fieldwork based research into transect travel methodologies. She is a registered landscape architect and contributes to the strategic planning, design and practice of urban and educational landscapes in Melbourne and beyond.

Jeff Malpas is Distinguished Professor at the University of Tasmania and Adjunct Professor at RMIT University, Melbourne, Australia. He was founder, and until 2005 Director, of the University of Tasmania's Centre for Applied Philosophy and Ethics. He is the author or editor of 21 books with some of the world's leading academic presses and has published over 120 scholarly articles on topics in philosophy, art, architecture, and geography. His best-known works include *Place and Experience* (Cambridge, 1999) and *Heidegger's Topology* (MIT, 2006). His work is grounded in post-Kantian thought and draws on a diverse range of thinkers, including, most notably, Albert Camus, Donald Davidson, Martin Heidegger, and Hans-Georg Gadamer. He is currently working on topics relating to the ethics of place, the failing character of governance, the materiality of memory, the topological character of hermeneutics, the place of art, and the relation between place, boundary, and surface.

Margaret Maile Petty is Professor and Head of the School of Design in the Creative Industries Faculty at Queensland University of Technology, Australia. Her research broadly investigates the discourse, production, and consumption practices of the modern built environment, with a particular focus on artificial lighting and interiors. She has published broadly in academic journals, such as the *JSAH*, the *Journal of Design History*, *Home Cultures*, *Interiors*, and *PLAT*, and is coeditor of *Cities of Light: Two Hundred Years of Urban Illumination* (Routledge, 2015) with Sandy Isenstadt and Dietrich Neumann, as well as of *Architectures of Display: Department Stores and Modern Retail* (Routledge, 2017) with A. Lasc and P. Lara-Betancourt.

Rebecca Preston's background is in design history and historical geography, and she is currently a research associate in the Department of History at Royal Holloway, University of London. Her interests lie broadly in the landscape, the built environment, and the life of cities and suburbs in nineteenth- and twentieth-century Britain; different kinds of living space are a related area of research. Recent publications include (with Lesley Hoskins) "The House and Garden: Villas and Terraces in England," in Jane Hamlett (ed.), *A Cultural History of the Home: The Age of Empire* (Bloomsbury, forthcoming 2017); "The Pastimes of the People: Photographing House and Garden in London's Small Suburban Homes, 1880–1914," *London Journal*, 39 (3), November 2014; and (coedited with Jane Hamlett and Lesley Hoskins) *Residential Institutions in Britain, 1725–1970: Inmates & Environments* (Pickering & Chatto, 2013).

Phoebe Robinson is a dancer/choreographer who has performed in numerous cities across Australia, as well as in New York, Berlin, and Japan, in works by Sandra Parker, Lucy Guerin, Neil Adams, Francis D'ath, and Kota Yamazaki. Phoebe has an established solo practice through which she has distilled a unique movement vocabulary. Her work emphasizes the drama that can be evoked through subtle and tiny gestures. Phoebe studied dance at the Western Australian Academy of Performing Arts (1997–2000) and completed a Master of Fine Arts (Choreography) at the Victorian College of the Arts,

University of Melbourne, in 2014. Previous to that, she spent a semester at the Universität der Künste Berlin in the MA Solo/Dance/Authorship in 2011. Since 2009 Phoebe has taught at Deakin University, Bachelor of Creative Arts (Dance), and at the Victorian College of the Arts, School of Dance.

Joel Sanders is the principal of the New York–based practice Joel Sanders Architect. He is also Associate Professor (Adjunct) at Yale University and was the director of the Graduate Program in Architecture at Parsons School of Design and an assistant professor at Princeton University. His work has been featured in numerous international exhibitions, including *Open House* at the Vitra Design Museum, *Glamour* at San Francisco MoMA, *New Hotels for Global Nomads* at the Cooper-Hewitt, National Design Museum, the Bienal de São Paulo in São Paulo, Brazil, and *Unprivate House* at New York's MoMA. Projects designed in his practice belong to the permanent collections of MoMA in New York City, San Francisco MoMA, and the Carnegie Museum in Pittsburgh, and his work has been showcased in numerous publications, including *Architecture*, *Interior Design*, *Architectural Record*, *The New York Times*, *Wallpaper*, and *A+U*. He received second place for his competition entry for Gangbuk Grand Park and first place for Seongbuk-dong Residences, both in Seoul, Korea. Sanders has received numerous awards, including five New York AIA Design Awards, a 2008 Interior Design Magazine Best of Year Award, an AIA Westchester/Mid-Hudson Chapter Honor Award, a Boston Society of Architects Research Grant, and two Design Citations from Progressive Architecture. He is editor of *Stud: Architectures of Masculinity* and frequently writes about art and design for various magazines and journals, including *Art Forum* and the *Harvard Design Magazine*. Monacelli Press released a monograph of his work, *Joel Sanders: Writings and Projects*, in 2005, and in 2011 released his coauthored book *Groundwork: Between Landscape and Architecture*, with Diana Balmori.

Diane Silverthorne has been an Associate Lecturer at Birkbeck, University of London, since 2008, teaching at undergraduate and postgraduate levels; she was appointed to her post at Central Saint Martins, University of the Arts London, in 2013. She is a published author on *fin de siècle* Vienna and on music, art, and Modernism; she is also a public speaker, notably for the South Bank Centre's *The Rest Is Noise Festival*. She is currently editing and contributing to an anthology on music, art, and performance for Bloomsbury. Diane qualified as an art historian at Birkbeck, specializing in the modern period, particularly the art and design of *fin de siècle* Europe. Her PhD dissertation on art, performance, and design in *fin de siècle* Vienna (AHRC sponsored) was part of a major research project on Vienna Cafe Culture 1900, under the auspices of Birkbeck and the Royal College of Art. Her publications include "Music and Immanence: The 1902 Beethoven Exhibition and the Vienna Secession" in *Music and Transcendence* (Routledge, 2015).

Penny Sparke is a Professor of Design History at Kingston University, London, and the Director of the Modern Interiors Research Centre. She studied French Literature at the University of Sussex from 1967 to 1971 and between 1972 and 1975 undertook research for her PhD in the History of Design at Brighton Polytechnic. She subsequently developed courses in, and taught, the History of Design to undergraduate and postgraduate students at Brighton Polytechnic (1975–1982) and the Royal College of Art (1982–1999). From 1999 to 2005 she was Dean of the Faculty of Art, Design & Music at Kingston University, and from 2005 to 2014 she was Pro Vice-Chancellor (Research and Enterprise). She has also participated in conferences, given keynote addresses, been a member of journal editorial boards, curated exhibitions, delivered visiting lectures, and broadcast and published in the field of Design History both nationally and internationally. Her most important publications include *An Introduction to Design and Culture, 1900 to the Present* (1986 and 2004); *Design in Context* (1987); *Electrical Appliances* (1988); *Italian Design from 1860 to the Present* (1989); *The Plastics Age* (1990); *As Long as It's Pink: The Sexual Politics of Taste* (1995); *Elsie de Wolfe: The Birth of Modern Interior Decoration* (2005); and *The Modern Interior* (2008). She has also supervised and examined many PhD candidates in her subject.

Eleanor Suess is Head of the Department of Architecture and Landscape, as well as Associate Professor, at Kingston University, London. She has a Bachelor in Fine Arts from the University of Western Australia (UWA), as well as architectural qualifications from UWA and the Bartlett, London. Eleanor qualified as a British Architect in 2004. She has more than ten years' experience in architectural practice in London, working for the award-winning practices Fashion Architecture Taste (FAT) and Proctor and Matthews Architects. Eleanor's main research interests lie in the intersection between architecture and art practice. She has exhibited interdisciplinary installation work at the Adelaide International Arts Festival and has done experimental film work in the United Kingdom, the United States, Australia, and Hong Kong. Her current research focuses on the use of artists' film for spatiotemporal architectural drawing and includes the production of experimental digital film as a form of architectural drawing. Eleanor is currently studying for an AHRC-funded PhD at Central Saint Martins, titled "Constructing the Architectural Moving Drawing: Transdisciplinary Practices between Architecture and Artists' Film."

Mark Taylor is Professor of Architecture at Swinburne University, Australia. His primary research focus is the history and theory of the modern architectural interior with an emphasis on cultural and social issues. His research on the designed interior is widely published in books and journals, and he has convened several conferences on the modern interior. His design work has been published in both professional and scholarly journals and has been exhibited nationally and internationally, including in the *Royal Academy Summer Exhibition*, London; in *Melbourne Museum*, Australia; and in the *2008 Venice Architecture Biennale, Australian Pavilion—Abundant*, Venice. Taylor is an editorial board member for *Architectural Design Research* and for *Interiors: Design, Architecture, Culture*, as well as co-editor of *Intimus: Interior Design Theory Reader* (John Wiley, 2006). He is editor of *Interior Design & Architecture: Critical & Primary Sources*, 4 vols. (Bloomsbury, 2013) and has recently coedited with A. Lasc and G. Downey, *Designing the French Interior: The Modern Home and Mass Media* (Bloomsbury, 2016).

Kerstin Thompson is Principal of Kerstin Thompson Architects (KTA), a Melbourne-based architecture, landscape, and urban design practice with projects in Australia and New Zealand. She is also as advocate for architecture in her role as member of the OVGA Design Review Panel, as well as occasional writer, curator, and jury member. Committed to design-based research and education, she is currently Professor of Design in Architecture at Victoria University of Wellington (New Zealand) and Adjunct Professor at RMIT and Monash Universities, Australia. KTA completed projects are across a range of sectors and have been extensively awarded and published. They include the Marysville Police Station and the Monash University Museum of Art and House at Hanging Rock, which won the AIA's Robin Boyd Award in 2014. Current projects include the Broadmeadows Town Hall, School of Art at Victorian College of the Arts, Deakin University Architecture + Building, Melbourne's Jewish Holocaust Centre, and the Masterplan to expand facilities at Arthur Boyd's Riversdale site for the Bundanon Trust. The practice's focus is on architecture as a civic endeavor, with an emphasis on the users' experience and enjoyment of place.

Nadia Wagner is a Lecturer in Interior Design at the Glasgow School of Art in Singapore. She is currently writing her PhD dissertation on atmosphere and smell in architecture at the University of Sydney.

Jude Walton is a Melbourne-based artist who works across film/video, installation, and performance, making site-responsive, time-based interventions, and more recently artist-made books. As an ensemble of works, they generate a poetics of ephemeral practice concerned with bodies, in place/s and time/s stretching over the past twenty-five years. Jude teaches theory and studio practice in performance in the School of Communication and the Arts, Victoria University, Melbourne. She is a key practitioner in current debates about dance as a gestural and mark-making practice and has a PhD based on the artists' book collection at the National Art Library of the Victoria & Albert Museum. She has given a number of performed lectures: *Between Text and Space* for "Writing Encounters at York," St. John University, York; and *Dancing the Book: Dust Detritus Remains* for the Faculty of Fine Arts Forum, Monash University (2008), and the National Art Library of the Victoria & Albert Museum, London (2007).

Dr. Patricia Wheaton has been involved in art and design history for many years through her undergraduate and postgraduate work specializing in designed objects and practices from the eighteenth to the twentieth centuries, particularly with regard to women's roles, the domestic interior, and the home environment. She was responsible for setting up and running a number of design-related courses at Kingston University, Brighton University, and University for the Creative Arts in the United Kingdom. For the last thirty years she has been dealing with designed objects in a more direct way through her continuing work for the jewelry department at Christie's Auction House in London. Her PhD was granted in November 2011, and her dissertation, titled "High Style and Society: Class, Taste and Modernity in British Interwar Decorating," examined class and social issues and the participation of women in the history of British interior decoration in the interwar period.

Introduction

Penny Sparke

> The complete building is the final aim of the visual arts. Their noblest function was once the decoration of buildings. Today they exist in isolation, from which they all can be rescued only through the conscious, cooperative effort of all craftsmen. Architects, painters, and sculptors must recognize anew the composite character of a building as an entity. (Walter Gropius *The Bauhaus Manifesto*, 1919)

For many years, architecture was positioned at the summit of the art and design hierarchy, and architects took on the role of working, not on only buildings' structures, but also on the detailing of the spaces within them, as well, sometimes, on the natural environments that surrounded them. While today many architects still assume those tasks, the last century has also seen the emergence of two new creative professionals: the interior decorator/designer/architect and the landscape designer/architect. While in some contexts that division of labor has done little to topple architects from their (self-appointed) position of "natural" superiority, the concepts of the interior and of the landscape have, in recent years, become the subjects of studies, embracing themes and ideas that sit outside those that have tended to dominate architectural history and theory (Rice 2006; Sparke 2005). As a result, that familiar hierarchy is, at least, being questioned. Some studies of interiors and landscapes have gone as far as to reposition architecture as merely a membrane, one that, as Kerstin Thompson explains in Chapter 8 of this book, rather than forming a barrier, becomes instead "an instrument to create and describe relationships between things."

The nature and meaning of that FLOW are the subject of this book. Rather than considering architecture as the dominant member of the interior/landscape/building relationship, it adopts a new perspective that sees all three operating in a close liaison within which they all play an equally important role. By focusing on the idea of FLOW, architecture is primarily seen as an enabler (or disabler) rather than as the determining element in the relationship. The concept of FLOW is frequently used metaphorically in this context. As a term, its origins lie in the movement of liquids, particularly water, whether in the form of a river that moves from its source to its mouth, of the sea's tide that ebbs and flows, or of water gushing freely from an open tap. Such are the properties of liquids that the concept of FLOW is defined by a sense of continuous uninterrupted movement and, above all, fluidity.

Where the relationship between architecture, interiors, and landscapes is concerned, there are many ways of reading FLOW, both literally and metaphorically. While architecture has traditionally been preoccupied with the resolution of form, interiors with space, and landscape with the picturesque, seeing them through the lens of FLOW emphasizes the ways in which they are interconnected and in which movement, whether real or imagined, between them takes place.

On the simplest and most literal level, FLOW can be understood as any movement (whether of people and things) through buildings that erodes the sense of a barrier between inside and outside. The idea of people moving freely is usually discussed in an urban context, but it can also be considered within buildings, especially complex ones. That freedom is often facilitated by the presence of transitional spaces—verandas, terraces, and so on—and the use of transparent and translucent materials, which help make the shift a smooth one, both physically and psychologically. Importantly, movement involves time, or duration, a dimension of architecture that is rarely discussed and that needs to be considered in any reflections on FLOW.

On a metaphorical level, when it is defined as the way in which the spaces within built structures can be seen as being seamlessly linked to the spaces outside them, FLOW need not involve actual movement (except that of the observer's eye). In this scenario it is almost as if the buildings' "boundaries" do not exist, or, even if they do, they act as a permeable or porous membrane that does not disrupt a sense of spatial continuity. The idea of spatial FLOW, which is discussed at length in this book, lies at the core of the debate about the relationship between interiors, landscape, and architecture. On one level, it is a difficult concept to grasp because it is both immaterial and intangible, but it is, nonetheless, a fundamental idea and, more importantly, an ideal that has underpinned the need to maintain a relationship between the natural and the built environment for centuries. Indeed, it goes to the heart of the reconciliation of those two environments.

The importance of this relationship means that FLOW is not just a satisfying visual feature of the environment but is also deeply rooted in our psyche. Interestingly, beyond the context of architecture, interiors, and landscape, the term *FLOW* is also frequently used to denote a psychological state, one that is, for instance, described in Mihaly Csikszentmihalyi in his book, *Flow: The Psychology of Happiness* (2002: 14). In that context, FLOW is used to denote a mental state in which a person performing an activity is "fully immersed in a feeling of energized focus, full involvement, and enjoyment in the process of the activity. In essence, FLOW is characterized by complete absorption in what one does." Although the term's full psychological meaning is beyond the focus of this book, it has implications for it nonetheless in the sense that spatial FLOW has a feeling of emotional "rightness" to it. Experiencing spatial FLOW is an open, joined-up sensation that reinstates a balance that has been disturbed by the excessive attention paid to architecture over the interior and landscape and the disruption between culture and nature. When FLOW is achieved, a sense of "completeness" is experienced once again.

Discussing the idea of FLOW brings a new critical language to the fore, one that relies on words such as *fluid*, *smooth*, *uninterrupted*, *continuous*, *dynamic*, *borderless*, *permeable*, *porous*, *transparent*, and *translucent*, many of them used metaphorically. Several of these terms were used by historians of interwar and post-1945 Modernist architecture, which set out to open the barrier between outside and inside that had been in place in the nineteenth century. The early-twenty-first-century iteration of FLOW that has inspired this book reharnesses this evocative vocabulary to take the Modernist project to the next logical stage, one, that is, in which architecture has all but disappeared and interiors and landscapes have joined together to form a single, reunited environment that sits beyond the control of the buildings that once defined them. Seen from this new perspective, many historical examples of FLOW—among them those that existed in countless vernacular buildings and environments, in the courtyard buildings of the classical world, in the picturesque gardens and country houses of the eighteenth century, and in many Modernist projects themselves—take on new meanings and a new relevance. Many of them are addressed in this book.

While it is primarily understood visually, FLOW also engages other senses, including touch and smell, and is experienced on many levels simultaneously. Ulrike Passe has noted the limitations of conventional architectural drawings in this context. They cannot, she explains, express the full behavioral content of spatial FLOW that is the movement patterns of air, its temperatures, and its smells. Architects, Passe claims, still define "space" aesthetically and functionally and ignore its other qualities, and she advocates the use of new computational tools, such as computational fluid dynamics (CFD), which have been developed to simulate the spatial behaviour of nonvisual phenomena, in order to address the possibility of integrating natural air and energy flows into architectural design representation (2009: 7).

Although the role of the interior is often understated in them, a few studies of the relationship between architecture and landscape have already been published. Anita Berrizbeitia and Linda Pollak's book, *Inside Outside: Between Architecture and Landscape* (1999: 14), is an early example, while, motivated by current ecological concerns, Diane Balmori and Joel Sanders's more recent *Groundwork: Between Landscape and Architecture* (2011: 5) addresses what they describe as an "interdisciplinary design perspective" in order to "heal the environment."

Perhaps the most important implication of FLOW is the emphasis on a set of new creative professionals who came to the fore at the point when an equal relationship between the interior, landscape, and architecture was being renewed. The specialist landscape architect emerged in the late nineteenth century a little after the interior decorator, who, in the years after 1945, morphed into the interior designer/architect. The result of these developments is that architects no longer have sole authority over the creation of inhabited spaces. One consequence is the emergence of a new discipline called "spatial design," which is accompanied by its own pedagogy. Spatial design crosses the disciplines of architecture, landscape architecture, landscape design, and interior design, as well as certain areas of public art, and it focuses on the FLOW of people between interior and exterior environments within both the private and public realms. A key preoccupation is with the notion of place, with an emphasis on place identity and the concept of *genius loci*.

In addition, although it has not yet penetrated the Academy, the relatively new activity of "interiorscaping," a hybrid process that sits in the interstices and overlaps between interior design and landscape design, has also emerged as a result of the renewed affinity between the interior and landscape. Interiorscaping is a natural consequence of the story, which began in the middle years of the nineteenth century, of the democratization of nature, including plants and flowers, being brought into the inside spaces of both private dwellings and public buildings. In brief, that narrative moves from the advent of the private greenhouse attached to middle-class residences, to the inclusion of plants and flowers as part of the interior décor of the home, to the use of them as markers of domesticity within public inside spaces (including hotels, department stores, exhibition halls, and ocean liners), to their presence, in the post–Second World War years, in shopping malls, airports, and office atria. With the advent of the "green revolution" of recent decades, which brought with it a return of plants in the home, the emergence of green walls in (and green roofs on) public buildings, and the use of full-scale trees in retail environments and elsewhere, the new professional, the interiorscaper, came into being. However, the assumption that interiors and landscapes are always designed by professionals has also been brought into question by FLOW because, at least in the context of domestic spaces, amateur inhabitants have the power to determine the nature of their indoor and outdoor spaces and environments.

The fact that landscapes, in their wild state, and interiors, in the form of caves and grottoes, were in existence for many years before the arrival of the built environment is sometimes used to support the idea of the preeminence of landscape and interior design over architecture. The interior provides shelter from the elements and from wild nature and, in its early incarnation, could be offered within the natural landscape. As such, human beings were in tune with the natural world even when they were sheltering from its dangers and excesses. Indeed, as Sing d'Arcy explains in Chapter 6 of this volume, an interior/landscape continuum was in place that did not require a relationship with architecture. When a three-way relationship did develop, arguably architecture threatened the two-way bond that had been in place before it. While many attempts were made over time to mitigate that threat, architecture's essential role was to create a barrier between what was within it and what was outside it, separating human beings from nature in the process.

On a larger scale, a serious threat to the link between humans and nature came with the linked processes of urbanization and industrialization. Within the era of modernity, that danger was at its greatest. It was compounded by the emphasis on mechanization and rationality. Inspired by the conditions of modernity, Modernist architects did not focus on the schism between human beings and nature but instead, or at least as historians have tended to narrate it, followed the momentum provided by technology and adopted the machine as their primary metaphor. Looking back at their work with the benefit of hindsight, however, and examining it through a new lens—one, that is, that emphasizes the environment and the world of the senses over that of technology and rationalism—new readings can be offered. Many examples of Modernist architecture, especially domestic buildings created on the outskirts of cities, among them Mies van der Rohe's Villa Tugendhat in Brno and Le Corbusier's Villa Savoye outside Paris, while not prioritizing nature, nonetheless valued the natural sites on which they were constructed. The use of terraces and large plate-glass windows served to facilitate an orientation that brought the outside inside. As the buildings still dominated their interior spaces and their exterior landscapes, the strategies utilized by the Modernists were primarily architectural in nature, but, nonetheless, the early stages of a determination to reunite the inside with the outside was being put in place. Enabled by the climate and advances in technology, these strategies were taken to a new level in the neo-Modernist domestic buildings constructed on America's west coast in the years after 1945. However, as Pat Kirkham explains in Chapter 18 of this book, Californian indoor/outdoor living was as much a myth as a reality.

In seeking to blur some of the boundaries between its inside and its exterior spaces, architectural Modernism was characterized by its dependency on a set of polarities, those, for example, of nature versus culture, architecture versus landscape, inside versus outside, interiority versus exteriority, and public versus private. To extend the discussion about polarities in the context of FLOW beyond Modernism, however, one could add those that exist between natural and synthetic materials, between the worlds of the sensorial and the rational, and in terms of the gendering of the new professions that arose on the back of a search for FLOW, those of male and female, masculine and feminine.

Inherent in the concept of FLOW as it is promoted today, however, is the need to move beyond these binaries and to embrace a new continuity that blurs the boundaries between them. As Kerstin Thompson explains again in her chapter, "what becomes more relevant is the interstitial, the space between traditional opposites." As part of that effort to establish continuity, new hybrids have emerged that are characterized by ambiguity. The idea of "tamed nature," for example, represented by the garden and indoor plants, sits in between the concepts of wilderness and the built environment, while the mechanisms of FLOW—terraces, balconies, verandas, front porches, plate-glass windows—are neither inside nor outside but both.

Importantly, also, a consideration of FLOW requires a discussion that extends beyond the Western industrialized world and embraces a wider geography. Fundamental to it is the specificity of climate and place. Case studies of FLOW from both the Northern and the Southern Hemispheres are presented in this book.

All these ideas and themes, and many others besides, permeate the pages that follow. The book presents its chapters in four parts: Engaging Nature, Mobility, Continuum, and Frames. While there is inevitably considerable overlap, or FLOW, between them, they focus on four key themes that arise from any discussion of this subject, as this introduction has already suggested. While the first tells about the importance of the healing of the nature/culture divide, the second reminds us of the fundamental significance of the concept of movement and duration in this discussion. The third gets to the heart of the issue, showing us what FLOW is and how it works, while the fourth shows that we are often offered a view of FLOW through a frame, one that enhances the essential ambiguity and transparency of the fluid relationship that can be seen to exist between interiors, landscapes, and architecture.

References

Balmori, D., and J. Sanders (2011), *Groundwork: Between Landscape and Architecture*, New York: The Monicelli Press.

Berrizbeitia, A., and L. Pollak (1999), *Inside Outside: Between Architecture and Landscape*, London: Rockport Publishers.

Csikszentmihalyi, M. (2002), *Flow: The Psychology of Happiness*, London: Rider.

Passe, U. (2009), "Designing Sensual Spaces: Integration of Spatial Flows Beyond the Visual," *Architecture Publications*, 4. Available online: http://lib.dr.iastate.edu/arch_pubs/4 (accessed January 31, 2017).

Rice, C. (2006), *The Emergence of the Interior*, London: Routledge.

Sparke, P. (2005), *The Modern Interior*, London: Reaktion.

1

Part 1
Engaging Nature

Richard Serra Clara Clara in the Tuileries, Paris 2008 Gini Lee

Introduction

Penny Sparke

One of the key discussions relating to the concept of FLOW has focused on the ways in which the defining processes of Western modernity—industrialization and urbanization—have seriously threatened its existence. Ever since those economic, social, and cultural processes caused a physical rift between the majority of the population of the Western world and the natural environment, we have been trying to reunite ourselves with the latter in a variety of ways. The loss incurred by that rift was, and remains, deeply felt, and countless strategies have been developed in an attempt to mitigate it.

Over the last century and a half, that loss has been one of the key challenges embraced by landscape architects and the architects and inhabitants of many of our built structures, the external walls of which frequently create a barrier that shuts nature out. The effect has often been to isolate us in a fabricated material and spatial environment that has little or no relationship with the natural world outside and that prevents and disrupts the possibility of FLOW. That challenge has generated many debates, many different strategic practices over the years, and many built structures. Sometimes the last are discursive constructions, created to offset the factors that prevent FLOW, and sometimes they achieve that effect un-selfconsciously through a simple response to local and climatic conditions and constraints.

Through a number of highly diverse case studies of subjects located within a wide geographical span, and situated across the period from the late nineteenth century to the present, this part of the book addresses just some of the countless ways and contexts in which FLOW has both manifested itself in the past and continues to show itself today. The chapters that follow address the implications for the creative professionals —the interior designers/architects, the landscape architects, and the architects—who either facilitate FLOW or are responsible for its absence. They also focus on a wide variety of built structures, situated in both public and private arenas and in both rural and urban spaces, that facilitate FLOW in a variety of ways. In addition, FLOW is seen to exist in certain urban and landscaped environments where built form is at a minimum. In addressing these subjects, the themes of gender, modernity, the local, the global, national identity, imperialism, and nature versus culture, among others, rise to the surface, determining the discussions about the ways in which FLOW is facilitated.

In his introductory chapter, "Human/Nature: Wilderness and the Landscape/ Architecture Divide," Joel Sanders from Yale University takes a broad-brush approach that sets the scene for the chapters that follow. He addresses the debate from the perspective of the current "global environmental crisis"—the inevitable result, arguably, of the rift created by the forces of modernity —and of its implications for the professional practices of architecture (which, he suggests subsumes the design of the interior) and landscape architecture. His main concern is the division that exists between them, one that, he contends, has exacerbated the disruption of FLOW. His essay focuses on the need to understand how the divide came about in the first place. Although, as he suggests, the human/nature polarity dates back to antiquity, Sanders's eye is on the role played by the American concept of "wilderness," formed in the nineteenth century and articulated in the writings of David Thoreau and John Muir. The divide is not merely physical, however; he maintains that it is also gendered, nature being frequently defined as feminine. The wilderness, he contends, with reference to the writings of Carolyn Merchant, was the "unruly woman" who needed to be tamed by men. Paradoxically, however, seen from another perspective, Sanders continues, the taming of the wilderness has been seen as emasculating.

The main focus of the essay is on the way in which the human/nature divide led to two separate professions and to the need for the emergence of the landscape architectural profession to complement the work of architects, the former being represented, in the United States, by a line of individuals from Frederick Law Olmsted, Jr., to Ian McHarg. Tracing their contributions through Modernism up to today's green revolution, Sanders ends by proposing a shift beyond the polarity of the wilderness model and toward a more unified, seamless view of architecture and the natural environment, both tamed and untamed, that makes FLOW possible.

In the second chapter, "Spatial Experience within the 'Colonial Bungalow,' the 'Tropical Modern,' and 'Critical Vernacular' House in South Asia, 1880–1980," Robin Jones takes us away from the Northern Hemisphere and employs his South Asian case study to address the way in which FLOW was a result of climatic conditions and local vernacular influences. The interior spaces in the colonial bungalow—a hybrid domestic building type, created in a specific geographical location at a particular period—engaged directly with the exterior, Jones claims. In his words, that building type attempted "to accommodate South Asian vernacular models of domestic space, including the relationship between interior and exterior, to European ideas of dwelling." Key to this was the importance of ventilation, which mitigated against the use of hallways, making the entrance into the interior of the bungalow a direct one. Also taken from the local culture was the use of multipurpose rooms, which gave the interior a high level of spatial fluidity, while the inclusion of verandas creating transitional spaces between the façades and the outdoors also facilitated FLOW. In his discussion of "tropical Modernism" and "critical vernacular architecture," Jones shows how hybridity remained in place and how architects continued to focus on the sensory nature of space, which, once again, encouraged FLOW.

Moving to Europe, in Chapter 3, "Continuities and Discontinuities: The House and Garden as Rational and Psychical Space in Vienna's Early Modernism," Diane Silverthorne, from Birkbeck, University of London, focuses on one of the most common ways in which inhabitants of domestic dwellings have linked nature to their homes and encouraged FLOW, that is, through engagement with their gardens. Her focus is on the ways in which an early Modernist artistic movement, the Vienna Secession, used that union, both literally in many of their nonurban homes and through representation in many of their paintings, as a marker of a belief in the *Gesamtkunstwerk*, that is, the complete work of art in which a synthesis was sought between garden, home, art, and life. Her emphasis is on the ways in which a number of late-nineteenth- and early-twentieth-century gardens created by Secession artists in suburban Vienna and the countryside beyond represented two seemingly conflicted themes within early Modernism, those of the rational and the psychic. She suggests that the idea of the garden linked to the home was central to the thinking underpinning the work of the Vienna Secessionists, who, she contends, sought a blurring of the boundaries between the countryside and the urban setting. Those ideas, as Silverthorne demonstrates, were represented in a variety of ways in many of the Secessionists' artworks.

The subject of the fourth chapter, "A Point of View: Christopher Hussey's Sense of the Picturesque," written by Patricia Wheaton, is located in interwar England. The chapter focuses on the work of writer and connoisseur Christopher Hussey, editor, from 1933, of *Country Life* magazine. The contribution of this chapter to the discussion about FLOW is the idea that, in the face of their contemporary destruction, Hussey looked back to the moment when, in the eighteenth century, the country house and its surrounding landscape were seen as inextricably linked and, together, inspired the idea of the "Picturesque." As Wheaton explains, for Hussey the most important thing was "the relationships flowing between them." At the same time, however, Hussey was also refining his taste for European Modernist architecture, many examples of which, among them Serge Chermayeff's *Bentley Wood*, he believed, were also at one with their surrounding landscape and respected the Picturesque aesthetic. While it was not always the case, Hussey saw, within architectural Modernism, an important strand that built on the ideas established in the eighteenth century and brought it into the age of the machine. By focusing on the concept of the Picturesque, as understood by Hussey, both as a quality of eighteenth-century English country houses and of certain Modernist buildings that worked in harmony with, rather than against, the landscape that surrounded them, Wheaton has highlighted the notion of FLOW as a continuing theme over an extended time period.

Still in the United Kingdom, but moving from the past to the present, from the private to the public sphere, and enlarging the scale from the domestic dwelling to the urban environment, Chapter 5, written by Chris Hay, an independent scholar, and Pat Brown, from Kingston University, is entitled, "Inside Out: Spectacle and Transformation." The thrust of their chapter is that some outdoor spaces can be understood as interiors and can express urban interiority. The authors claim that, following the 2012 Games, the Olympic Park, constructed in London's River Lea Valley, "was required, in effect, to begin to turn itself inside out . . . to turn a condition of intense interiority into its opposite, into, that is, one of exteriority." Specifically, this meant that it had to turn itself to look outward toward the city. The authors compare and contrast the park with another landscaped outdoor space that can also be understood as both an interior and an exterior, Gunnar Asplund's Woodland Cemetery in Stockholm. Both have barriers around them, but, while the former had a disruptive effect on the immediate landscape and had to redefine and reorient itself once its original (national/global) purpose had come an end, the latter emphasized continuity with the original site and was designed from the outset both as an inward-looking (local) space and as one that related to the urban community to which it related.

The sixth chapter, "The Allegory of the Cave: Speculations between Interior and Landscape for the Barangaroo Headland Cultural Facility," written by Sing d' Arcy from the University of New South Wales, remains within the scale of the urban and focuses again on the "interior" (in the basic sense of "shelter") that can be created "naturally" within an exterior environment. He examines an example of landscape regeneration in the form of a new park to be constructed on the edge of Sydney Harbour that will, in d'Arcy's words, "reference the topography of the site as it may have been in the early nineteenth century before its 'vandalism' throughout the twentieth." The "interior," which is created by the new landscape design that contains it, resembles a cave, an inside protective space, that is, that is created by nature rather than by human beings (as is the case with architecture). This case study serves to distance the idea of the "interior" from that of "architecture," seeing the former as a primordial concept that predates the latter. It also realigns the former with the world of nature, thereby reviving the concept of FLOW. The idea of the Renaissance grotto is also discussed, seen as an extension, rather than a disrupter, of nature. The grotto functioned, d'Arcy explains, as a link between artifice and nature and therefore sits somewhere between the cave and the architectural structure. The Barangaroo headland park is seen as operating in a similar way. D'Arcy concludes his essay by discussing the work of a cohort of students on the Bachelor of Interior Architecture course at the University of New South Wales who were given the Barangaroo Headland Cultural Facility as the starting point for a studio project.

Compiled by Jude Walton and Phoebe Robinson, from the University of Melbourne, the last chapter in this part, "45 Degrees," is a picture essay. It derives from work in a series of studies in physical spatial practice looking at bodies and the built environment, which was performed by dancer Phoebe Robinson and documented, in the form of a video, by Cobie Orger.

Chapter 1

Human/Nature: Wilderness and the Landscape/ Architecture Divide[1]

Joel Sanders

The global environmental crisis underscores the imperative for design professionals—architects and landscape architects—to join forces to create integrated designs that address ecological issues; however, long-standing disciplinary divisions frustrate this crucial endeavor. Architecture and landscape architecture have been professionally segregated since at least the late nineteenth century. They are constituted as independent fields, each with its own curriculum and licensing procedure. The challenge of developing a new model of practice—one that is both formally and programmatically sophisticated and environmentally responsible—requires that designers examine how this impasse ever arose. Although my remarks largely focus on what I refer to as the landscape/architecture divide in the United States from the nineteenth century until today, I would suggest they are relevant to this volume with its focus on the relationship between interior and landscape. As I have argued elsewhere, architecture and interiors are interdependent disciplines.[2] The building envelopes, understood in conjunction with the interiors they shelter, articulate the seams where inside and outside meet, and, as a consequence, they shape the way humans interact with one another and the designed environment.

The landscape/architecture schism can be traced back to antiquity and to another deep-seated yet suspect Western polarity: the opposition between humans and nature and thus between buildings and landscapes. One version of the human/nature dualism finds its home in an influential body of thought that arose in nineteenth-century America, the concept of wilderness. The idea of wilderness is so engrained in the American conscience—through literature, philosophy, and even notions of gender and sexuality—that it has effectively shaped the design approaches and even the codes of professional conduct that, in many ways, still define the relationship between architecture and landscape practice.

Scholars have traced the intellectual origins of American environmentalism to Henry David Thoreau and John Muir, American writers active in the second half of the nineteenth century who advanced the concept of wilderness. Indebted to eighteenth-century Enlightenment thinkers like Jean-Jacques Rousseau and Romantics like William Wordsworth, this generation of writers celebrated the ethical and spiritual benefits of living a life in unspoiled nature, uncontaminated by America's burgeoning urban industrial civilization (Nash 1967).

This account of the relationship between humans and nature marks a pronounced reversal in American thinking about landscape. Until the second half of the nineteenth century, the settlement of the American frontier was predicated on the Judeo-Christian belief that it was the responsibility of humankind to cultivate the wilderness, which was traditionally perceived to be a desolate place located on the margins of civilization and associated with terror and bewilderment.

This conception of wilderness not only perpetuated the age-old human/nature divide but also engrained ideas about the nature of gender. Relying on the long-standing personification of nature as a woman, feminist critics like Carolyn Merchant have shown that the rhetoric underlying the expansion and settlement of the American continent was founded on biblical accounts of the expulsion from Eden, the fall brought about by a woman. Wilderness was depicted as an unruly female to be subdued and ultimately cultivated through the labor of men, whose goal was to recover the paradise lost on earth. For feminists, this biblical injunction was reinforced by yet another gendered Western dualism that opposed material and immaterial, mind and body: rationalist thinking, considered a male prerogative, made possible the Scientific Revolution and a corresponding conception of Mother Earth as a passive body subjected to male domination through technology—a worldview that many eco-feminists argue persists today.[3]

Figure 1.1

Theodore Roosevelt and John Muir on Glacier Point, Yosemite Valley 1903. Library of Congress, Prints and Photographs Division LC-USZ628672.

By the mid-nineteenth century the American frontier had been settled. This impending loss of the majestic scenery of the American continent threatened America's national identity. Fueled by a surge in cultural nationalism and nostalgia for the rapidly vanishing frontier, early environmental activism represented a remarkable shift in wilderness thinking: the spiritual grounding of the young nation had come to depend on the preservation of the natural landscape. As Thoreau wrote, "In wildness is the preservation of the world" (Cronon 1996: 69).

By the turn of the twentieth century, the vanishing wilderness also paralleled the imperiled male masculinity. Associated with yet another authentically American trait—rugged individualism—wilderness was regarded as a source of masculine vigor and vitality. The home of the frontiersmen and the cowboy, wilderness represented a safe haven, a refuge where men could resist the emasculating, domesticating forces of urban culture. Theodore Roosevelt famously championed the establishment of America's first national parks because they countered "flabbiness and slothful ease" and promoted that "vigorous manliness for the lack of which in a nation, as in the individual, the possession of no other qualities can possibility atone" (Nash 1967: 150) (Figure 1.1).

Not only did wilderness form the foundation of American environmentalist thinking, but it also exerted a direct and profound influence on the subsequent development of two overlapping but increasingly diverging fields, architecture and landscape architecture. The dualistic conception of humanity and nature only reinforced the long-standing Western conception of buildings as constructed artifacts qualitatively different from their ostensibly natural surroundings. If buildings were different from landscapes, then a new type of landscape professional was required to fill the gap and complement the work of architects.

In 1899, a diverse group of gardeners, horticulturalists, and designers, under the leadership of Fredrick Law Olmsted, Jr., established a professional academy, the American Society of Landscape Architects (ASLA). Over the years, wilderness core values have resurfaced in various guises, connecting the work of a first generation of nineteenth-century American landscape architects led by Olmsted, who were directly influenced by their wilderness peers, to three generations of twentieth-century Modernist critics and landscape designers, including Henry Russell Hitchcock, Garrett Eckbo, Charles Rose, and Ian McHarg.

Yet another undercurrent of wilderness thinking connects this lineage of landscape practitioners. By positing that the human is entirely outside the natural, wilderness presents a fundamental paradox. The historian William Cronon writes, "If we allow ourselves to believe that nature, to be true, must also be wild, then our very presence in nature represents its fall. The place where we are is the place where nature is not" (Cronon 1996: 80–1) (Figure 1.2). Wilderness, then, presents designers with a particularly thorny dilemma: how to reconcile the ideal of untouched nature with the imprint of humans and human design. The guilty conscience fostered by this conundrum has haunted American landscape architects, and the dilemma was compounded by the negative connotations of designed nature: decoration, domesticity, and femininity. The result was a deep and persistent suspicion of designed nature that still endures.

Figure 1.2

Emanuel Gottlieb Leutze, *Westward the Course of the Empire Takes Its Way*, mural study, U.S. Capitol, 1861. Smithsonian American Art Museum, Washington, D.C. / Art Resource, NY.

The pioneering work of Frederick Law Olmsted betrays the paradoxes at the heart of wilderness thinking. Unlike Muir, who turned his back on cities to find redemption in the pristine American landscape, Olmsted fully embraced making nature accessible to urban citizens. Olmsted sought to legitimate the emerging profession by differentiating it from gardening, insisting that it was an art and not a trade. In a letter, he wrote that he had personally elevated landscape architecture from "the rank of a trade, even of a handicraft, to that of a profession—an Art, an Art of Design" (Treib 1993: 19).

Nevertheless, Olmsted's conception of landscape architecture as design proved inconsistent with the guiding premise of his aesthetic philosophy: communion with nature depended on exposing people to a simulacrum of natural scenery unspoiled by evidence of human intervention (Figure 1.3a and 1.3b). Upholding the notion of a nature/culture polarity, Olmsted conceived of Central Park as a natural oasis inscribed within the dense New York metropolis, one that could offer the weary urbanite refuge from the industrial city through the rejuvenating effects of the visual contemplation of nature. In a passage that exemplifies yet another long-standing Western duality, the mind/body split, he writes, "As what is well designed to nourish the body and enliven the spirits through the stomach makes a dinner a dinner, so what is well designed to recreate the mind from urban oppressions through the eye, makes the Park the Park" (McKibben 2008: 125). For Olmsted, Central Park was not a place for active recreation, as it is today, but a place for visual observation. In later projects, like Prospect Park and the Boston Riverway, he again grappled with the ostensible incompatibility between nature and metropolitan design. Although they were massive infrastructural projects requiring advanced technology, engineering, and design, Olmsted disguised their constructed character by using a pastoral vocabulary that viewers assumed to be natural.

At the outset of the twentieth century, Olmsted was the acknowledged leader of a growing new profession. Only thirty years later, however, a new generation of landscape architects had lost its way, its efforts stymied by the supposed incompatibility of nature and design. The catalogue for *Contemporary Landscape Architecture and Its Sources*, an exhibition curated by Hitchcock at what was then called the San Francisco Museum of Art in 1937, underscored the crisis surrounding the profession's inability to devise a compelling new Modernist landscape vocabulary. The San Francisco curators narrowly defined the problem of the modern landscape as belonging to residential garden design. In the process, Hitchcock grafted principles from architecture onto landscape architecture. Transferring modern architecture's famed prohibition against ornament to its sister discipline, he advocated that landscape designers renounce their propensity for decorative ornamental planting and instead concentrate on functional concerns. Conflating two design professionals— the interior decorator and the gardener—who he saw as threatening the integrity of buildings by adorning them with ephemeral materials, Hitchcock cautioned against the use of flowers, writing that flower beds "serve primarily a decorative purpose, like curtains or upholstery indoors, subordinate to the useful general purpose of the terrace" (Hitchcock 1937: 19).

This identification of both interior design and garden design with decoration clearly tapped into deep-rooted disciplinary assumptions tinged by gender prejudices. In a similar vein to the criticisms made by male architects about interior decoration, gender prejudices also shaped cultural perceptions of landscape, a practice that also relies on the most ephemeral of materials—trees, plants, and flowers—to adorn the stable constructions of architects. Unlike architecture, a cerebral enterprise apprehended intellectually, gardens, like tactile interiors, elicited visceral pleasures stimulated by the textures, colors, and scents of material Mother Nature. If, in a strict Modernist view, all of landscape, whether cultivated or untamed, was considered an accessory to architecture, then gardens were even more inconsequential. As they repudiated ornament based on its association with feminine adornment, Modernists like Hitchcock also condemned decorative plantings, which they equated with womanly fashion, artifice, and deception. While International Style architects focused on pressing social issues, landscape designers, like interior designers, devoted their attention to the inconsequential and devalued domain of the female homemaker. In short, the discipline of landscape could redeem itself only by transcending its own tainted history as a superficial pastime affiliated with women. These prejudices would soon be reiterated by subsequent generations of landscape professionals.

Figure 1.3a and Figure 1.3b

Frederick Law Olmstead, *Riverway*, Boston, Massachusetts, view during and after construction, 1892 and 1920. Courtesy of the National Park Service, Frederick Law Olmsted, National Historic Site.

Ironically, Hitchcock's exhibition upheld the preeminence of architecture by arguing that landscape designers should extend architectural principles from indoors to outdoors: "Gardening on roof terraces and in close conjunction with houses is not so much a separate art as a sort of outdoor architecture" (Hitchcock 1937: 15). Imposing another key tenet of modern architecture on landscape—functionalism—he contended that designers must treat garden terraces as literal extensions of the interior, as "rooms that promote exterior functional activities" (Hitchcock 1937: 15). He maintained that outdoor spaces immediately adjacent to the house should be treated architecturally, but those farther away from the building should be left intact. This approach was exemplified in such prewar domestic masterpieces as the Villa Savoye and the postwar Farnsworth House, both of which conjure up the image of the isolated building set in a pastoral setting. They were both conceived as suspended objects that, through the new technologies of the curtain wall and the steel frame, leave nature deceptively unspoiled.

Architecture has appropriated a responsibility once shared with landscape design—the framed view. While buildings in the West have largely been conceived of objects independent from the landscape, architects working in concert with gardeners have employed devices—like French doors leading to porches aligned with trees and hedges—that articulate a smooth transition between inside and outside. But now divorced from the ground plane, the elevated house allows detached spectators confined within the interior to observe carefully composed views of an ostensibly pristine landscape (Hitchcock 1937: 15, 18).

It was the responsibility of a next generation of American landscape architects—Garrett Eckbo and James Rose—to find a way to reconcile the designed landscape with the nature/culture mentality underpinning modern architecture. Preoccupied with the burden of generating a viable direction for Modernist landscape, they seemed stymied by a professional inferiority complex. They shared the conviction that their discipline's legacy of creating pretty pictures composed with ornamental plantings must be overturned by embracing modern architecture's core values.

These two landscape architects practiced in California. Allying themselves with a loosely defined California school of Modernist landscape designers like Thomas Church and Lawrence Halprin, they sought an alternative to the Modernist paradigm of the isolated machine in the garden. Instead, they endeavored to take advantage of the West Coast's gentle climate and relaxed lifestyle to marry architecture and landscape in a way that facilitated indoor-outdoor living (Figure 1.4). But these practitioners had few role models in their own field. Instead the works of architects like Frank Lloyd Wright, Rudolph Schindler, and Richard Neutra, as well as the Case Study architects, represented a departure from the prevailing conception of architecture as a self-contained object building with nature as a foil.

Figure 1.4

Thomas Church, *Donnell Garden*, Sonoma, California, 1948. Photo by Charles A. Birnbaum, The Cultural Landscape Foundation.

These resourceful designers looked outside their discipline to fine art. They absorbed the influence of maverick early European landscape designers, including Gabriel Guevrekian and Pierre-Emile Legrain, and like contemporaries Roberto Burle Marx and Isamu Noguchi, they were indebted to Cubism and Surrealism. The outcome was a series of modest residential designs that borrowed bold abstract forms and motifs from a variety of modern art sources, including Theo Van Doesburg, Joan Miró, and Jean Arp.

But this fertile period of small-scale experimentation was short-lived. Eckbo and Rose, like many of their postwar peers, gradually withdrew from taking on the residential commissions that were the bread and butter of many noted American landscape designers: Charles Platt, Warren Manning, and Ruth Dean at the turn of the century and Thomas Church in the 1950s. Small-scale residential projects came to be regarded as the domain of the amateur female homemaker, due in part to the emergence of mass-market publications like *House Beautiful* (Harris 2002: 180–205). Eckbo and Rose shifted their focus to large-scale commissions like university campuses, corporate office parks, and suburban subdivisions, joining the ranks of a generation of corporate landscape firms that would dominate the profession for years to come. By the 1970s, the ASLA awards reflected this shift: only five of two hundred awards went to residences.

Another postwar practitioner, Ian McHarg, partnered with state and federal agencies to tackle the infrastructural challenges of formulating ecologically minded master plans that could transform entire metropolitan regions. He outlined his ecological approach in *Design with Nature*. For McHarg, writing in 1969, Olmsted's worst predictions had been realized—rapacious capitalism aided by remarkable technological advances had tipped the precarious balance between nature and civilization, resulting in environmental casualties in America's polluted, slum-ridden cities. McHarg compared city dwellers to "patients in mental hospitals" consigned to live in "God's Junkyard" (McHarg [1969] 1995: 20, 23).

McHarg also wrestled with the issue of reconciling nature and design, although he pursued a different course from Olmsted, who smoothed over the paradox of constructing nature by concealing art, engineering, and infrastructure with a design vocabulary that appears to be natural. Likewise, McHarg departed from Modernists like Tunnard, Steele, Church, Eckbo, and Rose, who strived to wed functionalist precepts to abstract form making derived from the fine arts. Instead, McHarg turned to the natural sciences. Not really interested in new materials or technologies, he nevertheless shared the preoccupations of contemporaries like Buckminster Fuller and Frei Otto, who, following in the footsteps of nineteenth-century designers like Viollet-le-Duc, Ernst Haeckel, and René Binet, were interested in the underlying laws of form generation in nature.

Natural scientists were for McHarg what engineers were for Le Corbusier. In a quasi-functionalist argument reminiscent of Le Corbusier's *Towards a New Architecture*, he advised designers to study and emulate the morphology of plants and animals, not human works of engineering (McHarg [1969] 1995: 170). By identifying the natural sciences as a bridge between the constructed and the natural, McHarg made a more convincing claim for the integration of science and design than his functionalism-inspired predecessors. No longer specific to architecture, science became the legitimate purview of the landscape architect, who was now capable of generating seemingly inevitable designs grounded in the logic of science that integrated the built and the natural without resorting to art.

McHarg pioneered an ecological methodology that encouraged designers to consider a range of interconnected environmental factors—climate, water, flora, and fauna. Nevertheless, his comprehensive regional proposals, generated through a process-oriented approach grounded in the supposedly objective logic of the natural sciences, largely evaded design. His master plans were too large, conceptual, and abstract to engage issues of form, space, materials, and the human body in the way traditional garden designs once did. While McHarg's design approach coincided with and reflected the process-oriented, ecological values that dominated the late 1960s and the 1970s, his philosophy nevertheless betrays the same struggle to come to terms with the supposed incompatibility of nature and design that preoccupied two generations of American landscape designers before him. McHarg revisited many wilderness-inflected themes inherited from his predecessors: a dualist way of thinking that views nature as a vulnerable feminine entity that must be protected from the predatory interests of humans, including architects; a professional bias against designed nature, decoration, and feminine artifice; and a preference for large-scale problem solving based on a deterministic design approach justified by science.

One of the consequences of this way of thinking is a mistrust of the designed environment, a legacy that continues to haunt many design professionals. The legacy of wilderness core values inhibits alliances not only between architects and landscape architects but also between interior and landscape designers. Its dualistic worldview conceives of interiors, like architecture, as a human endeavor, an art that intrinsically exists in opposition to the natural. Moreover, engrained disciplinary biases further undermine the marriage of interiors and landscape. In the same way that interiors are literally subsumed within the building shell that separates inside from outside, interior design is considered a subordinate branch of architecture. Interiors and landscapes, two fields devalued because of their pejorative association with femininity, domesticity, and decoration, must be controlled and regulated by the master discipline, architecture. In short, architects and the buildings they make both literally and figuratively impede the marriage of two fields: architecture, like a stern but well-meaning parent, forbids the union of its potentially unruly offsprings, interiors and the brash interloper, landscape.

The residue of wilderness thinking—in particular, its dualistic disciplinary worldview and its preference for science over aesthetics—also has environmental consequences, strongly shaping the parameters of green design today. In the first two decades of the twenty-first century, two types of design professionals—architects and landscape architects—and two sectors of the construction industry—builders and landscapers—have developed parallel strategies for making buildings and landscapes more sustainable. Products and materials are generally designed to replicate the environmentally irresponsible ones they replace: solar panels are attached to sloped or flat roofs, renewable materials clad the interior and exterior of conventional buildings, and organic fertilizers and indigenous plantings are eco-friendlier ways of improving the acres of traditional lawns and shrubs that adorn buildings conceived as isolated objects.

In short, green design fosters a product-oriented mentality that generally evaluates materials and techniques on the basis of performance and efficiency, rarely taking into consideration issues of form and program. Moreover, by taking disciplinary divisions for granted, sustainable design unwittingly reinforces one root of the problem: the dualistic paradigm of the building as a discrete object spatially, socially, and ecologically divorced from its site. As a consequence, this American ideal—itself derived from wilderness thinking—inhibits designers and manufacturers from treating buildings and landscapes holistically as reciprocal systems that together impact the environment.

Might it be possible to jettison these outmoded and environmentally irresponsible prejudices and instead reimagine buildings, interiors, and landscapes as mutually interactive entities? Relinquishing wilderness values will allow designers to adopt the more complicated viewpoint advanced by progressive scholars and scientists: a recognition that nature and civilization, although not the same, have always been intertwined and are becoming more so. Climate change reveals that there is not a square inch of the planet that does not in some way bear the imprint of humans.

It is important to adopt a more complex understanding of the relationship between nature, science, and technology. Common ground must be sought between technophobia and technophilia. Environmental problems can be resolved only by considering nature as both a scientific and a cultural phenomenon. Realigning deep-rooted preconceptions and conceiving of culture and nature, and, as a consequence, buildings, interiors, and landscapes, as deeply interconnected entities will allow designers to usher in a new model of integrated practice, a way of working that reunites three fields of inquiry that should never have been divided.

This new mentality will allow representatives of three disciplines now accorded equal status to forge productive continuities between interior and exterior. Designers are encouraged to pay attention to the interface—the seam, or overlap, where indoors and outdoors meet. A critical awareness of the fluid connection between natural and synthetic, as well as between exterior and interior space, motivates designers to think about scale, form, and materials in entirely new ways: materials become the connective tissue that enacts the passage between interior, building envelope, and landscape. The scale of the human body becomes the crucial common denominator that bridges the intimate scale of interiors with the expansive scale of the outdoors. Considering the spatial and material junctures that link inside and outside through the lens of ergonomics, these can generate new ways of thinking not only about form but also about program, positioning human activities, both inside and outside, in a way that coincides with twenty-first-century notions of what it means to live with nature.

Endnotes

1. This chapter is an abridged version of an essay included in the book *Groundwork: Between Landscape and Architecture* by Diana Balmori and Joel Sanders (2011).

2. In "Curtain Wars: Architecture, Decorating and the Twentieth-Century Interior" (Sanders 2002), I argued that deep-seated cultural prejudices resulted in the problematic professional split between two inseparable fields, architecture and interiors. This essay extends this way of thinking to account for yet another arbitrary professional divide between architecture and landscape. In my view, "architecture" refers to both the hard and soft surfaces that clad both the interior and exterior of buildings and that together enable the performance of human identity.

3. For two influential feminist accounts of the intertwined relationship between nature, science, capitalism, and gender, see Carolyn Merchant, *The Death of Nature: Women, Ecology and the Scientific Revolution* (1980), and Val Plumwood, *Feminism and the Mastery of Nature* (1993).

References

Balmori, D and J. Sanders (2011), *Groundwork: Between Landscape and Architecture*, New York: The Monacelli Press.

Cronon, W. (1996), *Trouble with Wilderness*, New York: W. W. Norton.

Harris, D. (2002), "Making Your Private World: Modern Landscape Architecture and 'House Beautiful,' 1945–1965," in M. Treib (ed.), *The Architecture of Landscape, 1940–1960,* Philadelphia: University of Pennsylvania Press.

Hitchcock, H. R. (1937), *Contemporary Landscape Architecture*, San Francisco: San Francisco Museum of Art.

McHarg, I. ([1969] 1995), *Design with Nature*, New York: John Wiley.

McKibben, B. (2008), *American Earth: Environmental Writing Since Thoreau*, New York: Library of America.

Merchant, C. (1980), *The Death of Nature: Women, Ecology and the Scientific Revolution*, New

York: HarperCollins.

Nash, R. F. (1967), *Wilderness and the American Mind*, New Haven: Yale University Press.

Plumwood, V. (1993), *Feminism and the Mastery of Nature*, London: Routledge.

Roper, L. W. (1973), *FLO: A Biography of Frederick Law Olmsted*, Baltimore: John Hopkins Press.

Sanders, J. (2002), "Curtain Wars: Architecture, Decorating and the Twentieth-Century Interior," *Harvard Design Magazine (HARDSoft CoolWARM . . . Gender in Design, plus Classic Books Part II)*, 16 (Winter/Spring): 14–20.

Treib, M. (1993), *Modern Landscape Architecture: A Critical Review*, Cambridge: MIT Press.

Chapter 2

Spatial Experience within the "Colonial Bungalow," the "Tropical Modern," and "Critical Vernacular" House in South Asia, 1880–1980

Robin D. Jones

This chapter discusses how space was organized and experienced within the "colonial bungalow," the "tropical modern" house, and the "critical vernacular" house in South Asia (India and Sri Lanka). The "colonial bungalow" in South Asia evolved during the nineteenth century as a hybrid structure that combined awkwardly local building practices and uses of space with European notions of dwelling. During the second half of the twentieth century, the development of "tropical modern" and subsequently "critical vernacular" forms of architecture in India and Sri Lanka (after independence in 1948) referenced Modernist idioms as well as "indigenous and historic spatial concepts, elements and architectural details and construction methods" (Perera 1999: 144).

The chapter discusses the sensory experience of space within these buildings, particularly in relation to the boundaries between architecture and the exterior. Its arguments draw from recent critical literature on postcolonial architecture in Asia (Perera 1999; Jazeel 2006; Lu 2010; Pieris 2007, 2013). In addition, it refers to recent writings by David Howes, Constance Classen, and others from within the so-called "sensory turn" in cultural studies (Howes 2005).

The "colonial bungalow", previously the subject of an uncomplicated, postimperial nostalgia, has recently undergone more critical appraisals that problematize this building form and the European colonial and local identities that it produced (King 1984; Collingham 2001; Glover 2004; Chattopadhyay 2006; Jones 2007).

The work of South Asian architects during the period after independence, including that of Charles Correa (India) and Geoffrey Bawa (Sri Lanka), negotiated between the spatialities of the precolonial vernacular, the colonial, and the modern. Two significant attributes are evident in their later work: an emphasis on the haptic experience of space and, deriving from vernacular traditions, careful consideration of the relationship between the inside and outside of their buildings. In fact, it has been suggested that a key contribution of these architects lies in these areas of heightened embodied experience within their domestic buildings rather than in the production of visually prominent structures.

Prior literature on late-twentieth-century architecture in South Asia can be divided into two main approaches. The first presents straightforward, somewhat celebratory narrative histories of the architects practicing in the region in the postcolonial era, as exemplified in the writings of, for example, David Robson on Bawa (2002). The other approach analyzes architectural developments in the region from more critically informed perspectives and from a range of disciplines, including cultural geography, urban planning, architectural history, and anthropology (Perera 1999; Jazeel 2006; Vale 2008; Lu 2010; Pieris 2007, 2013).

The "Colonial Bungalow" in South Asia

The "colonial bungalow" in South Asia evolved as a structure with a medico-cultural purpose: its intended function was to protect the health and help support the lifestyle of ex-patriot Europeans living in tropical regions (Figure 2.1). However, this conceptualization of the bungalow as a protective shell to shield and support the European body from hot and humid climates was more of an aspiration than something actually realized on the ground. These structures (together with the colonial urban house in South Asia), for the most part designed and built by local craftsmen, were often criticized by their European occupants as "inept copies of English residences" (Chattopadhyay 2006: 119–20). Perhaps it is more helpful to interpret these dwellings as attempts to accommodate South Asian vernacular models of domestic space, including the relationship between interior and exterior, to European ideas of dwelling.

As the architectural historian Will Glover suggests, one defining characteristic of the colonial bungalow, from a European perspective, was the porosity "between the interior rooms . . . and the . . . exterior" (2004: 75). This porosity resulted from a number of local causes, chief among them the bungalow's indebtedness to and evolution from the local, Indian house form, especially the desire for ventilation in a hot climate (Glover 2004). This need for ventilation inside the bungalow militated against the use of hallways "to separate and channel . . . activity from one space" to another (Glover 2004: 76). Because this standard feature of middle-class houses in Britain was lacking, entry into the bungalow usually was made directly from the outside, without any intervening zone of transition between inside and out. Contemporary commentators noted that the occupants' privacy was often regularly invaded and their sense of being inside was continually challenged because of this arrangement.

Figure 2.1

"Magai Bungalow, Teerhoot"
[Champaran District, N. India],
c. 1880. Author's collection.

Moreover, the need to open the interior rooms of the bungalow to cooling breezes meant that the scale of rooms was often larger than equivalent rooms in Britain. Such rooms were also constructed with multiple door openings in the walls to allow air to circulate. This climatic necessity added to the sense that space flowed unchecked from one room to another in a manner completely unlike that found in European middle-class homes. Consequently, the difference between the private and more public spaces within the bungalow was blurred. From the evidence of inventories, we know that the majority of rooms in nineteenth-century Anglo-Indian bungalows and houses did not have specific functions (Jones 2007: 132–3). This feature derived from local practice and reflected how the use of space in the vernacular courtyard house depended on climate, time of day, gendered use, and domestic activity rather than the European model of assigning space to a particular function or to a particular gender.

The nineteenth-century bungalow in India also often failed to adequately shelter the European body from the effects of the local climate. In fact, the prevailing climatic conditions outside, on many occasions, directly affected the inhabitants inside. In 1856, Thomas Machell, a British planter living in the rain-soaked hills of Coonoor, south India, described in words and images the climatic intrusions into his bungalow. In an illustrated letter to his relatives in Europe, which included a sketched plan of his bungalow, he characterized the qualities of its different rooms. In his narration, the function of each room was deemed less important than the ways in which these rooms affected him physically. For instance, he described them variously as a "dark, damp hole," a "dressing [room] wet as a pond," and a "damp bedroom always" (Jones 2007: 78–9). As argued elsewhere, "the British experience of India [during the colonial period] was intensely physical" (Collingham 2001: 1).

Prior scholarship has suggested that the arrangement of space in the colonial bungalow was an inversion of the traditional spatial organization of local homes in South Asia. The rooms in such houses, in both India and Sri Lanka, were usually arranged around a central, internal courtyard (*uthan, mida midula*), and daily domestic activities took place around that space. The traditional, local house looked inward, therefore, and usually presented a series of blank walls to the outside world. As Iftekhar Ahmed has suggested, within vernacular South Asian houses "the courtyard functions as a bounded, open-to-sky private area almost akin to indoor space" (2012: 52). The internal courtyard also fulfilled the need for thermal comfort in hot and humid climates; it was virtually "an extension of indoor living" and allowed a variety of activities to take place (Ahmed 2012: 52).

The colonial bungalow, built for Europeans in South Asia, reversed this relationship and projected an open and outward-facing aspect. Instead of the locally preferred open space or courtyard at the center of the dwelling, in the colonial bungalow that open space was, over time, transferred to the outer walls of the structure and took the form of a verandah. While the open space of the local courtyard was filled with one or two inner and usually windowless rooms, the outer rooms of the colonial bungalow were usually flanked by one or more verandahs, which cooled the air in the immediate vicinity of the dwelling and offered at least the perception of transition between inside and outside.

The notion of the colonial bungalow as a protective space to shield the European body from the physical effects of living in South Asia was continually compromised. For instance, following local practice, servants often worked and even slept on the verandah of the bungalow. Additionally, it became a space for conducting business or was used as an outside room. These factors reduced its usefulness as a barrier between the interior space of the bungalow and the outside (Glover 2004: 76). As the architectural historian Swati Chattopadhyay has suggested, the interior of the Anglo-Indian dwelling "functioned according to different rules from home." As she writes, "no locks or bolts on the doors, [indicated] too plainly that Indian doors were not supposed to be shut. Without the possibility of closing off rooms, the boundary between the house and the outside world became ineffective" (2006: 92). This induced a sense of uncertainty about the exterior limits of the dwelling, a blurring of boundaries between inside and outside and a resultant compromise of the European occupants' sense of interiority.

The "Tropical Modern" House in South Asia

The phrase *tropical modern* combines two contradictory concepts—the notion of the exotic but also the disease-ridden and deadly tropics and their antithesis, the purportedly Western, health-giving, and rational modern way of life. The term originally derived from the writings of European architects who practiced in "the [former] colonial tropics." In 1953, the Conference on Tropical Architecture was held at University College, London, and, as Hannah Le Roux has suggested, "was a critical event in the development of an idea of a specific approach to architecture" in the tropics (2003: 342). In 1954, the Architectural Association in London established a specialist six-month course in Tropical Architecture; in October 1953 and January 1954, *Architectural Design* published two special editions on Tropical Architecture edited by Otto Koenigsberger (Le Roux 2003: 343); and in 1956 Maxwell Fry and Jane Drew produced an influential book on the subject, *Tropical Architecture in the Humid Zone.*

   The term *tropical modern* linked a number of dualities: the non-European "other" and Western rationalism, the timeless and decadent East and the progressive West, and the organic East and the man-made West. The term *tropical modern* and its implied narratives masked the informal continuation of the colonial project and its residual networks in Africa and Asia in the years after independence. As Perera has suggested, "architectural modernism [was] not just European, but was also constructed within the premises of Euro-centrism, undermining the social and cultural values of non-European people and recognizing only climatic difference in relation to temperate Europe" (1999: 118). The term gained currency in West Africa, where, for example, a number of European architects were practicing in the 1950s and 1960s. It was also in this region that the engineer/"constructor" Jean Prouvé introduced his prefabricated, aluminium and steel "maison-tropicale" to Niamey and Brazzaville in Niger—the ultimate Modernist tropical bungalow (Huppatz 2010: 32-44).

   After independence, however, the context for the development of the built environment in South Asia was different. Unlike in the former colonies in West Africa, few Western Modernist architects practiced in the South Asian region after independence, although there were some notable exceptions: Le Corbusier (assisted by his cousin Pierre Jeanneret, together with Maxwell Fry and Jane Drew) planned the modern city of Chandigarh, the new capital of the Punjab, a region created after the partition of India in 1948. In 1958, the American designers Ray and Charles Eames were invited by President Nehru to advise on the state of Indian design (Mathur 2011: 34–53). The American architect Louis Kahn designed the National Assembly Building in Dhaka, Bangladesh (1962–1974), as well as the Indian Institute of Management in Ahmedabad, India (1962).

CEYLON

ANDREW BOYD, Architect

THE NORTH FRONT. The rendering is white; external
woodwork is painted grey; front doors are Chinese red.

Figure 2.2

"Houses at Colombo," designed
by Andrew Boyd, 1939. F. R. S.
Yorke, *The Modern House* (1934,
5th edition 1944), London:
Architectural Press, p. 100.

On a more domestic scale and within the smaller landmass of Sri Lanka, an
English tea researcher turned architect, Andrew Boyd, designed several tropical
Modernist houses in Ceylon in the 1930s and 1940s. Two of these were illustrated in
the British architectural press (Boyd 1940: 5–6) and also in later editions of F. R. S.
Yorke's *The Modern House* ([1934] 1944) (Figure 2.2). The houses presented a white
rectangular boxlike structure to the street. Rational, Modernist concepts were used
in the orientation, plan, and design of the buildings to enhance the well-being of the
occupants. The orientation of Boyd's houses was north-south to avoid excessively hot
sun; the two-slope roof with vertical surface between created a line of ventilation;
and there was through ventilation in all the main rooms. The materials were a mix
of modern and traditional (reinforced concrete ribs, insulation board, lime-rendered
brick). At the same time, the Architectural Association–trained Sri Lankan architect
Minette de Silva brought a version of Western Modernist building practices and idioms
to the island, although she acknowledged some local traditions of the use of space
and ornamentation.

Tropical Modernism attempted to introduce the underlying principles of Euro-American Modernism to colonized, or recently colonized but newly independent, regions. It was an attempt to translate a set of ideas and built forms that had been developed in the West and apply them in a rational and scientific manner in a radically different context. However, in South Asia, local conditions and climate challenged such an approach, and some local architects (as well as the few European architects working in that region) began to develop a different way of building.

"Critical Vernacular" Architecture in Sri Lanka

This new approach has been described by Perera and others as the development of a "critical vernacular architecture" (2010: 76), which was the "result of a consciousness of the inappropriateness of colonial and modern architecture of the West in a culturally different, extra-European, post-colonial" situation (Perera 1999: 146). A Danish architect, Ulrik Plesner, working in Sri Lanka in partnership with Bawa during the 1950s and 1960s, commented on the few Modernist experiments in the island since the 1940s: "most of the new buildings were a reflection of western ways, climatically unsuitable and visually indifferent . . . it was a process of clearing away the shabby asbestos roofing, the bare bulb lighting, the disastrous flat roofs, the imported rubbish, the slimy black mouldy walls without drip ledges, the admiration for the second rate from Europe" (quoted in Perera 1999: 147). In other words, the chief features of the Western, Modernist house—white-painted geometric shapes, flat roof, and sharp, crisp corners—were completely inappropriate for the tropical and monsoon conditions of South Asia, where nature and climate literally assaulted the building. At a time when Modernism was rejecting historic models, Plesner's architectural training in Denmark emphasized the human experience of natural materials, conventional construction methods, and ideal building or object types (Jones 2015: 8–12).

During the postindependence period, South Asian architects, such as Bawa in Sri Lanka and Correa in India, began to experiment by reconfiguring, in a contemporary idiom, the indigenous dwelling space by drawing on the features and plans of vernacular, precolonial buildings. These architects referred to "indigenous and historical spatial concepts, elements and architectural details and construction methods" (Perera 1999: 144). As Shanti Jayawardene has suggested, Bawa's work "implied a sharp break with the then modes of the 'international style' which were reaching a high point in neo-colonial fluency around [the] 1950s and 60s" (quoted in Perera 1999: 147).

In the design of their domestic buildings, architects such as Bawa and Correa began to refer back to the "open-to-sky" aesthetic of precolonial building practices. In addition, the visual aspect of a building was downplayed in favor of the sensory experience of space, including the spatial flow through the building and the disruption of clear distinctions between interior and exterior, thereby deemphasizing the boundaries between the two. In an essay entitled "Blessings of the Sky," Correa wrote that "in India, the sky has profoundly affected our relationship to built form and open space. For in a warm climate, the best place to be in the late evening and early morning is outdoors" (quoted in Brown 2009: 23). Plesner, Bawa's architectural partner, wrote about the moment of revelation that the traditional, hipped roof of vernacular buildings was more appropriate than the Modernist flat roof in the tropics. The "big roof" was the essential feature of the vernacular building and allowed for the creation of a loose and free-flowing plan beneath: "with the discovery of the universal big roof, things fell into place . . . openness under big roofs became the key to beauty, comfort, economy, ecology, pleasure, as, in fact, it still is" (quoted in Filler 2013). Reference to vernacular forms meant that architects such as Bawa emphasized the significance of the hipped and tiled roof, with eaves extending to form colonnaded verandahs, and the incorporation of "open-to-sky" spaces within the plan around which rooms were arranged. These features allowed for an almost uninterrupted flow of space from interior to exterior within the envelope of the building.

For example, Bawa's house for the textile designer Ena de Silva (1962) in Colombo, Sri Lanka, now demolished, was designed around a large internal courtyard with the interior spaces of rooms open to and flowing into that space. The de Silva house has been described as a modern reinterpretation of vernacular Sinhalese domestic space, that is, the traditional *walawa* or elite courtyard house (Jazeel 2006: 8).

It has been argued that a defining characteristic of the critical vernacular house in South Asia is the "illusion of infinite spatiality." Such buildings also elicit in the occupant a potent sense of "emplacement" or the "sensuous inter-relationship between body-mind-environment" (Howes 2005: 7). This sense of "emplacement" is invoked by the plan of the critical vernacular house, which creates a series of disaggregated, free-flowing but bounded spaces within the building, some of which are open to the sky. Instead of walls and doors signifying transitions from zone to zone, as occupants move through the building they experience different spaces through subtle transitions of light, temperature, and flow of air. Once inside the building, occupants experience a sense of porosity between inside and outside spaces.

Instead of these houses being primarily spaces for the eye, they refer to other sensory experiences. As Correa wrote of architecture in a warm climate: "one steps out of the 'box' to find oneself . . . in a verandah, from which one moves into a courtyard . . . the boundary lines between these various zones are not formal or sharply demarcated, but easy and amorphous. Subtle modulations of light, of the quality of ambient air, register each transition on our senses" (1982: 31).

This chapter has discussed the shifting spatial experiences within the "colonial bungalow", the "tropical modern," and the "critical vernacular" dwelling. It concludes by suggesting that the development of critical vernacular architecture in South Asia offered an alternative to Western Modernism's production of architecture as an idealized vision and the dominance of the visual realm in recent Western architectural discourse (Jazeel 2006: 11). It did so by reconfiguring "indigenous and historic spatial concepts and architectural details" (Perera 1999: 144).

This architectural shift led to the production of a more varied, emplaced, and richer sensory experience of domestic space. Finally, to paraphrase the architect and writer Juhani Pallasmaa, the disaggregated spaces of Correa's and Bawa's domestic buildings do not present a "disembodied Cartesian idealism of the architecture of the eye"; rather, "they are structured around sensory realism" (Pallasmaa 2005: 71). Through the blurring of boundaries between interior and exterior, the haptic qualities of these spaces are foregrounded. Correa's and Bawa's buildings, particularly their domestic ones, become architectures of sensing or sense-scapes (Howes 2005: 143). In fact, they may best be described as "sensory agglomerations, conceived to be appreciated in their actual physical and spatial encounter" (Pallasmaa 2005: 71).

References

Ahmed, I. (2012), "The Courtyard in Rural Homesteads of Bangladesh," *Vernacular Architecture*, 43 (1): 47–57.

Boyd, A. (July 1940), "Houses, 2," *The Architectural Review*, 98 (524): 5–6.

Brown, R. M. (2009), *Art for a Modern India, 1947–1980*, Durham: Duke University Press.

Chattopadhyay, S. (2006), *Representing Calcutta: Modernity, Nationalism and the Colonial Uncanny*, Abingdon, UK: Routledge.

Collingham, E. M. (2001), *Imperial Bodies: The Physical Experience of the Raj, c. 1800–1947*, Cambridge: Polity Press.

Correa, C. (1982), "Architecture in a Warm Climate—Open to Sky Space," *MIMAR 5: Architecture in Development*, 5: 31–35.

Filler, M. (2013), "Under Sri Lanka's Big Roof," *The New York Review of Books*, May 29. Available online: http://www.nybooks.com/blogs/nyrblogs/2013/may/29/sri-lanka-bawa-plesner (accessed October 19, 2015).

Glover, W. (2004), "'A Feeling of Absence from Old England': The Colonial Bungalow," *Home Cultures*, 1 (1): 61–82.

Howes, D., ed. (2005), *Empire of the Senses: The Sensual Culture Reader*, Oxford: Berg.

Huppatz, D. J. (2010), "Jean Prouvé's Maison Tropicale: The Poetics of the Colonial Object," *Design Issues*, 26 (4): 32–44.

Jazeel, T. (2006), "Bawa and Beyond: Reading Sri Lanka's Tropical Modern Architecture," *South Asia Journal for Culture*, 1 (1): 1–22.

Jones, R. D. (2007), *Interiors of Empire: Objects, Space and Identity within the Indian Subcontinent, c. 1800–1947*, London: Manchester University Press.

Jones, R. D. (2015), "Ulrik Plesner and the Impact of Post-war Scandinavian Design in Sri Lanka," *Domus Sri Lanka*, 14: 8–12.

King, A. D. (1984), *The Bungalow: The Production of a Global Culture*, London: Routledge.

Le Roux, H. (2003), "The Networks of Tropical Architecture," *The Journal of Architecture*, 8 (3): 337–54.

Lu, D., ed. (2010), *Third World Modernism: Architecture, Identity and Development*, London: Routledge.

Mathur, S. (2011), "Charles and Ray Eames in India," *Art Journal*, 70 (1): 34–53.

Pallasmaa, J. (2005), *The Eyes of the Skin: Architecture and the Senses*, Chichester: John Wiley.

Perera, N. (1999), *Decolonizing Ceylon: Colonialism, Nationalism and the Politics of Space in Sri Lanka*, New Delhi: Oxford University Press.

Perera, N. (2010), "Critical Vernacularism: A Locally Produced Global Difference," *Journal of Architectural Education*, 63 (2): 76–8.

Pieris, A. (2007), *Imagining Modernity: The Architecture of Valentine Gunasekera*, Pannipitiya and Colombo: Stamford Lake (Pvt) Ltd. and Social Scientists' Association.

Pieris, A. (2013), *Architecture and Nationalism in Sri Lanka: The Trouser under the Cloth*, London: Routledge.

Robson, D. (2002), *Geoffrey Bawa: The Complete Works*, London: Thames and Hudson.

Vale, L. (2008), *Architecture, Power and National Identity*, London: Routledge.

Yorke, F. R. S. ([1934] 1944), *The Modern House*, London: The Architectural Press.

Chapter 3

Continuities and Discontinuities: The House and Garden as Rational and Psychical Space in Vienna's Early Modernism

Diane V. Silverthorne

"Natural beauty," Theodor Adorno states in *Aesthetic Theory*, is "suspended history, a moment of becoming at a stand-still. Artworks that resonate with this moment of suspension are those that are justly said to have a feeling for nature." Yet, like modernity, "this feeling is . . . fleeting and ephemeral" (1997: 70, 71). To make his point, Adorno cited the German Enlightenment philosopher Wilhelm von Humbolt, who reproached a magnificent craggy landscape for its lack of trees and a city for its lack of mountains. As Adorno remarked, fifty years later the same landscapes would probably have seemed delightful (1997: 71).

Landscapes, whether bounded as gardens or unbounded, existing in the indeterminate spaces between the further reaches of the urban landscape and the "natural beauty" of surrounding country, may be described as historically specific. Cultural historian Carl Schorske's account of *fin de siècle* Vienna's gardens captured the changing outlook of Austria's cultivated middle class in the critical years that precipitated the end of the Austro-Hungarian Empire (1981). Garden spaces were suggestive of competing strains of Modernism, on the one hand "the possibilities of rationality as a guide to life," and on the other "a sensitivity to psychic states" (1981: 25). Both these states were widely reflected in painting and music as well as in literature. At the center of writer Adalbert Stifter's *Indian Summer* (1857), the Rose House and its garden estates acted as the embodiment of the unified impulses of nature and culture. Andrian-Werburg's *The Garden of Knowledge* (1895) emphasized the crisis of *fin de siècle* Vienna in the central figure's self-infatuation. Poet and playwright Hugo von Hofmannsthal wrote of the hedonistic utopian beauty of the rococo garden (Schorske 1981: 281–311).

Robert Rotenberg's social history of three hundred years of Vienna's gardens defines them as socially and politically specific (1995). Gardens were a system of signs that "entered people's conversation about their understanding of nature, the city, social power and their experiences within these realities" (1995: 6). The term used for the features that surrounded the city's built environment was *die Landschaft* (the landscape), which was divided into various subtypes (1995: 26). Rotenberg defines a series of historically and socially specific greenspaces, including the *fin de siècle* "gardens of reform" and "gardens of reaction," which fulfilled "the dream of a return to the preindustrial world" (1995: 148–87, 215).

In *fin de siècle* Vienna, Modernist art, literature, and music often embraced the notion of "the garden in the home," as well as the garden *and* the home. *Ver Sacrum* (Holy Spring), the art periodical of the Vienna Secession (1898–1903), was used as an experimental two-dimensional medium for new forms of domestic architecture, interiors, and garden design. Photographs of the Vienna Secession's early exhibitions show, through the placement of strategically situated laurel trees in pots, cane chairs, and the display of fine and applied arts, that a synthesis of art, life, home, and garden was considered the new art.

Composer Arnold Schoenberg was an essential and central figure in Vienna's Modernism. His development of a new musical language that embraced the further reaches of dissonance may be traced through three significant works, each situated in enclosed landscapes. Notably, *The Book of the Hanging Gardens* (op. 15),[1] a cycle of songs based on Expressionist poetry by Stefan George, establishes a tension between the socially-ordered nature of the garden and the uncontrollable passion of two lovers. It was composed to evoke only sound and mood. Similarly, the impressionistic landscapes of Gustav Klimt are notable for their indeterminate mood and their sense of interiority. This chapter considers these various overlapping private and public landscape types of *fin de siècle* Vienna as constructions of rational life on the one hand, exemplified by the work of Secessionist artist Carl Moll, and on the other, as psychical states driven by an inner necessity, as in Schoenberg's Expressionist music and the art of Vienna's Expressionist painters.

Constructions of "*fin de siècle* Vienna" as the birthplace of early Modernism have often relied on the centrality of the coffeehouse and its culturally charged "spaces of interiority" for histories of exceptional developments in the arts. Yet, as recent literature demonstrates, Vienna's "spaces of interiority" were not fixed but rather permeable (Gronberg 2007; Ashby, Gronberg, and Shaw-Miller 2013). The coffeehouse space was in constant dialogue with external events and other cultural spaces in many ways including the proliferation of little magazines, newspapers, and avant-garde periodicals. Similarly, Vienna's urban spaces were in constant dialogue with the surrounding countryside. As Stefan Zweig described, the city's houses "dissolved themselves in gardens and fields, or climbed in gradual rises in the last green wooded foothills of the Alps. One hardly sensed where nature began and where the city ended" (1964: 13).

The blurring of boundaries between city and surrounding landscape was given greater emphasis by the annual bourgeois *Sommerfrische* (summer migration) to the mountain resorts surrounding the city. At times, the population of mountain and lakeside could be said to mirror the mythicized creative circles of Vienna's coffeehouses. Gustav Klimt summered with his cousin and close companion Emily Flöge on the Attersee; Arnold Schoenberg and family spent their holidays with the Zemlinskys at Gmunden, and for two significant years, with the young painter Richard Gerstl.[2] A publicity poster designed by Secessionist Alfred Roller that advertised the new mountain railway suggested the wind-borne transportation of fashionable Vienna in a series of Baroque-like layers upwards toward the heavenly mountain spaces of unpolluted "natural beauty" (Figure 3.1). In the performance of this annual leave-taking of city for country many of Vienna's writers, artists, and other intellectuals continued to work on their various artistic projects, as Tag Gronberg has shown in her analysis of these more permeable and interconnected spaces (2007). Theirs was not a break with the city for a more authentic rural existence, but rather a continuum. However, a reaction against Vienna's *Ringstrasse* (Ring Street) apartments of the 1860s, as well as the spatial ambiguities of the *Ringstrasse* itself, led to a yearning for gardens as comfortable, enclosed spaces and a return to *Biedermeier* ideals.

The *Biedermeier* period of the early nineteenth century was laden with the values of *Gemeinschaft* (community), to which were ascribed an appreciation of quiet pleasures and simply-designed domestic interiors. Later in the century, the Viennese yearning to experience "country life in a home" connected family life and modern domestic architecture to *Biedermeier* ideals and a nostalgia for the past reinvented in the modern suburb (Rotenberg 1995:100–2). What was needed was an antidote to city living and the neo-Renaissance-style urban apartments of the *Ringstrasse,* with their grand staircases and small living rooms. Instead, in their place, as described by Hermann Bahr, they longed for "real country cottages, which looked as if they have sprung out of the living soil, like peasant's houses and acacia trees" (Vergo 1993: 125). *Biedermeier* ideals were enshrined in the revival of Vienna's cottage quarter in the 1870s, which was swiftly populated by many of its musical, literary, and artistic figures, as well as the new modern domestic architecture of the Wiener Werkstätte garden villa suburb of *Hohe Warte* (High Viewpoint), designed by Josef Hoffmann and Koloman Moser (Figure 3.2). Commissioned by Secession colleagues and friends, *Hohe Warte* villas shared common features as well as adjoining plots of land: white roughcast facing, a top-floor studio with views to the Vienna Woods and the mountains beyond, and living spaces extended by terraces and gardens. Hoffmann's new villas and the lifestyle they embraced were celebrated in the pages of the periodical of the same name. The stated aim of *Hohe Warte* (1906–1909) was to cultivate "artistic education and urban culture," suggesting a confident middle class asserting its own values (Lux 1904–5: 145–55). Its main focus was the domestic interior, although its content encompassed a much broader set of interests, from jewelry to reform dress, exhibitions, criticism on the lyric and dramatic arts, as well as garden design.

Figure 3.1

Alfred Roller: Schneebergbahn bei Wien, 1898. MAK—Austrian Museum of Applied Arts / Contemporary Art. Photo: © MAK/Georg Mayer.

In 1908, the interpenetration of house, garden, and culture was also celebrated in the first *Kunstschau* (Art Show), a public exhibition of the fine and applied arts displayed in neoclassical pavilions designed by Hoffmann, and specially landscaped gardens by Paul Roller. Perhaps the *Kunstschau* might be described as the forerunner of the Ideal Home Exhibition in London. Citing William Morris, the catalogue described the ideal garden in terms of control and order, exemplifying the rationality of cultured modern man: "large or small, the garden should look well-ordered and rich: it should be closed-off from the outer world: it should in no way imitate the purposes or accidents of nature, but look like something which one could see nowhere else but in a human dwelling" (Schorske 1981: 326).

Morris says garden should be isolated

Figure 3.2

Josef Hoffman, Hohe Warte:
Moll and Moser House. MAK—
Austrian Museum of Applied
Arts / Contemporary Art.
Photo: © MAK/Georg Mayer.

Biedermeier values embodied in the organic elision of garden and home, and
the staging and presentation of the cultured bourgeoisie as modern man, were also
marked by a series of portraits by Secession founder and patron Carl Moll of his villa
and garden at 8 Steinfeldgasse. The paintings were square-format, connecting the
commonly used design motif of the Vienna Secession and *Wiener Werkstätte* (Vienna
Workshop) with the intentional control of the domestic spaces of house and garden, in
a spirit of fastidious orderliness. Nature, like the house, was to be tamed and managed,
the sublime in nature embraced and then squared away. Moll's *Self Portrait (In My
Studio)* (1906), which was part self-portrait, part showcase for the new domestic
interior, gives only an indication of the garden beyond. Muted light falls on the artist's
admirably high forehead from an unseen window. It accents his intellectualism, an
embodiment of the German idea of *Bildung* (self-cultivation), a term with particular
significance in the late nineteenth century that suggested the virtue of learning and
high culture (Schorske 1981: 292). The light casts its pale blue shadows on the wall
behind. The stillness of the study, with the male figure in a professional suit and
surrounded by strategically placed artworks, implies timelessness: the ephemeral
and contingent, marked by the candle under glass. The same luminosity highlights
the drift of white curtains, a style favored by the *Wiener Werkstätte*. In contrast,
the attenuated figure of an androgynous youth by Belgian sculptor Georg Minne
(the frequently-exhibited artist of the Secession), a sculpture acquired and displayed
by Moll in his painting, is deadly white. It seems to conflate young life and a more
troubling anxiety beyond the untroubled boundaries of the home.

Two further Moll paintings of the garden and patio outside are empty of people yet suggest their controlling presence. In *Terrace of the Villa Moll* (1903), the patio clearly demarcates the border between framed space outside, an extension of the home, and the indeterminate space beyond. Rhythmically spaced cube planters and the carefully tailored laurels give no indication that the mountains may be viewed in close proximity to the suburban garden. Geraniums stand ready to be uprooted to make way for the next planting. A 1905 garden view, *The Artist's House on the Hohe Warte*, is of an artfully humble garden table, seemingly recently vacated. A flurry of blue hydrangeas merges with a glowing and translucent sky. A "Madonna and Child" in an elevated niche set into the walls of the house oversees the garden. It is a space of containment, regulated by a spiritual force, but one that is also open to the beauties of God's vast creation. The calm serenity of Moll's interior spaces, home, and garden, a refiguring of *Gemeinschaft* society, was marked by order, a sense of wholeness or completeness. Pointing to rational man in "The Metropolis and Mental Life," Georg Simmel wrote: "Metropolitan man develops an organ protecting him against the threatening discrepancies of his external life. He reacts with his head instead of his heart. Intellectuality preserves subjective life against the overwhelming power of metropolitan life" (2007: 184).

Paradoxically, in view of Simmel's sentiment, the utopian vision of family life in the suburbs could only be made possible through participation in the wealth-making, industrialized city beyond its bounds. The denial of the city's existence was central to the idealization of this mode of existence (Johnson 1999: 14–37).

I now turn from rational to psychical man, and to garden spaces as subjective states in the landscape paintings of Vienna's early Expressionists, which appear to "breathe the air from another planet."[3] The experience of Vienna's urban spaces was described by writer Robert Musil as a series of glittering, conflicting sensations of sounds and silence, light and dark, of deep, narrow streets, "of irregularity, change, forward spurts, collisions of objects and interests, punctuated by unfathomable silences made up of pathways and untrodden ways, of one great rhythmic throb as well as the chronic discord and mutual displacement of all its contending rhythms" (1997: 4). These more dissonant, subjective states may be discerned in the urban landscape paintings of Richard Gerstl, whose short-lived career has been noted mainly for his portraiture of the male figure. His urban landscape, *On the Danube Canal* (1907), a work painted from Gerstl's studio in Vienna's Liechtensteinstrasse, is suggestive of Musil's "unfathomable silences" and "rhythmic throb." Strong, coloristic daubings have the expressive intensity of a Van Gogh. They mark the city's anonymous, semi-cultivated garden spaces between the vibrating efflorescence of apartment buildings, commercial enterprises, and the canal bank. The work suggests the subjective experience of the city, those things that are not represented in this urban scene, or at least only by expressive implication. What is not represented is the spectacle of the crowd. The buildings radiate with an elemental glow or aura, which also commonly emanates from the subjects of early Expressionist portraits, a ghostly light indicating the soul made manifest (Harrison 1996). In contrast, Gerstl's painting of the garden of the Liechtenstein Palace is one step removed from the deep, narrow streets. It suggests a haven of order, an enclosed and regulated space overlooked by and encroached on by the looming buildings.

Gerstl's disconcerting *Nude in the Garden* (c. 1907) seems attended by the innocence of a prelapsarian state combined with a nightmare-like Freudian intensity. The naked male figure watering his plants is seemingly oblivious to the crowd gathered at the garden fence. Thick, gestural painterly effects blur the painting's sense of reality. A uniformed soldier in the crowd waves a flag, an incontrovertible sign of Vienna's adherence to rules of social hierarchy and superficial politesse. Perhaps no other space, other than the Vienna café, which acted as a more socially permissive space, permitted the representation of figures with such intensity. Suspended between reality and utopia, the garden allowed for Freudian displacement and the portrayal of instinctual life "transformed into sensory vividness" (Freud 2005: 99).

A different perspective of Freud's sensory vividness is represented by Gerstl's garden portrait of the composer Schoenberg and family (1908). The artist rejected realism in favor of a furious dazzle of color and light, freighted with the intensity of experience, perhaps Gerstl's ill-fated affair with Mathilde Schoenberg. Figures and ground dissolve and dematerialize. "We must feed our ideas with locusts and wild honey, not with history," declared the German artist Franz Mark in correspondence with fellow painter August Macke in 1910 (Harrison 1996: 145). Here garden landscape elides with portraiture, complying with the Expressionist imperative to "utterly spiritualise and dematerialise inwardness of feeling" (Harrison 1996: 145). The bounded space of garden has become unbounded; the frame of the painting, or the garden itself, no longer holds. The painting may be seen as a critique of the *Biedermeier* mania for floral displays in a multiplicity of forms and media, including lush garden beds, paintings, and as a favored motif on every household interior surface (Rotenberg 1995: 106).

I turn now to Egon Schiele, who, like many of Vienna's cultural figures, left his birthplace in rural Austria for the city, experiencing this separation as a continuing exile, often expressed in a yearning for gardens and the pleasures of open spaces. Schiele is best known for the extreme gestural states of his portraiture, his near-naked figures pinned for examination, like botanical specimens, to empty space, neither interior nor exterior. The artist was also a prolific landscape painter dating from the time of his student years in the small town of Klosterneuburg, just outside Vienna. Prolonged stays in similarly rural places punctuated his artistic life. From Krummau, he wrote to his patron, Dr. R, "I want to tell you soon about my wonderful little summer home and my lush flower garden. I am looking forward to it!" (Leopold Museum 2008: 69). This vision, of garden as home, an escape from society for the restoration of the self, provided Schiele with the means for the projection of its opposite: landscape as a veil for dissidence and dissonance. Death and nature are inevitably symbiotic partners in *fin de siècle* Vienna. Krummau gave birth to Schiele's studies of "Dead Towns" and depictions of "Autumn Trees," a series of paintings that dispensed with any real sense of the garden as a cherished place for more ambiguous, denuded, or desiccated spaces. They critique gardens as framed and utopian space in favor of the construction of nature as something other. Space is emptied out. Notions of interiority and death transposed to the seemingly neutral spaces of landscape become, in this transition, neither neutral nor innocent.

In Neulengbach, Schiele was "enchanted by his new surroundings." His house was "isolated at the edge of town in the middle of meadowland, with a view of a wooded hill topped by a castle" (Whitford 1996: 99). In *Self-Portrait with Black Vase* (1911), instead of regulated pots of tulips, the vestiges of garden in the home were represented by the attenuated, denuded twig emerging horizontally, against nature, from the black, anthropomorphic vase. They are suggestive of the atomization of life, not its unification, of transience and death, not permanence and security. This was home and garden as ugliness liberated, an art whose "surface was broken" to reveal the realities of a less governable universe (Schorske 1981: 362).

For my last example, I return to Vienna's city spaces. In 1908, Schoenberg exchanged his dark apartment in the Liechtensteinstrasse for a "larger and nicer house in Hietzinger Haupstrasse" (Stuckenschmidt 1977: 128). His desire to move coincided with a yearning to live in the country and work in fresh air. Between 1908 and 1911 the composer painted intensively. His interest in using his immediate domestic surroundings was evident in *Street Scene at Night* (c. 1911) and *Night Landscape* (1910). Neither the airiness of Schoenberg's new home in the suburb, nor his pleasure in it, is reflected in these works. Where Moll's house and garden reflect light, tranquillity, and ease, Schoenberg's studies suggest the impossibility of finding ease, even in the quiet suburbs.

In all, these various and diverse illustrations of *fin de siècle* Vienna's garden spaces appear to act both as containment and as a liberating space for the exploration of rational and psychical man.

Endnotes

1. Known as *Fifteen Songs of Stefan George*, op. 15.

2. Composer Alexander Zemlinsky, Schoenberg's brother-in-law, and family. Gerstl's affair with Schoenberg's wife Mathilde during this period is well documented. See J. Lloyd, I. Pfeiffer, and R. Coffer, eds. (2017), *Richard Gerstl*, Chicago: University of Chicago Press.

3. From George's poem, "The Book of the Hanging Garden," often cited as signifying Schoenberg's break with tonality.

References

Adorno, T. (1997), *Aesthetic Theory*, ed. G. Adorno and R. Tiedeman, trans. R. Hullot-Kentnor, Minneapolis: University of Minnesota Press.

Ashby, C., T. Gronberg, and S. Shaw-Miller, eds. (2013), *The Viennese Café and Fin-de-Siècle Culture*, New York: Berghahn Books.

Freud, S. (2005), "On Dreams," in Anna Freud (ed.), *Vintage Freud: The Essentials of Psycho-Analysis*, trans. J. Strachey, 81–125, London: Vintage Books.

Gronberg, T. (2007), *Vienna: City of Modernity, 1890–1914*, Oxford: Peter Lang.

Harrison, T. (1996), *1910: The Emancipation of Dissonance*, Berkeley: University of California Press.

Johnson, J. (1999), *Webern and the Transformation of Nature*, Cambridge: Cambridge University Press.

Leopold Museum, ed. (2008), *Egon Schiele: Letters and Poems from the Leopold Collection 1910–1912*, Munich: Leopold Museum with Prestel.

Lux, Joseph August (1904–5), "Biedermeier als Erzieher," *Hohe Warte*, 1: 145–55.

Musil, R. (1997), *The Man Without Qualities,* trans. S. Wilkins and B. Pike, London: Picador.

Rotenberg, R. (1995), *Landscape and Power in Vienna*, Baltimore: The John Hopkins University Press.

Schorske, C. E. (1981), *Fin-de-Siècle Vienna: Politics and Culture*, New York: Vintage Books.

Simmel, G. (2007), "The Metropolis and Mental Life," in M. H. Whitworth (ed.), *Modernism, Blackwell Guides to Criticism*, 182–9, Oxford: Blackwell.

Stuckenschmidt, H. H. (1977), *Schoenberg: His Life, World and Work*, trans. H. Searle, London: John Calder.

Vergo, P. (1993), *Art in Vienna 1898–1918*, London: Phaidon.

Whitford, F. (1996), *Egon Schiele*, London: Thames & Hudson.

Zweig, S. (1964), *The World of Yesterday,* Lincoln: University of Nebraska Press.

Chapter 4

A Point of View: Christopher Hussey's Sense of the Picturesque

Patricia Wheaton

This chapter explores the work of Christopher Hussey, whose writing for the magazine *Country Life* from 1921, and as editor from 1933, provides a distinct viewpoint, that of a connoisseur and architectural historian rather than a professional architect; his work therefore has a pronounced cultural and social perspective. As Marcus Binney has explained, "As a writer on architecture he was overshadowed by the big names developing architectural history as an academic discipline—Wittkower, Summerson and Pevsner—but the breadth of his connoisseurship probably exceeded theirs" (2007: 166).

The architectural landscape between the wars was in turmoil stylistically, politically, and economically. While younger architects were continually searching for a new, national aesthetic for the next generation, there was at the same time a resurgence of interest in eighteenth-century Neoclassicism amid worries about the destruction of the British landscape and the escalating demolition of historic country houses, which engendered renewed concern for preservation and planning. Hussey's enduring interest in classical architecture of the Regency period reflected his views of the English country house and its relationship to the landscape, believing, as he did, that close affinities existed between the eighteenth century and his own time. For him one of the vital ingredients of Regency planning was the notion of the "picturesque," seen as underpinning the composition of the entire setting and described by David Watkin as representing "the triumph of illusion where the styles of other ages and cultures are tried on like theatrical costumes and where architecture is designed like scenery and gardens like paintings" (1982: 12).

In practice, the notion of the picturesque was wholly concerned with visual values, the outcome of a new attitude paralleled by Neoclassicism and the Romantic movement in painting. It was informed by principles of architecture devised by Sir Uvedale Price in his *Essay on the Picturesque, as Compared with the Sublime and the Beautiful* (1796) and was carried forward into the realm of aesthetic psychology by Richard Payne Knight's *Analytical Inquiry into the Principles of Taste* (1805). Throughout the nineteenth century, architects had been inspired by such writers, romantically conceiving that buildings should be enjoyed in visual terms as part of a landscape setting, the unity of the composition accruing value through its asymmetrical massing. Hussey embraced the concept, adding his own volume, *The*

Picturesque: Studies in a Point of View, in 1927, in which he pioneered the notion that the picturesque proceeded from painterly visions of artists such as Claude Lorraine and Niccolo Poussin, which were delivered to architecture in the form of buildings in the landscape.

Hussey's own country house, Scotney Castle in Kent, was inherited from his uncle, though he did not take possession until 1952, when he was age fifty-three. As a child he had spent regular holidays there, and though he was not always comfortable in the family's company, the house and its surroundings became his constant inspiration, providing the roots from which his appreciation of the ideal of the picturesque was formed. He wrote to his wife after he took her there for the first time after they were married in 1935, "It was such an adventure—taking you to *Scotney*. That scene, you know, means a lot to me—background, retreat, never-never land; and I am shy of showing it to people in case they hurt me by reacting wrongly" (Cornforth 1988: 70). Such sentiments validate Hussey's visual awareness learned from his parents (both competent artists) and his own enthusiasms for drawing and painting houses, gardens, and the countryside. Communication through writing and painting befitted someone who, throughout life, suffered from a pronounced stutter.

Figure 4.1

The new house, entrance front, *Scotney Castle,* Kent (1835–1843). Anthony Salvin (architect). Reproduced by kind permission of *Country Life* Picture Library CL 07/06/2007.

The Scotney estate principally comprised two houses united by a landscape. In the valley, surrounded by a moat, nestled the romantic ruins of the medieval castle, and at the top of the hill stood the newer house built in 1837 for Hussey's paternal grandfather Edward Hussey III by Anthony Salvin, an architect who had made his name designing country houses in the Elizabethan Revival style (Figure 4.1). This house was built from the golden streaky sandstone that was quarried locally. The entrance front was dominated by a crenelated central tower, while tall chimneys and scenic massing of various gables gave variety to the façade and animation to the roofline. The garden front was plainer and sparsely detailed, and the whole house was elevated on a grassy mound to afford it the most advantageous sight lines; the tall bay windows with sliding sashes framed the setting and offered unrestricted views south and east over the garden and down to the castle beneath (Figure 4.2).

Hussey's passionate fascination with the picturesque had begun at Scotney around 1924, his watershed moment occurring while contemplating the alluring views from the library down to the castle. He had always assumed the vista to be a natural one, but he suddenly realized that what he was actually seeing was the clever connivance of his grandfather's architect. Here was an entirely contrived environment devised first and foremost for the pleasure of visually savouring the landscape. He wrote,

Figure 4.2

View from the balcony of the new house to the ruins of the castle below, *Scotney Castle*, Kent. Reproduced by kind permission of *Country Life* Picture Library CL 09/09/1999.

> Through the windows of that room you see in a valley below, a castle, partly
> ruined on an island in a lake. A balustrade cresting a cliff forms the foreground,
> a group of Scots firs and limes the side-screens. Beyond, a meadow melts in
> the woods rising to a high skyline . . . it formed the perfect picture . . . The
> very scene before me so far from being happy co-incidence, must have been
> planned on picturesque principles. (Garnett 2007: 11)

His surmise was supported by the fact that he uncovered in his grandfather's library a
yellowing volume of Sir Uvedale Price's *Essay on the Picturesque* (1796). This was the
first time that Hussey could put a name to his own aesthetic motivations, being rather
taken aback that they were, "no more than the product of heredity and environment"
(Cornforth 1988: 73). This was proof that the picturesque as an aesthetic theory was
already understood by his ancestor a hundred years before.

Hussey's discovery of picturesque theories was fundamental to the development
of his intellectual approach, which extended far beyond the writing-up of country
houses for *Country Life* but encapsulated his ideas on the history of landscape design,
the role of architecture in the landscape, and the relationships between them. It is
therefore surprising to discover that, at roughly the same time that he was displaying
his romantic proclivities for the picturesque at Scotney, he was being seduced by his
reading of the first copy, in French, of Le Corbusier's *Vers une architecture* (1923).
Noel Carrington, his colleague at *Country Life* and cofounder of the DIA (Design and
Industries Association), remembered being passed the same rather dog-eared copy
showing evidence of Hussey's keen perusal. At the end of 1923 they both joined the
63 Club in London's Oxford Street, an enthusiastic but short-lived group that aimed to
bring Le Corbusier's rational theories of a mechanical, standardized aesthetic to a wider
audience. Other members included Frederick Etchells (translator of Le Corbusier's work)
and Serge Chermayeff (at the time working on interior decoration for Waring & Gillow).

On a tour of Bavaria and northern Germany in 1928 and 1931, Hussey began to see
early developments in European Modernism at first hand. He wrote to his friend Billa
Cresswell,

> Keep your eyes open for the modern German architecture. It is immensely
> interesting. We have nothing to compare with it here. Of course judged by
> classic or picturesque, or any other standards, it is "ugly." But so is everything
> else new. Often it is highly effective and sometimes thrillingly adventurous. The
> great thing is that it is serviceable and expresses the spirit of today. Whether it
> is architecture is another thing. (Cornforth 1981: 1368)

Significantly, 1931 was the same year that Hussey wrote an article for *Country Life*
on the first truly modern house to be built in England, namely, High and Over at
Amersham. Architects Amyas Connell and Basil Ward had both trained in the classical
tradition, and their client, Bernard Ashmole, was professor of classical archaeology at
London University. Hussey believed that such backgrounds had considerable bearing on
the concept of the building.

The affinities of "High and Over" lie with the Mediterranean, and ultimately with the practical ideals of classic civilization. It is natural at first sight, the building should startle. But the more one studies the whole arrangement the more reasonable a building does it reveal itself to be. It may sound paradoxical but it is a pure expression of the classic mentality. (Hussey 1931: 303)

The house was perched on the hilltop, its novel Y-shaped plan topped with aircraft-wing canopy screening north-east winds, while a continuous strip of steel-framed, plate-glass windows allowed maximum light to enter the house, which afforded panoramic views over the 13-acre landscape to the old town of Amersham. Arbiters of taste with perfect comprehension of the classical past like Hussey, brought up on a diet of proportion and moderation, could only admit that the house had some contemporary merit and believed that the planning authorities had a duty to allow such experimental architecture to go ahead. High and Over, he maintained,

Figure 4.3

High Cross Hill, Dartington Estate, Devon (1932). Howe and Lescaze (architects). Reproduced by kind permission of *Country Life* Picture Library CL 11/02/33.

is sound and stimulating architecture. . . . There is nothing in its clean level lines nor in its whiteness that does not harmonize with the rolling chalk uplands. It does in fact conform carefully to the contours of the site. But bears no pretence to having grown out of the soil . . . but says frankly "I am the home of a twentieth century family that loves air and sunlight and open country." (Hussey 1931: 307)

Hussey understood that adjustments had to be made in the light of present circumstances related to new standards of living and possibilities afforded by new materials and technologies. He accepted the fact that such changes would inevitably result in various forms of machine production and standardization. The only downside of this continual search for conformity, he argued, was when it was used inappropriately across the board and taken to extremes. He felt that such features would not sit comfortably with the English psyche. In 1933 Hussey reported on what was to become a supreme example of modern architectural logic in Britain. High Cross Hill in Dartington, Devon, was designed by architects Howe & Lescaze and built for W. B. Curry, scientist and headmaster of the Dartington Hall estate school, which was developed as a pioneering education center for the arts by Americans Mr. and Mrs. L. K. Elmhurst. In Hussey's opinion, it was "probably the most extreme instance in England of the functional type of house associated with the name of Corbusier" (Hussey 1933a: 147) (Figure 4.3). After the first shock of its originality, he was overwhelmed by the notion of a house scientifically and uncompromisingly designed to meet the material requirements of the age.

> Even while the heart still hankers after seemly houses that fit into their landscapes and our preconceived notions as perhaps, we used to feel about those new-fangled streamlined motor-cars that had nothing in common but their purpose as the wagonettes and landaus with motor engines that for a time kept up a bowing acquaintance with their prototypes, and disguised the fact that a revolution in transport had taken place. (Hussey 1933a: 147–8)

Hussey's and *Country Life*'s sponsorship of the exhibition *British Industrial Art in the Home* at Dorland Hall, Lower Regent Street, from June to July 1933 emphasized his continuing determination to promote British industrial products and the serious role that he envisaged for modern architecture and design in Britain's housing regeneration. The year 1933 was a defining moment for Hussey; planning the exhibition had taken eight years, and he had assumed the editorship of *Country Life*. The second exhibition at Dorland Hall was organized in 1934, and this time Oliver Hill took the lead. Toward the latter years of the 1930s evidence suggests that Hussey was growing disenchanted with the extremes in modern architecture that were being demonstrated by the younger generation. Architectural historian David Watkin contended that Hussey was becoming increasingly impatient with advanced modern movement practices, "for their totalitarian insistence . . . and lack of sensitivity to local conditions" (1979: 88).

While such radical practices may have represented a bridge too far for Hussey, there were still a growing number of architects in Britain who believed that such progressive themes would eventually lead to the improvement of the material conditions of the whole society. Commenting on the state of modern architecture in the interwar period, theorist and architectural historian Anthony Jackson, for example, recognized the significance of the modern house purely as "a statement of a rationalist approach that could raise standards and cut costs" (1970: 64), while architect Raymond McGrath enthused that "the future is in the hollow of our hands. In the wide windows of the twentieth-century house are framed the white towns of tomorrow" (1934: 210). Hussey, however, was critical of such a viewpoint, believing it to be uncompromising, even fanatical, in its total disregard for landscape and the English context. The middle path, which in Hussey's view had been attempted successfully in Britain in the 1930s in one or two cases, had been the keynote of the 1933 exhibition and served to show a clear pathway for the industrial arts as the main ingredient of a solid and progressive national style. He wrote, "Its [industrial art's] scope is extremely wide and only the narrow-mindedness of enthusiasm can maintain that because we have a new technique therefore the rich idiom and associations that compose our aesthetic heritage must be wholly jettisoned . . . there is room for both; the original and the adapted form" (Hussey 1933b: 682).

Figure 4.4

Bentley Wood, Halland, Sussex (1937–1938), south front. Serge Chermayeff (architect). Reproduced by kind permission of *Country Life* Picture Library CL 02/11/40.

The house that Serge Chermayeff completed in 1938 for his own residence, Bentley Wood in Halland, Sussex, was perhaps the finest example of a modern living space and a significant contribution to immediate prewar domestic housing in the International Style. It was described by Professor Charles Reilly as "lovely, crystal white and golden cedar . . . a regular Rolls Royce of a house" (1938: 479). It was widely reported on, both in professional architectural journals and in decorative arts magazines, including two articles by Hussey for *Country Life* (1940a, 1940b). In previous examples we have seen Hussey's constant preoccupation with the importance of country houses responding to context (Figure 4.4). At Bentley Wood on a wooded slope overlooking the South Downs, the terrain could not have afforded a better opportunity to engage with the landscape. The long rectangular building was a study in proportion, constructed principally of a timber frame sitting on a brick plinth, with a regular line of six balconied bays glazed on the ground floor and glazed and set back on the bedroom floor. The cream-painted windows and buff-colored brick and red cedar cladding (weathered to silver-grey) complemented its place in the woodland setting. The terrace extended at right angles to the stark outline of the house, which provided a visual contrast to the landscape beyond. From the inside the occupants had uninterrupted views through floor-to-ceiling glass sliding doors set in recessed tracks, with stone paving blurring the inside/outside boundaries.

Hussey admired the way the house and the land worked together in framing the open space, believing that it demonstrated the underlying visual sense of the picturesque that had so continually animated his vision. There was also the added advantage of a Henry Moore sculpture, *Recumbent Figure* (1938), positioned at the furthest point of the garden, which formed a point of contemplation, just as the ruins at Scotney had done, standing well away from the building while acknowledging relationships between them. After his initial visit, Hussey wrote that he was "stimulated by its sanity and freshness, by its courageous but reverent restatement of basic values" (1940a: 303). He also took the opportunity to restate his views on the importance of garden design in developing connections to modern architecture while preserving the natural character of the site:

> The general effect aimed at here might be described as a fragment of an idyllic landscape of which the gentle contours and the tree groupings provide the contrasts needed by the austere lines of the building. . . . The house itself is conceived as part of the garden, in that the ground-floor windows fold away completely so that terrace and living rooms are thrown into one. The terrace is extended at the side of the house to an out-of-doors dining space which is continued as a "green gallery" southwards screened to the east by the long windbreak wall of buff brick. (1940a: 303)

The warmth of Hussey's reaction to Bentley Wood confirmed once more that what he valued most, the picturesque setting, need not be sacrificed to modernity but was the inheritor of it. He believed that the designer of the house not only demonstrated a constructive imagination, a functional response to the plan upholding traditional principles of materials, but also displayed Chermayeff's appreciation of the English landscape, which in this house was fully reconciled with the modern aesthetic. Could Bentley Wood have been for Hussey some satisfactory resolution of the picturesque in modern architecture that he had first encountered through the windows of the library at Scotney? He was ready to accept that nature sometimes needed a little prompting so that vistas could be framed to the best advantage. In the modern setting at Bentley Wood, modern sculpture addressed the need for a focal point to the distant view from the house, while the right angles of the house and wall produced a constructional framework, a scenic device for the view toward the house.

There were, of course, dissenting voices to Hussey's view of Modernism, seeing it as a regressive stance within British architecture rather than a fully appreciative discovery of Modernism's functional pluses. It is acknowledged that Hussey's attempts to draw parallels with classicism and the picturesque continually informed his enjoyment of the country house. However, what I believe he expressed in his writing for *Country Life* was a determination to adapt to the contemporary world, to utilize Modernism's redeeming qualities in order to discover a modern aesthetic for the nation and to move its architecture forward. Connections with the past were made in order not to lose sight of the traditional aesthetic values of place and context that had provided a sure haven for design throughout British history.

References

Binney, M. (2007), "Scotney Castle," *Country Life*, June 7: 166.

Cornforth, J. (1981), "Continuity and Progress," *Country Life*, October 22: 1368.

Cornforth, J. (1988), *The Search for a Style: Country Life and Architecture 1897–1935*,

London: Andre Deutsche with *Country Life*.

Garnett, O. (2007), *Scotney Castle: The New House*, interim guidebook, London: The

National Trust.

Hussey, C. ([1927] 1967), *The Picturesque: Studies in a Point of View*, Hamden: Archon Books.

Hussey, C. (1931), "High and Over, Amersham, Bucks," *Country Life*, September 19: 303–7.

Hussey, C. (1933a), "High Cross Hill, Dartington, Devon," *Country Life*, February 11: 147–9.

Hussey, C. (1933b), "Dorland Hall Exhibition: British Industrial Art in the Home, 20th June to 12th July 1933," *Country Life*, June 24: 682.

Hussey, C. (1940a), "Bentley, near Halland, Sussex," *Country Life*, October 26: 303–7.

Hussey, C. (1940b), "Bentley, near Halland, Sussex: A Modern Country House II," *Country Life*, November 2: 388–93.

Jackson, A. (1970), *The Politics of Architecture: A History of Modern Architecture in*

Britain, London: The Architectural Press.

Knight, R. P. (1805), *An Analytical Inquiry into the Principles of Taste*, London: T. Payne.

Le Corbusier (1923), *Vers une Architecture*, Paris: Editions Crès.

Le Corbusier (1927), *Towards a New Architecture*, trans. F. Etchells, London: John Rodke.

McGrath, R. (1934), *Twentieth-Century Houses*, London: Faber & Faber.

Price, Sir Uvedale (1796), *An Essay on the Picturesque, as Compared with the Sublime and the Beautiful*, London: J. Robson.

Reilly, Professor C. (1938), "Bentley Wood," *The Architects Journal*, September 22: 479.

Watkin, D. (1979), "Architectural Writing in the Thirties," *Architectural Digest*, AD Profile 24 49 (12): 84–9.

Watkin, D. (1982), *The Buildings of Britain*, London: Barrie & Jenkins.

Chapter 5

Inside Out: Spectacle and Transformation

Chris Hay and Pat Brown

This chapter considers the relationship between inside and outside by exploring interiority on an urban scale. We examine a particular interior/exterior condition situated in east London. The environment in question is the former Olympic Park, created to act as the principal venue and primary focus for the London 2012 Olympic and Paralympic Games held in the United Kingdom that summer for a period of just over one month.

We are interested in this particular environment because, according to its promoters, it was originally designed to stage a global spectacle and, once the games were over, to act as a catalyst for the long-term transformation of a relatively poor part of east London. The scale of the ambition was made clear in the Lower Lea Valley Framework Report, which included the Olympic site. The report stated that "the overall aim of regeneration in the Lower Lea Valley is for it to become a vibrant, high quality and sustainable mixed use city district that is fully integrated into the urban fabric of London set within unrivalled parkland and a unique network of waterways" (Mayor of London 2007).

The Olympic Park therefore has had two distinct roles. The first was a short-lived one in which an international event took priority, and the second is a long-term one in which it is being transformed to provide a context for physical, social, and economic change. The second role will stretch over a much longer time frame, and the development of the various sites that are marked on the post–Olympic master plan 2030 will depend on the vagaries of the market conditions in which "regeneration" currently operates within the United Kingdom.

We suggest that, to achieve both of these aims, the park had to turn itself inside out once the games were over. A condition of intense interiority was turned into its opposite, one of exteriority, so that the park, now in legacy mode, could better act on, and increasingly stimulate change in the surrounding city.

tes the marked disjunction between the park and the city that
d during the games themselves. We make a comparison with
ietery, Stockholm, the subject of a shared paper for the Flow
considered the cemetery interior and the exterior city as both
separate and mutually dependent. In contrast, the exterior of the Olympic Park is
treated as territory ready to be appropriated and then colonized. This situation raises
questions about the overall ambition of the park and its immediate periphery and
neighborhoods; it also questions on whose terms the regeneration of the latter is
being offered.

The Olympic Park: Place

The Olympic Park is situated in the River Lea Valley. The river "was once celebrated as
a fishing stream" (Ackroyd 2007: 48). However, by the 1850s, this bucolic scene was
overtaken by rapid and unplanned development, and the conditions were such in and
around the now Olympic area that in 1855 Alfred Dickens, brother of Charles, was
commissioned by the General Board of Health to recommend improvements to public
health in the light of a situation in which "open ditches carried both domestic and
industrial refuse, roads were unpaved and where Cholera was rife" (Powell 1973).
  Beneath the site,

> there are the stones from the Roman road to Colchester and bones of people
> who died in the Great Plague, but it was the 19th century varnish and soap
> makers and rubber plants around the River Lea, and print works, iron foundries,
> fertilizer factories and distilleries around Bow Creek and the Thames Junction
> Branch of Eastern Railways that made the whole area a receptacle of waste.
> (O'Hagan 2012: 39)

A century of industrial use and misuse followed, leaving a landscape "of industrial
parks that have taken the place of the 'stink industries' upon its banks" (Ackroyd
2007: 48).
  The River Lea is 68 kilometers long, and in its southern reaches, where the
Olympic Park is sited, it flows through what were seen as "some of the most deprived
communities within London," where, for example, "unemployment is high and health
poor" (Rose 2005). These statistical indicators underpin the case for regeneration.
They also obscure the many ways the area was used, formally and informally, and the
diverse habitats that existed prior to the enclosure of the Olympic site.
  These complexities have been documented by Juliet Davis in her study *Inside the
Blue Fence*, in which she noted that there were "208 businesses operating on the site
and 782 separate parcels of land under different ownerships and . . . the site supported
a diverse range of cultural, recreational and productive uses" (Davis 2008: 11). A
blue fence bounded the Olympic construction site, defined the first outer edge of the
Olympic Park, and was thus an indicator of its interiority and otherness.

The Park as Interior

In *The Ten Books of Architecture*, Vitruvius imagines that fire, as a result of an accidental burning, creates a clearing in the forest (Vitruvius 2009: 37). He suggests that architecture arises out of making space, of clearing space, and of recognizing an interior, a place, that is, separated from the world outside, a condition of "profound interiority" (Dripps 1999: 3).

This manipulation of the ground described by Vitruvius links interiority and landscape. We can see how these conditions manifested themselves in one of the most celebrated of the twentieth century's landscapes, namely, the Woodland Cemetery in Stockholm. Realized between 1914 and 1940 by Gunnar Asplund and Sigurd Lewerentz and contained within a 3.6-kilometer stone wall, this is an interior, we argue, that orchestrates experience and performance in the context of mourning. Separated from, yet profoundly connected to, the life of the city that surrounds it, the landscape mediates between everyday life and the act of remembrance. The cemetery is inclusive, available to all and connected fundamentally to its community and place. It is a place where ceremony and ritual are both collective and individual; it is simultaneously a place of refuge and prospect.

We argue that the Olympic Park shares many of these features. Both places are heterotopias, examples of counterspaces "that interrupt the apparent continuity of normality and of everyday life" (Dehaene and De Cauter 2008: 4). They both have very particular relationships to time and to place. While the cemetery relates to timelessness and eternity, in contrast the Olympic Park is concerned, in its primary manifestation, with the fleeting, transient moment.

Following the stripping that took place on the site for the games, and after a period of reconfiguration and further building, the park, now renamed Queen Elizabeth Olympic Park, is intended to be both a destination in its own right, like London's Hyde Park, and a part of the city that surrounds it.

The relationship between the Olympic Park and the city beyond contrasts profoundly with that between the Woodland Cemetery and Stockholm. The cemetery, while distinct, enclosed, and interior, has a rapport and an inclusive exchange with the communities of the city outside. In contrast, the Olympic site was exclusive in its Olympic guise and since then has sought to reengage with its neighborhoods and the everyday routes beyond it. Its first ambition to be a unique destination and its later ambition to encompass everyday commonplaces are of completely different orders. These have resulted, we believe, in an ambiguity or ambivalence in the park that was built into its conception.

Both interiors, that of the cemetery and that of the park, were and remain enclosed by barriers, by a wall in the case of the cemetery and by a temporary security fence in the case of the park. These interior conditions "are contingent upon a precise mechanism of opening and closing" that both separates and conjoins (Dehaene and de Cauter 2008: 6). Each one is a world within a world, one that contains an orchestrated series of experiences arranged in particular sequences to enable people and events to ebb and flow in as seamless a way as possible. These landscapes are theaters in which the success, or otherwise, of events depends on the precise articulation and integration of front and back of house.

We suggest that both landscapes are textile surfaces on which the surface of the land is arranged to accommodate setting and communicate occasion. Reference can be made here to the writings of the nineteenth-century architect and theorist Gottfried Semper, in particular to Semper's theory of dressing: "the dressing (of the building) becomes a veiling camouflage or artistic mask, that is most relevant" (Semper 2004: 50).

We find the idea of dressing a persuasive one. Both vertical and horizontal planes can be dressed. Both interiors within buildings and interiors outside them can be dressed, and dressed appropriately, to conjure experience and distil meaning.

Dressed for the Occasion

One can see this concept of dressing at work in the Olympic Park. By considering time in section, as well as in plan, one can make explicit the accumulation of changes that have both taken place and are still to come. The surface decking, or dressings, that sit on the surface of the site were renewed prior to the games and then remade in the postgames period. The particular dressing for the Olympic occasion involved the radical horizontal separation of dressing from the ground beneath. The soil, the edaphic layer and growing medium at the interface between geological time and weathering, was replaced. The story is one of arsenic, asbestos, and heavy metals. The London Olympic home ground in the Lower Lea Valley accommodated industrial manufacturing that resulted in an accumulation of pollutants. This soil was stripped and capped, sent to a soil hospital, and reconstructed *ex situ*. It was then replaced to create a human health layer as a security blanket to cover the underlying industrial pollution and abandonment in order to stage a show of athleticism and spectacle above.

The sheering of the horizontal planes of the site was arguably as fundamental a separation of inside and out as the vertical barriers erected to regulate site entry and exit. It was less visible than the surface barriers, but just as explicit in defining what was acceptable in the interior and what was not. Where Olympic delivery was the main objective and the final goal preordained, the very nature of nature was denied. Natural processes were constrained in pursuit of a controlled scene of predictable and measurable costs in terms of care and content.

Figure 5.1

Final construction of the
Olympic Park, April 2012.
Wikimedia Commons, E G
Focus.

Dressing continues in the post-Olympic phase, in which surfaces and buildings are treated to express a particular intention, either the global or the local. One can see the global at work in the South Park, designed by James Corner Field Operations and Make Architects, who proposed a "compelling urban destination, for local, national and international visitors" (Field Operations n.d.). This area of the park offers, among its external spaces, a hub building that contains a café, event spaces, and a shop. The pavilion is composed of "vertical and horizontal planes that enclose both internal and external spaces, the spine walls of which provide the ideal location for art and media projections" (Make Architects n.d.). Its abstract language, an updating of the International Style of the interwar years of the twentieth century, ensures that its dressing complements the global aspirations of the major structures around it.

In contrast, the North Park, designed by Land Use Consultants and Erect Architects, is conceived as local. Here the park addresses "ecological processes linking into the surrounding riverine landscape" (Land Use Consultants n.d.). Primarily for children and families, this area of the park also contains its own hub building, with a similar program to that of the South Park. "The building is treated as an extension of the landscape, where interior and exterior spaces relate to each other" (Erect Architects n.d.), and this time the structure is clad, or dressed, in weathered hardwood.

This separation of global and local is somewhat artificial, as both spaces simultaneously embody these possibilities. However, both parks are dressed for the occasion, as was the Olympic stadium, which was clothed in an exterior wrap, funded, rather controversially, by the Dow Chemical Group.

Remembering and Forgetting

There are profound differences in approach between the cemetery and the Olympic Park. We note that interior practice, when concerned with altering existing buildings, shares with landscape practice "existing conditions" that have to be considered as part of the design process. They are both practices of adaption. The Woodland Cemetery, for example, was created from what was already there. The existing was valued and adjusted, thus ensuring continuity between past, present, and by extension the future. Considered in this manner, interiors and landscape can be thought of as works in progress, part of the passage of time and never actually complete. The Woodland Cemetery exhibits precisely these characteristics. The design values the preexisting, including the existing intelligence present in the site, such as soil conditions, and the biological register. The proposal also draws on ideas present in society, such as equality in the face of death. The design is therefore rooted not only physically but also socially. The landscape expresses shared values and continuity. It is concerned with remembering.

Figure 5.2

The Woodland Cemetery, Stockholm, April 2012. Wikimedia Commons, Arild Vagen.

Figure 5.3

Olympic Park: Post Games transformation, July 2016. Chris Hay.

In contrast, the design of the Olympic Park started through processes of forgetting. The existing, in almost all its manifestations, was removed. As Iain Sinclair has noted, "it has not been a good year, the devastation of the ecology of the Lower Lee Valley [*sic*], with the loss of allotments, unofficial orchards behind abandoned lock keepers' cottages, native shrubs, wildlife habitats, disturbed the balance of a substantial chunk of London" (Sinclair 2011: 167). The local was deleted and the site became a blank slate on which to inscribe the Olympic ideal and an instant of perfection for the opening ceremony on July 27, 2012.

An Imperial Vision

The games were awarded to London partly on the basis of the city's plans for a legacy. This idea went far beyond the adaptation of Olympic-sized venues and the Athletes Village, the legacy of Barcelona, for example. According to the British foreign secretary, Jack Straw, "London's bid was built on a special Olympic vision that will not only be a celebration of sport, but also a force for regeneration. The Games will transform one of the poorest and most deprived areas of London" (Straw 2005). This was a considerable ambition, and one that, we argue, is likely to be made more difficult by the discontinuity between global ambition and local realities.

Our concern is that, in order to be acceptable to an international audience and to express the national ambitions that are inevitably bound up in mounting the Olympic

Games, the park and its buildings can be considered as similar to a nineteenth-century imperial outpost that has been imposed on the local condition. According to Edward Said, "Imperialism after all is an act of geographical violence, through which place is explored, charted, and finally brought under control" (Said 1994: 271). We suggest that an analogous process has been at work in the creation of the Olympic Park. This interior world is inevitably disconnected from the city that surrounds it. These are buildings and spaces that are expressions of national ambition, and as such they are akin to imperial spaces, such as those described by the urban historian Janet Abu-Lughod, to whose account of imperial Cairo Said refers.

> At the end of the 19th century Cairo consisted of two distinct physical communities, divided one from the other by barriers much broader than the single little street that marked their borders. The city's physical duality was but a manifestation of the cultural cleavage. . . . Neither parks or street trees relieved the sand and mud tones of the medieval city, yet the city to the west was adorned with French formal gardens. One entered the old city by caravan, the new by railroad. In short, on all critical points the two cities, despite their physical contiguity, were miles apart socially and centuries apart technologically. (Said 1994: 155–6)

This picture can be transposed to present-day London, with Hargreaves Associates' gardens for the Olympic site, which were designed in part to reflect national plantings of competitor countries (Hargreaves 2011), much like the formal French gardens of imperial Cairo. In both cases the landscape proposals reflect the imperial or Olympic ideal and have little connection with the local. They are extrinsic rather than intrinsic to the sites in question.

Interestingly, similar planting strategies were used to stage both the Great Exhibition of 1851 and an imperial event in the Pageant of London held in Sydenham, south London, in 1911. One of the attractions of the latter was an electric railway that took visitors through representations of the empire's dominions, passing "realistic scenery, colonial life and activity" (Driver and Gilbert 1991: 121).

In both parks, created some hundred years apart, there was a desire to connect the center with the periphery, the imperial capital with its colonies (in the case of the London Pageant) and the Olympic center (London) with the Olympic family of nations. This resulted in the construction of environments that did not immediately draw on their locations for their identity but rather sought to supplant them to express imperial ambition or Olympic spectacle. The local was cleared to make space for the "internal colonization of the home country" (Mitchell 2002: 17).

The Olympic Park depends on the application of political power for land acquisition, by compulsory purchase orders in a process akin to the way in which "empires move outward in space, as a way of moving forward in time. . . . [T]he 'prospect' that opens up is not just a spatial scene but a projected future of 'development'" (Mitchell 2002: 17).

Conclusion

This chapter has explored the relationship between inside and out by examining the concept of interiority on an urban scale and, in particular, the interior condition of the Olympic Park in east London. We are interested in this urban interior because it has been designed to stage spectacle on a global scale and, subsequently, to act as a catalyst for the transformation of a relatively poor part of east London. We have compared this contemporary urban landscape with the Woodland Cemetery, Stockholm, which also contains elements of spectacle and ritual and is integrated, in its own particular way, with the city of which it is a part.

We have sought to raise correspondences and differences between the two interior conditions and have argued that the relationships between inside and out in the case of the cemetery have ensured continuity of rapport over an extended period of time. When seeking to find analogous relationships in the case of the Olympic Park, we note that they are less distinct and more ambiguous. Here, in place of relationships of mutual support, the values that were so clearly encoded into the park's surfaces have begun to reach out, supplant, and subsequently colonize those of the city that surrounds it. The park has indeed turned inside out, and the ongoing effect of this is causing a major rewrite of the history of the Lea Valley and of east London, beyond the bounds of the Olympic Park.

References

Ackroyd, P. (2007), *Thames: Sacred River*, London: Catto & Windus.

Davis, J. (2008), *Inside the Blue Fence: An Exploration*. Available online: http://www.lse.ac.uk/LSECities/citiesProgramme/pdf/citiesLAB/citiesLAB_davis.pdf (accessed January 14, 2017).

Dehaene, M., and L. de Cauter, eds. (2008), *Heterotopia and the City: Public Spaces in a Post Civil Society*. London: Routledge.

Dripps, R. P. (1999), *The First House: Myth, Paradigm and the Task of Architecture*. Cambridge: MIT Press.

Driver, D., and D. Gilbert, eds. (1991), *Imperial Cities*. Manchester: Manchester University Press.

Erect Architects (n.d.), Photos of Timber Lodge at Queen Elizabeth Olympic Park. Available online: http://www.erectarchitecture.co.uk/projects/community/125-p-qeop-timber-lodge-and-tumbling-bay.html (accessed January 14, 2017).

Field Operations (n.d.), "South Park Plaza at Queen Elizabeth Olympic Park." Available online: http://www.fieldoperations.net/project-details/project/south-park-queen-elizabeth-olympic-park.html (accessed January 14, 2017).

Hargreaves, G. (2011), Lecture at the Landscape Institute AGM, London, October 13.

Land Use Consultants (n.d.), "Tumbling Bay Playground." Available online: https://landuse.co.uk/portfolio-items/tumbling-bay-playground-stratford/ (accessed January 14, 2017).

Make Architects (n.d.), "The Podium." Available online: http://www.makearchitects.com/projects/queen-elizabeth-olympic-park-podium/ (accessed January 14, 2017).

Mayor of London (2007), "Lower Lea Valley: Opportunity Planning Framework." Available online: https://www.london.gov.uk/file/8202/download?token=n4ezfLUz (accessed January 14, 2017).

Mitchell, W. J. T., ed. (2002), *Landscape and Power*, Chicago: University of Chicago Press.

O'Hagan, A. (2012), "Diary," *London Review of Books*, 34 (3): 39. Available online: http://www.lrb.co.uk/v34/n03/andrew-ohagan/diary (accessed January 14, 2017).

Powell, W. R., ed. (1973), "West Ham: Local Government and Public Services," *British History Online*. Available online: http://www.british-history.ac.uk/vch/essex/vol6/pp96-112 (accessed January 14, 2017).

Rose, D. M. H. (2005), "Report to the Secretary of State for Trade and Industry." Available online: http://www.gamesmonitor.org.uk/files/Inspectors%20recommendation%20to%20Secretary%20of%20State-3875798-1.pdf (accessed January 14, 2017).

Said, E. W. (1994), *Culture & Imperialism,* London: Vintage Books.

Semper, G. (2004), *Style in the Technical and Tectonic Arts* [German original c. 1860–62], Los Angeles: Getty Research Institute.

Sinclair, I. (2011), *Ghost Milk: Calling Time on the Grand Project*, London: Hamish Hamilton.

Straw, J. (2005), "London 2012 Olympic Bid," House of Commons Debate, July 6, 2005, c404. Available online: https://www.theyworkforyou.com/debates/?id=2005-07-06a.404.0#g404.1 (accessed January 14, 2017).

Vitruvius, P. (2009), *On Architecture* [c. 40 BC], trans. R. V. Schofield and R. Tavernor, London: Penguin.

Chapter 6

The Allegory of the Cave: Speculations between Interior and Landscape for the Barangaroo Headland Cultural Facility

Sing D'Arcy

Figure 6.1

View of the amphitheatre, 2011. Sophie Metcalfe's proposal for Music Acoustic Sounds Australia, Barangaroo, Sydney, Australia. Courtesy Sophie Metcalfe.

Barangaroo is the name that has been given to the redevelopment of the 22-hectare platform that skirts the harbor on the northwestern edge of central Sydney. As with its partner on Bennelong Point (where Sydney Opera House is located), the marriage of architecture, politics, and place has proven highly controversial. In what has been described as the "project of a generation" (Moore 2009), a park is being constructed *ex nihilo* at the northern end of the site. The design of the park references the topography of the site as it may have been in the early nineteenth century before its "vandalism" throughout the twentieth as the result of the city's industrial development (Moore 2009). Inhabiting the void on the verso side created by this act of landscape reconciliation will be a cultural facility that has yet to be assigned a program.

The cavelike structure of the cultural facility has resulted in a scenario in which the possibility of the iconic building as an architectural object has been denied. Instead the interior has become the spatial protagonist, sheltered by the landscape above. Since this was an opportunity to explore the possibilities of a productive collaboration between landscape and interior, final-year students from the Bachelor of Interior Architecture course at the University of New South Wales were asked to develop a program and a spatial response to this condition, one that was free from the conventional notions of interior/exterior as dictated by floor and facade. Through an analysis of the discourse and precedent of the cave and grotto as allegory, this paper seeks to explore not the controversy itself, but rather the potential that this rare confluence between landscape and interior can offer as a speculative proposition.

"Buildings Are the Very Reverse of Rocks"

Thomas Whately's observation (1770: 116) would confirm the opinion of most architectural critics of the Barangaroo Headland Park and cultural facility. The absence of architecture is the absence of building. From Vitruvius to Marc-Antoine Laugier, architecture is framed as diametrically opposed to the cave and the savage stages of human development associated with it; as Karsten Harries put it, "the forest is allowed to triumph over the cave" (1998: 115). David Gissen's work on subterranean spaces in architectural thought highlights the view that these dank spaces have generally been considered "fundamentally deficient spaces of human habitation" and "metaphorical space[s] of ignorance" (Gissen 2009: 30–1). The perceived inadequacies of the cave typology undoubtedly contributed to its alienation from mainstream architectural discourse. Gülsüm Baydar Nalbantoğlu, however, sees the purely interior, unstructured, and invisible nature of the cave as resulting in a topos that inherently "defies proper architectural analysis and conventional technologies of representation. The latter is constructed, visible and objectifiable. Architectural truth has come to mean leaving the cave behind" (1997: 89). The sentiment of this statement was recently echoed by Chris Hay and Pat Brown, who stated that "contrary to the 'product' or 'object,' landscapes and interiors confound creative representation" (2011: 6). Daniel Huppatz saw the legacy of the interpretation of the cave, even in the contexts of contemporary design theory, as contributing to "a disciplinary distinction between architecture and interior design" (2010: 143).

If we take the distinction as proposed by Huppatz, one whereby the interior embraces its primordial connection with the earthbound shelter, it can lead to what Gissen cited as the "potential new form of sensation" (2009: 36). While it is possible to cast the conception of the Barangaroo cultural facility in terms of the primordial return, it could also be read in the light of the tradition of the mythical grotto within the landscape, in what Diana Balmori saw as "Intermediate Structures" that articulated "the relationship between art and nature, and between divergent architect and landscape languages" (1991: 38). The design of grottoes during the Renaissance and particularly the Baroque periods drew on this paradoxical nexus between artifice and nature to create "ingenious architectural machines" and "ingenious architectural metaphors" (Hofer 2011: 205). The grotto operated as *machina* in the Baroque sense of a device or design that creates surprise, wonder, or a state of emotional affection in the person who experiences it, rather than the contemporary notion of a purely mechanical operation. While the rhetorical imperative of the Barangaroo cultural facility may not be as explicit as those of its seventeenth- and eighteenth-century counterparts, there is an inherent metaphoric, symbolic, and rhetorical program to the project, most notably the act of environmental restoration ("Barangaroo's Headland Park" 2011). In Nina Hofer's analysis of the seventeenth-century Grotte de Téthys at the Palace of Versailles, she stated that the grotto-as-machine, both metaphorically and architecturally, figures as a "moment of productive cooperation between natural forces and the actions of man. In such company, the machine is hardly artificial. It belongs to and extends nature" (Hofer 2011: 285).

I would argue that the metaphoric construction of the Barangaroo Headland Park has been cast in a similar vein by its proponents. There is no attempt to conceal the artificiality of the green reinstatement; rather, it celebrates the ingeniousness of the design it fulfils in a *deus ex machina* moment, "an historic opportunity to recreate the archipelago of headlands that once defined Sydney's inner harbour" ("Barangaroo's Headland Park" 2011: 2). This is an act that could not be achieved through purely conventional architectural means, as demonstrated by the Opera House and Bennelong Point. The design, while unfamiliar, is still recognizable as a work of architecture. The participation of landscape has been denied: its potential is subsumed into the concrete platform and skirt at the service of the building above. Whereas in this instance architecture overcomes landscape in a celebration of expression, the collaboration between interior and landscape has the ability to create "spaces of architectural overcoming," which "disrupt the striated, hierarchical methods of architectural production" (Smith 2005: 51).

It is at this crux that the Opera House and other works cited as cavelike, such as Eric Mendelsohn's Einstein Tower, Gottfried Böhm's Neviges Mariendom, or most palpably Han Poelzig's Grosses Schauspielhaus, differ from the approach put forward in this chapter. Compared with Peter Cook's 1964 Mound, Emilio Ambasz's Fukuoka scheme, or MVDRV's recent Galije project, which negate the architectural presence of their massive programs by burying them under vegetated embankments, the previously cited examples inherently rely on the separation of site and architecture rather than on "architecture and landscape as a single, collusive environment" (Spens 2007: 12). This form of disruption is manifest in the Barangaroo Headland Park cultural facility project, as the landscape/interior collaboration denies any possibility of an iconic civic building in the traditional sense—no recognizable facade, no recognizable form—and as such denies the gaze of an easily consumable and readily marketable brand (Jones 2011: 121). While this typology may rattle conventional notions of architectural production and representation, it cannot negate the fact that the monumental interior is also inherently embedded in, and the consequence of, the very same systems of politics and consumption (Pimlott 2007: 239).

The Studio Project

Design studio projects in university interior architecture programs rarely venture beyond the standard confines of the determined limits of an extant urban context, an architectural envelope, or a specified program. The Barangaroo Headland Park cultural facility, as the 2011 graduation studio project for the students in the Bachelor of Interior Architecture course at the University of New South Wales, offered them the opportunity of such a venture. Cathy Smith saliently observed that, when interiors and landscape are practiced outside of architecture, "projects reveal that environment-making is on open-ended speculative process" (2005: 51). It is in this context that I undertake an analysis of the studio projects. Rather than analyzing isolated schemes as stand-alone works, I refer to particular approaches in relation to aspects of the interior/landscape collaboration as discussed in the first section of this chapter.

Design Response

With over fifty students taking part in the design studio, the projects presented a diverse range of responses. While all the individual programs developed by the students were conditioned by the civic and cultural nature of the scheme, the design responses to each program saw three main approaches: landscape as container for the interior—the shell; interior as subtraction of landscape—the cave and grotto; and lastly, landscape and interior as continuous ribbon—the fold.

The Shell

Of the three typological approaches, "the shell," in which the program and its spatial manifestation were conceived as independent from the landscape above, is perhaps the most problematic. On the one hand, it provided a relatively straightforward spatial strategy to the accommodation and elaboration of the program, and subsequently of the interior architecture, in many cases producing quite spectacular and arresting designs, while on the other hand, it prompted a schismatic situation whereby the relationships between site, context, program, and space refused conventional reading or resolution. For a number of the students, this dualism between the process and product came to be their undoing, with the schemes being little more than generic containers for an anonymous scheme. Yet for others, the paradox of an absent architectural context, the landscape/interior situation, "site/non-site," and a sprawling, rambling promenade of infinite space and program opened the path to a critical and highly inventive speculation of the condition of the monumental interior and the genre-blur that is inherent to it (Spens 2007: 14).

Mark Pimlott identified this type of underground museum interior as a globalized hybrid of the shopping center, museum, and commercial office, one that is characterized by its spatial continuity, adaptability, and universality: "The type has aspired to be universal, to be all places and contain all contents . . . a continuous interior of totalized consumption" (2007: 239). In many ways Pilmott's description of the type aligns with Koolhaas's notion of "junkspace," of which interiority and continuity are defining elements (Koolhaas 2010: 137). Inherent to this approach taken by student projects was the clear acknowledgment and celebration of the complete artifice of the landscape above. "Air, water, wood: everything is enhanced to produce a Hyperecology sanctimoniously invoked for maximum profit" (Koolhaas 2010: 149). By taking this as a standpoint, it allowed the validation and exaggeration of the schism; rather than seeing it as a pristine natural landscape in which to insert a sensitive and discrete interior, students took the view that it was little more than a roof with some trees on top, a giant volume akin to a shopping mall or an airport with an open-ended cultural program.

While critics such as Miles Glendinning (2010: 167) are scathing in their criticisms of such designs that subscribe to the cult of the consumption of spectacle, individualistic extravagance, and ephemeral display, I would argue that, by freely speculating on such proposals, our next generation of designers is able to test its position on what role it and its designs will play in the shaping of the future built environment. Debate and reflection underpinned the design studio exercise and explicitly laid bare the theoretical and moral minefields often involved in the development of such projects linked to the mechanism of politics and power, as is the Barangaroo redevelopment.

Bojan Basara's Museum of Australian Sport sought to provide a facility to showcase the contribution of indigenous Australians to the nation's sporting heritage through an exhibition-style museum, as well as to provide a venue for the demonstration of new sport forms. Rather than responding to the language of the landscape above, Basara took the shell as a black-box site in which to create new interior urban networks and sports spaces to enact, to view, and to socialize. The enormity of the space was not viewed as an impediment, but rather as providing the opportunity to develop a hybridized interior that juxtaposed seemingly incongruous spatial models and diverse programmatic elements. The development of program and space manifests Koolhaas's dictum that Junkspace does not pretend to create perfection, only interest (2010: 149).

The Cave

The novel situation presented by an interior defined by a landscape proved to be a major source of inspiration for many of the students. Instead of taking the path of a clean separation between the massive park suspended above and a disconnected program below, the majority of schemes took the analogy of the cave as a starting point, and some schemes as their end point as well, in what Gissen termed "sites of uncharted and immense particularity" offering a "unique and underexplored spatial milieu" (2009: 30). The analogies ranged from geological processes involved in the formation of caves and their morphological traits, to the tectonic possibilities of stone and the tradition of subterranean interiors, to the sensorial experience of darkness, awe, and mystery for which caves and grottoes are so often admired.

Many of the students' projects actively addressed the subterranean context of the site. The landscape and interior were unified as one solid mass of stone, space being formed in an act of excavation. Naturalism was rejected in favor of tectonic formalism, a clear sign that this was a human endeavor, carefully planned and executed. Hubert Damisch posed the notion that these types of subterranean projects inherently lack the hallmarks of the classical architectural tradition. He described the Egyptian labyrinth as "this edifice lacking façade and forecourt, profile and contour, without a 'skyline,' and whose external aspect reveals nothing of its internal structure or plan, comprehensible only after the fact" (2001: 29).

The designs of Yunisa Sugianto's "Multicultural Exchange in Visual Arts" take their cues not from the glazed transparency of Sydney architecture, but rather from the labyrinth, embedding, as it does, a monolithic scheme into the rock of a new headland. Sugianto's project carves out a carefully choreographed series of chambers. Each afforded a different treatment of scale, materiality, and illumination according to programmatic hierarchy.

Whereas the Katsalidis Fender MONA project involved the excavation of some 60,000 tons of rock and sand to create the labyrinthine interior (Lohrey 2011: 216), Sugianto, like Basara, relished in the artifice and fiction of the headland recreation to construct a rhetorical and allegorical framework to suit. A-Yun Han and Mingjun Jennifer Ryu positioned their projects on the very extreme range of program and spatial conception. They proposed spaces that, unlike the rigorously worked examples above, posited hazy visions of jewel-encrusted grottoes.

In Han's scheme, the pearl-like shells that litter the interior landscape are spectacular in their reflectivity, strangeness, and complexity. They are much akin to a *galerie des glaces* in a Baroque palace or to more recent grottoes such as the one in Herrenhausen by Niki de Saint Phalle or Callum Morton's ingenious machine in Tilburg. Ryu's tenebrous, formless interior defies an immediate or total reading. The ceiling, walls, and floors reflect and blur image, prompting the persons experiencing them to immerse themselves in the program of sensory art, whether willingly or not: "The memory of the primordial caverns with the glittering walls haunts the later, manmade analogues of the sacred natural grotto" (Stafford and Terpak 2001: 72). The interior in Ryu's project creates a complete new world of artifice, spectacle, and affect that returns to Hofer's "grotto-as-machine" concept. The interior is devised to act on our senses, to prompt emotional responses of wonder, novelty, and surprise.

The Fold

In the two previous sections we saw how interior and landscape were treated as either disparate components, as in the shell example, or integrated but still maintaining the dyad of exterior as landscape and interior as the inverse of that space, as in the cave examples. The last grouping of schemes I wish to analyze sought to create a new condition in which landscape and interior were continuous and integrated both spatially and programmatically.

One of the most arresting propositions is Sophie Metcalfe's "Music Acoustic Sounds Australia (MASA)." It refers to the porosity of Sydney sandstone and specifically the cantilevered rock shelves that define the harbor's edge. This scheme comfortably relates to the earlier examples of designs inspired by geological processes, morphology, and tectonics, yet the design of MASA opens itself up to the park and to the city, actively engaging with the immediate surroundings. MASA develops the programmatic relationship to space and landscape in a less curated manner than many other projects. This allows for a greater degree of permeability throughout the schemes, a fact which I argue is a result of the unique relationship with the landscape in which it participates.

Conclusion

There is little doubt that the controversy that has dogged the Barangaroo development will continue well after the headland park and its indeterminate cultural facility are built. What program or programs will be accommodated is still to be determined. Irrespective of the final reality of the venture, the UNSW Interior Architecture studio project provided an opportunity for students to participate in the debate—a role not normally assigned to interior architects, let alone students. Beyond the political realities of both the studio and the scheme, the investigation of the development of interior spaces within the contexts of landscape proved to be a highly rewarding experience. The mediation of façade, while still present, was less powerful when presented as a rock edge, one meter of soil, or a harbor edge, albeit artificial conceits. This liberation encouraged a playful and speculative approach to the design process, resulting in a product of exceptional quality. Caves, long considered dank, dark spaces antithetical to architecture, have also acted as the "multidisciplinary womb: birthplace of art, graphic communication, interior design, multimedia design, information design and virtual reality" (Huppatz 2010: 138). While it may seem curious, and perhaps paradoxical, to complete a university education in interior architecture by returning to the primordial roots of the cave, this exercise has proven that, once designers and the world in which we design are unchained from the conventional ways of seeing, new synergies can be formed from what may previously have been regarded as the most improbable of situations.

References

Balmori, D. (1991), "Architecture, Landscape, and the Intermediate Structure: Eighteenth-Century Experiments in Mediation," *Journal of the Society of Architectural Historians*, 50 (1): 38–51.

"Barangaroo's Headland Park Gets Underway" (2011), Media release from the Barangaroo Delivery Authority. Available online: https://resource.barangaroo.com/hc/article_attachments/115015073807 /20110303%20Barangaroo's%20headland%20park%20gets%20underway.pdf (accessed 12 January 2018).

Damisch, H. (2001), *Skyline: The Narcissistic City*, Stanford: Stanford University Press.

Gissen, D. (2009), *Subnature: Architecture's Other Environments*, New York: Princeton Architectural Press.

Glendinning, M. (2010), *Architecture's Evil Empire? The Triumph and Tragedy of Global Modernism*, London: Reaktion Books.

Harries, K. (1998), *The Ethical Function of Architecture*, Cambridge: MIT Press.Hay, C., and P. Brown (2011), "Interior Topography and the Fabric of Terrain," conference paper presented at *Flow 1*, May 12–13, London: Kingston University. Available online: http://eprints.lincoln.ac.uk/4676/ (accessed January 13, 2016).

Hofer, N. (2011), "Charging the Waters: The Grotte de Téthys as Versailles's Initial Metaphoric Ground," *Architectural Research Quarterly*, 15 (3): 249–60.

Huppatz, D. (2010), "The Cave: Writing Design History," *Journal of Writing in Creative Practice*, 3 (2): 135–48.

Jones, P. (2011), *The Sociology of Architecture: Construction Identities*, Liverpool: Liverpool University Press.

Koolhaas, R. (2010), "Junkspace," in A. Sykes (ed.), *Constructing a New Agenda: Architectural Theory 1993–2009*, 134–151, New York: Princeton Architectural Press.

Lohrey, A. (2011), "High Priest: David Walsh and Tasmania's Museum of Old and New," in R. Koval (ed.), *The Best Australian Essays 2011*, Collingwood: Black.

Moore, M. (2009), "Storming the Headland," *Sydney Morning Herald*, September 19. Available online: http://www.smh.com.au/national/storming-the-headland-20090918-fvc8.html (accessed January 13, 2016).

Nalbantoğlu, G. B. (1997), "Limits of (in)Tolerance: The Carved Dwelling in the Architectural and Urban Discourse of Modern Turkey," in G. Nalbantoğlu and W. Chong Thai (eds.), *Postcolonical Space(s)*, 89–100, New York: Princeton Architectural Press.

Pimlott, M. (2007), *Without and Within. Essays on Territory and the Interior*, Rotterdam: Episode Publishers.

Smith, C. (2005), "Spaces of Architectural Overcoming," *IDEA Journal*, 6 (1): 51–59.

Spens, M. (2007), "From Mound to Sponge: How Peter Cook Explores Landscape Buildings," *Architectural Design*, 77 (2): 12–15.

Stafford, B., and F. Terpak (2001), *Devices of Wonder: From the World in a Box to Images on a Screen*, Los Angeles: Getty Research Institute.

Whately, T. (1770), *Observations on Modern Gardening Illustrated by Descriptions*, 2nd ed., London: T. Payne.

Chapter 7
45 Degrees

Jude Walton and Phoebe Robinson

Deeply mesmerizing and meditative, *45 degrees* is a live dance performance and a film that was cast and choreographed using the minimal architecture of a stairwell and the void it produces. Performed by Phoebe Robinson with video documentation by Cobie Orger, this work is one in a series of studies looking at bodies and the built environment. Directed by Judith Walton,[1] *45 degrees* takes an architectural form, in this instance a set of stairs at the Melbourne University School of Architecture, as a mold for the dance.

The film reveals two perspectives of the work, back and front, screened side-by-side. One view is molded by the architectural form of the stairs, while the other is referenced by a string line drawing the angle of 45 degrees in space.[2] The string is a way of redrawing the architecture of the stairs, since it has a similar provisional quality as the initial plan drawings, diagrams, and sketches for the building.

In the left frame, the gravitas of the heavy structure of the stairs compresses the dance, while in the right frame Phoebe dances with just the string line, as a mere light reference to the void below the stairwell. This performance demonstrates an embodied way to apprehend a building in terms of scale: length, breadth, height, and volume. The string in a sense produces a pattern of or for the architecture and provides a dimensionally acceptable mold for the dance, wherein Phoebe attempts to reenact her kinesthetic experience of moving under the stairwell.

Notes

1. Within this series, Judith Walton also directed *Lehte* and *Lehte II* at Heide Museum of Modern Art in 2014 and 2015.

2. Video link: https://vimeo.com/46333113

Figs. 7.1–7.8

45 Degrees, 2012. Photograph Cobie Orger.

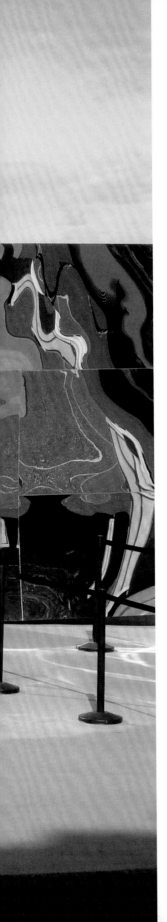

2

Part 2
Mobility

MONA, Hobart 2012 Gini Lee

Introduction

Gini Lee

Mobility theory espouses a social and a spatial practice where the flow in its many forms appears as a constant and underpinning dynamic confirming the understanding that people, and the places they live in, are subject to constant change, even in the face of the apparent solidity and stasis characteristic of the constructed world. In the social studies arena, mobilities research is regarded as a transdiciplinary field concerned with spatial mobility that reaches across human and nonhuman geographies, territories, and everyday situations. In the urban and architectural world that encompasses cities and the movement of people and objects, mobility concepts are typically framed through the dynamics of urban infrastructures, flow lines, and technologies of connectivity. For *Flow: Interior, Landscape, and Architecture in the Era of Liquid Modernity*, the papers curated under Mobility are seen to interrogate the complex relations between inside and outside, interior and landscape. The authors and practitioners offer diverse ideas, theories, and everyday examples that expand notions of spatial and material mobility in the context of design academia and realized practice.

Mobility is a multidimensional concept that, like the other parts in this book, on nature, continuum, and frames, critically enables multilateral thinking as it projects compelling dichotomies that invoke the potential for mobilities theory to influence spatial operations in places of diversity. Moving between nomadism and stasis and between situated, bounded space and the space of flows and systems, design theory and practice negotiate forms of mobility that are simultaneously grounded and intangible. Andrea Kahn demonstrates this fluidity in her writing on the nature of site conditions as she seeks to define the processes that characterize our relational interactions with urban space. Mobile ground is proposed as one of Kahn's five concepts for urban site thinking and as a negotiated "field of action." Observation of the flow back and forth among the various human (and nonhuman) players in urban development, place occupation, and everyday life reveals the perceptual lenses that inform site transformations across variable operational fields. Kahn's definition below focuses on the urban condition but equally senses the combinations of strategy, open-endedness, and flexibility of action and interaction as essential to encouraging fluid interior and landscape perspectives in site practices (the ~~urban~~ strikethrough is my emphasis).

Inscribe a *mobile ground* where ~~urban~~ sites are understood as dynamic and provisional places, as points of departure to parts unknown rather than as places of arrival of fixed address. Conceiving of ~~urban~~ sites as mobile foregrounds their provisional condition, reminding designers that sites remain subject to change beyond their control. On mobile ground, ~~urban~~ design actions are best considered in strategic terms—focused on framing ~~urban~~ relations and structuring ~~urban~~ processes. Mobile ground describes a space of progression, slippage, and continual revaluation, where diverse realities tip over, into and out of each other. It is where site boundaries and site images shift, bend and flex, depending on who is looking. (Kahn 2005: 289–90)

Elias Constantopoulos's paper, "The Indignant Beton," demonstrates Kahn's observations through a three-part discussion that flows between the realities of daily life in contemporary Athens and the development of the architectural project that navigates conceptually between solidity and transparency, and materially between concrete and glass. Challenging the duality implicit in the stasis of home life with the civic space of the street, the "Indignant Beton" flows across tangible and intangible material, merging the spatial and social forms of the Athenian topography. The palimpsest of the personal is argued alongside the external dynamics that impel the desire to leave the concrete interior of one's home, to occupy the square in an indignant mood. Occupied civic space is thus transformed into a new home where the irate are able to connect, communicate, and navigate the politically charged event in a space built for a purpose but now attaining meaning beyond the purely civic. Constantopoulos writes on the interior dwelling as a contributor to the expansion of multiple concrete apartment boxes and intersecting street lines that drape and flow across the hillsides of his city. Despite the anonymous reality of the apartment, he seeks reconciliation with modernity through architectural form and materiality. Yet, beyond the unrealized architectural promise, the mobile ground in this city is to be found in the political consequences of community indignation and the need to congregate through the agency of an activated mobile ground that draws people to move out from the home to the street and thus to the square.

Mobilities theorists do not conflate their constructs with the well-known theories of nomadism, flow, and deterritorialization (Deleuze and Guattari 2013/2003) or the distinctions that arise in the metaphorical devices that accompany the social perspectives defined by the "liquid" spaces of flows and the "solid" spaces of places (Castells 1996). Instead they embrace the coexistence of mobilities and immobilities. Sheller's overview of mobilities theory "places an unprecedented emphasis on (im)mobility, moorings, dwelling and stillness as much as movement, speed, or liquidity" (Sheller 2011: 1). Spatial mobility is a component of the field that includes investigations into the degree of sedentary/stasis and mobile/nomadic interactions of people with their socio/spatio/temporal worlds. Space and place geographies provide the physical context for the practices of movement that traverse between places of stillness and pause and those of mobility where the performative routines overlie and influence ground conditions alongside more virtual connections.

Traversing across space and time is a quality of the form of experimental filmmaking described as structural film and revealed in Eleanor Suess's exploration of Canadian director Michael Snow's *Wavelength* (1967). A film without an apparent narrative plot, *Wavelength* utilizes tactics that constitute the basis of structural film: fixed camera position, flicker effect, loop printing, and rephotography. It is the slow and relentless exposure to the material, aural, and haptic qualities of a single room and the events that take place in it over time that provides the audience's deep immersion in the site and the situation. Much of the film concerns stillness and slowing the speed of the room to allow the durational and temporal qualities of night and day to provoke a new awareness of the material qualities and small changes in the room and its atmospheres. Suess's interest in the relationships between the processes of filmmaking and the production of an architectural moving drawing conflates the static form of the drawing and the mobility of filmic narrative.

The process of apprehending the subject interior as an architectural representation of the room alongside architectural elements contributing as actors in the tableau is suggested as a device to enable recreation of new experiences beyond the moment of viewing and is further expanded in Suess's exhibition work *Projective Views* as a counterpoint to her theoretical examination of Snow's oeuvre. Utilizing the window as the change element—the juxtaposition of views between the real-time spatial view and the projected facsimile of an alternative space far away—produced a conflation of time and space, between the real, haptic, and aural experience of the gallery and the miniaturized yet compelling occupation of the space of here and of there. Developing the idea of the architectural device as a model and facsimile of real space is a scale- and narrative-shifting tactic to advance spatial mobility across dimensions.

Mobilities concepts embrace the corporeal and the imaginative, the concrete and the abstract, and, most importantly, the relational dynamics that enable the active coexistence of these seemingly opposing states. The literature reveals a lexicon for mobility that includes compelling words such as *network*, *turbulence*, and *flow* alongside equally ameliorating terms like *dwelling*, *pause*, and *stillness* (Sheller 2011). The key element of mobilities thinking suggests that these dual concepts are interdependent, just as the mobile phone network depends on the sequence of ground-based phone towers to function. Simmel's concept of urban metabolism suggests that cities are reliant on the movement of human interactions in combination with the immobility of object forms for their shape and identity (Sheller 2011).

Through mobile ground thinking, dichotomous concepts are dissolved; situations are no longer either/or, but rather negotiated as both, potentially devoid of hierarchy, and more creatively and effectively responsive to disruption and change. Grounding mobility requires the interaction of complex systems that embrace the physical and the social, as well as the networked and constructed elements of cities, places, buildings, interiors, and landscapes. Pertinent to the understanding and ongoing life of historical properties are the contemporary spatial and material qualities of these places and the apprehension of their "use value" today. The heritage place and/or curated situation/event are built upon precedence and the collection of knowledge and artifacts housed within the archive or ever present in the trace palimpsest embodied in the structure.

Transformation, erasure, material, and narrative juxtapositions are the processes that inform the trajectory of places and their people over time. The transformation of the spatial and social structure of the Republican Home in Santa Fé de Bogotá is the subject of Patricia Lara-Betancourt's tracing of the shifts in lifestyle in the nineteenth-century home due to changing political and economic fortunes. In many ways the traditional home, characterized by flowing hallways, inner courtyards accessed by all, and an openness to the flow of people from the street into the inner sanctum and its attendant gardens, was turned inside out by new bourgeois concerns for comfort and privacy, separation from daily mundane activities, and a desire for an interior lifestyle modeled on European precedent. Imported concepts required new methods for negotiation of the basic colonial structure of the house and an attendant flexibility in the social structure of the house forced by new spatial proclivities. The houses' open address to the civic nature of the city was overwritten by imported styles and goods suited to global prosperity and a more mobile worldview.

Revealing change over time takes an alternative form in Gini Lee and Dolly Daou's visual essay derived from an installation mounted in the FLOW 2 Melbourne exhibition. *A Place Out of the Archive: Reprise under [the Condition] of Flow* (2012) is first a journey through content extracted from the Architecture Archive, followed by a series of tours revisiting these important civic places to record the material and spatial conditions of their working interiors, as places of heritage interest and intrigue. Revisiting again and rephotographing in the same way through an intention to blur the interiors into a contemporary color field produced abstract impressions of the atmospheres and interactions. This experiment in the presentation of flows across the temporal boundaries of the cultural and spatial again produces a palimpsest where the layers seek to collapse distinctions between what was once there, what is now, and what the future might hold.

Ole Jensen adopts Shane's concepts of armature and enclave in his exploration into the meaning of urban mobility, hoping to expand upon the normative opinion that regards the fixity of enclaves as bounded territory (sedentary) and the seeming mobility of armatures as linear and transit systems (nomadic) (Jensen 2009: 140). Challenging the dichotomy inherent in these basic definitions, Jensen suggests that both systems display elements of openness to their surroundings where borders are often permeable to the crossing of the networks and flows afforded by armature infrastructures. Architects KTA diagram their enclaves and armatures as combined and overlaid assemblages producing spatial devices to confront the inferred oppositional frame between ground and field. Across three projects, Kerstin Thompson expands upon KTA's transdisciplinary thinking and practice-based understanding of the critical relational aesthetics and processes that inform collaborations between interior and exterior, public and private, architecture and landscape. KTA see their architectural elements as bridging concepts that collapse distinctions between spatial flow and enclosure and public and private occupation. The other theoretical dichotomy, between sedentary place-based thinking and nomad flow and mobile thinking, sees Jensen paraphrasing, on the one hand, Sennett's concerns for material and environmental alienation from the here and now produced by constant bodily circulations, and, on the other, contrasting to the freedom implied in the expanded territory of the nomad (Jensen 2009: 141–2). KTA's response appears to confirm that the architectural project is one that embraces mobility and grounded works simultaneously. Through enunciating the importance of challenging disciplinary boundaries, their works adopt a mobile, nonhierarchical perspective that mediates between inside and outside, enclave and armature, public and private, designer and occupant.

The dynamics of mobility/mobilities thinking on conceptualizing spaces require critical interaction with and commitment to transdisciplinary design scholarship and practice, especially where the coexistence of bounded fixity (of place) and open-ended mobility (of armatures and systems) occurs. Mobilities practices that embrace complementary technologies and theories derived from experimental and temporal practices eschew narrative, seek connectivity across disciplinary boundaries, and establish trajectories across space and time. Ultimately, these research and practice works are offered to the FLOW program without their authors' preknowledge of mobility as a construct. Yet the curation of these works for publication brings to presence the emergence of an expanded disciplinary practice in motion between interior and landscape.

References

Castells, M. (1996), *The Rise of the Network Society: The Information Age: Economy, Society, and Culture*, vol. 1, Oxford: Blackwell.

Deleuze, G. & Guattari, F. (2013) *A Thousand Plateaus : Capitalism and Schizophrenia*, London: Bloomsbury Academic.

Jensen, O. B. (2009), "Flows of Meaning, Cultures of Movements: Urban Mobility as Meaningful Everyday Life Practice," *Mobilities*, 4 (1): 139–58.

Kahn, A. (2005), "Defining Urban Sites," in C. J. Burns and A. Kahn (eds.), *Site Matters: Design Concepts, Histories, and Strategies*, New York: Routledge.

Sheller, M. (2011), "Mobility," *Sociopedia.isa*. Available online: http://www.sagepub.net/isa/resources/pdf/Mobility.pdf (accessed January 31, 2017).

Chapter 8

Spatial Continuums: Linear, Radial, and Clustered Architectures in Practice

Kerstin Thompson

Spatial Flow

A key pursuit in the practice of Kerstin Thompson Architects (KTA) is to create a flow between interior and exterior space: to achieve transitional and intermediary relationships between interiors and landscapes. In our experience, this spatial flow is best enabled by a proactive and determined collaboration between the disciplines of architecture and landscape architecture. Three case studies demonstrate how this approach has expanded the spatial opportunities and consequences for the projects, inviting greater civic opportunity, a revitalized public realm, and ecological repair.

Thinking within an expanded field of spatial consequence inevitably challenges the nature of physical boundaries, real or implied, and their dubious nature, especially as they pertain to "the site." Where exactly lies the "in" or "out" of a site within the context of urbanism or ecology?

> The carpet is twelve feet by eighteen, say. That gives us 216 square feet of continuous woven material. Is the knife razor-sharp? If not, we hone it. We set about cutting the carpet into thirty-six equal pieces, each one a rectangle, two feet by three. Never mind the hardwood floor. The severing fibres release small squeaky noises, like the muted yelps of outraged Persian weavers. Never mind the weavers. When we're finished cutting, we measure the individual pieces, total them up—and find that, lo, there's still nearly 216 square feet of recognisably carpet like stuff. But what does that amount to? Have we got thirty-six nice Persian throw rugs? No. All we're left with is three dozen ragged fragments, each one worthless and commencing to come apart.
> (David Quammen in Park 2006)

Quammen's brutal rendering of the "severed fibres" of a divided Persian rug is analogous to the effect on our cities and landscapes of the deluded thinking that somehow inside can be separated from out. It is all the more compelling reason for the imperative of flow in the making of our constructions.

Each project therefore has a design intent that operates across interior and exterior space to achieve a spatial continuum. In the House and Landscape at Lake Connewarre this continuum is *linear* (Figure 8.1); in MUMA it is *radial* (Figure 8.3) and in Carrum Downs Police Station *clustered* (Figure 8.5); It manifests through the synthesis of geometry, materiality (vegetation /building) and tectonic to direct the degree of opening/closure and opacity/transparency.

Employing these spatial devices gives rise to interstitial spaces in which traditional opposites such as public and private, architecture and landscape, figure and ground, inside and out, can be negotiated.

For Lake Connewarre, the creation of private amenity provided an opportunity to enhance the public realm by repairing the ecology of the lake's edge. The development of house and landscape yields private retreat and public contribution.

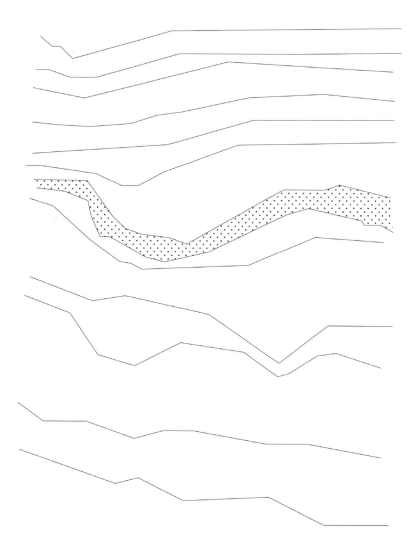

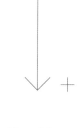

Figure 8.1

LINEAR—House and Landscape at Lake Connewarre with arrow indicating increase from exotic to indigenous plantings.

Figure 8.2

House and Landscape at Lake Connewarre. View towards restored landscape from breezeway. Photo Kerstin Thompson

The design of the House and Landscape at Lake Connewarre was a catalyst for the repair and restoration of degraded farmland, forming a vital link with adjacent sites and the extended environment (Figure 8.2). The masterplan is organized as an ecological gradient into a series of lateral bands of buildings and vegetation to amplify and repair the latent ecology evident between the hinterland and lake's edge. The architecture of the house, conceived as one of the bands, operates at a territorial scale as a thickened wall and marks the threshold between the revitalized hinterland and intertidal landscapes.

In MUMA (Monash University Museum of Art), the typically insular experience of the museum is opened up visually to connect with the adjacent Ian Potter Sculpture Forecourt. In doing this, the museum becomes integral to the everyday and public experience of the campus.

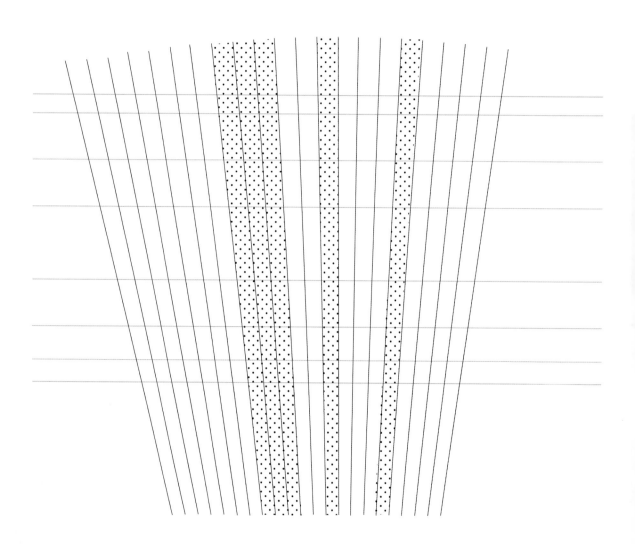

Figure 8.3

RADIAL—MUMA & Ian Potter Sculpture Forecourt.

The relationship between the museum interior and the landscape of the Forecourt is reinforced through a shared geometry. The radial geometry of the existing building is extended out into the center of the campus and coupled with a new geometry of parallel lines running east–west. In combination, these order the galleries, the internal and external circulation, and the concrete plates that define a series of major and minor gathering and outdoor exhibition areas. Vistas between inside and outside are formed within the radials. These enable exchange between the more privileged and internal program of the museum with the broader public realm and daily life of the campus. By transforming the boundary conditions between museum and forecourt, art infiltrates and activates the surrounding landscape to enhance the campus grounds and provide it with a cultural and social focus (Figure 8.4).

Figure 8.4

MUMA (Monash University Museum of Art). View from Ian Potter Sculpture Forecourt into museum interior. Painting by Howard Arkley. Photo Trevor Mein.

With Carrum Downs Police Station, the usually confined and cellular workspace of a police officer is transformed into a more collective zone enhanced by a garden aspect, natural light, and air.

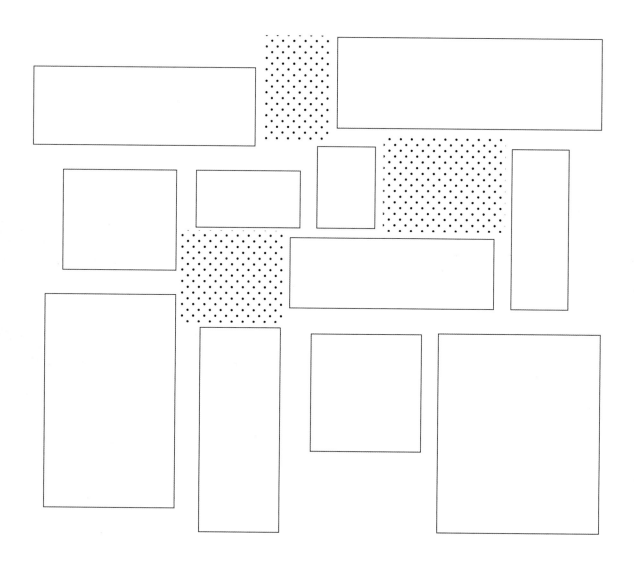

Figure 8.5

CLUSTER—Carrum Downs
Police Station.

Figure 8.6

Carrum Downs Police Station. Cluster of programmatic elements distinguished through different color brickwork.

A rethink of the station typology as a community rather than an institution, Carrum Downs is imagined as a mini-city. Instead of the usual long corridors and separate cellular cubicles, a cluster of programmatic elements, each figured as an individual volume and distinguished materially through the use of different colored brickwork, is the basic organization for functional and garden spaces. The cluster is united by the roof and by the generous circulation areas created in the interstitial spaces. By providing spaces of overlap for informal interactions in the workplace, this alternative typology encourages knowledge and social exchange between organizational divisions (Figure 8.6).

In each project, the interior and exterior goings-on are arranged in such a way as to bridge private life with public life. What might have been an autonomous inner world instead explicitly connects to the broader situation to enable meaningful overlaps and exchanges between these different conditions, producing a richer and more integrated experience of place. In this scenario buildings and landscapes are ideally contingent upon, and enhancing of, each other and of the ecological system within which they operate. The relationship between site and construction, interior and exterior, public and private is one of mutual dependency and benefit. (Figure 8.7)

Figure 8.7

Scaled relationships:
CLUSTERED, RADIAL, LINEAR.

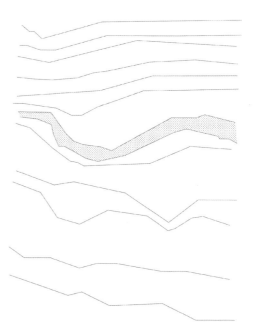

Disciplinary flow

Disciplinary boundaries had to be challenged in order to expand the conceptual underpinnings and spatial flows of these projects. From KTA's experience collaborating on these projects with landscape architects Fiona Harrison, Simon Ellis and Tim Nicholas, we identified three critical tactics for achieving disciplinary and, as a consequence, spatial flow.

Tactic 1: Commence the collaboration between the disciplines at the project initiation stage. The most formative stages for defining the project opportunity and design direction—site analysis and generation of core principles and intents—should be done together.

Tactic 2: Establish the relationship between the two disciplines as one between equals on the understanding that the disciplines are mutually defining and share the conceptual power, especially early on, so that one is not "leading" the other.

Tactic 3: Foster an expanded territory for thinking and speculating between the disciplines by challenging spatial and disciplinary binaries and biases.

These tactics counter what typically occurs: that architecture, with architect as primary consultant, takes the role of project leadership and then invites other disciplines to contribute to the project once the conceptual framework has been established. In this scenario, the vision is inevitably architectural in its thinking and landscape is only brought in to support or challenge this. As such, landscape figures as the relatively benign fluff around the edges of the building. Or conversely, it resists this diminutive role and thereby triggers a power struggle by introducing an alternate and contrary landscape vision as parallel universe. Neither of these outcomes is especially productive in terms of a working process or conducive to spatial and ecological flow. This hierarchical mode of collaboration can be summed up by the still pertinent words of Meyer and Corner:

> ..Architecture and nature are juxtaposed as opposites. Architecture is the positive object and nature, the neutral open ground plan patiently awaiting the building's arrival to give it a presence, to give it a form. (Meyer:14 1994)

Similarly, when a binary is operative, and where one discipline is presumed to take precedent over the other, the outcome can be compromised:

> The power struggle between disciplines results in landscape playing the role of receptacle of ideas rather than being embraced as an active and generative force in design. (Corner: 1999)

The premise that landscape and architecture are equals, in dialogue, is inherent to our preferred way of working. It's through this dialogue, which simultaneously directs and applies specific disciplinary knowledge toward a shared problem that common spatial continuums are most effectively yielded.

From this, particularly in Connewarre and MUMA, the cross-disciplinary thinking deployed at the generative stage of the project and the equal instrumentality granted both disciplines produces an expanded field of spatial consequence: one that takes account of and designs with a more comprehensive array of forces, conditions and intents for the subject site and project and that culminates in a richer, more integrated and sustainable experience of place.

References

Corner, J. (1999), "Introduction," *Recovering Landscape: Essays in Contemporary Landscape Architecture*. New York: Princeton Architectural Press.

Meyer, E. (1994), "Landscape Architecture as Modern Other and Postmodern Ground," H. Edquist and V. Bird (eds) *The Culture of Landscape Architecture*. Melbourne: Edge Publishing.

Park, G. (2006), *Theatre Country: Essays on landscape and whenua*. Wellington: Victoria University Press.

Acknowledgments

Aspects of this paper have been developed from one written with Fiona Harrisson entitled Material conversations: inside and outside of landscape and architecture for SAMVAD: Dialogue 2011 conference, Ahmedabad, India.

Chapter 9

Light Events: Interior and Exterior Space in Michael Snow's *Wavelength* (1967)

Eleanor Suess

The temporal, and constantly changing, relationship between interior and exterior is contingent upon the time of day, week, and year along with the tectonic quality, function, and inhabitation of each space. The manifold complexity of these temporal relationships is rarely represented through the conventional static media of spatial recording and production: architectural drawings imagine such spaces frozen at a single point in time. Interior and exterior are two distinct spatial conditions that cannot be inhabited simultaneously, and the relationship between an interior and its external world is dependent upon one's position at any given time. Through a specifically architectural analysis of Michael Snow's seminal film *Wavelength* (1967), this chapter addresses an interior position and its relationship to an exterior view and the implied world beyond the space of the room. As such, this film is appropriated as a form of architectural drawing, in particular, an "architectural moving drawing" capable of "drawing" time as well as space. I will also argue that the film/drawing can act propositionally, to construct architecture, through its filmic screening and active reading as architectural drawing.

Structural Film

The majority of research on film and architecture deals with the role of architecture as a dramatic element in narrative cinema, or with the emergence "of architecture that is 'cinematic'—that is, theatrical in effect and thematic in nature" (Lamster 2000: 2). However, architectural space usually acts subserviently[1] in dramatic cinema's focus on human narrative (particularly in mainstream commercial films). Gilles Deleuze explains that "cinema was constituted as such by becoming narrative, by presenting a story, and by rejecting its other possible directions . . . the 'cinematograph' became 'cinema' by committing itself to a narrative direction" (Deleuze 1989: 25, 293), but I argue that it is the *alternative* direction of cinematographic practice, that of artists' film, that may offer techniques to allow architecture to be foregrounded. Artists' film[2] (also known as experimental or avant-garde film) is a form of art practice that emerged from the divergence of cinematographic practice from early forms of film production. While "cinema" was developing into a form of entertainment, of storytelling, early experimental films "were rooted in the cubist revolution pioneered by Braque and Picasso [. . . and] New theories of time and perception in art . . . led artists to try to put 'paintings in motion' through the film medium" (Rees 1999: 10).

One area of experimental film that became prevalent in Europe and North America in the 1960s and 1970s was *structural film*, a term coined by the American critic of avant-garde film, P. Adams Sitney. Describing North American work, Sitney defined structural film as "a cinema of structure . . . and it is that shape which is the primal impression of the film . . . what content it has is minimal and subsidiary to the outline," and he highlighted four characteristics: "fixed camera position . . . , the flicker effect, loop printing, and rephotography off the screen" (Sitney 1974: 407–8). Countering and extending Sitney's reductive definition and term, London-based experimental filmmakers Peter Gidal and Malcolm Le Grice placed emphasis on the concerns of the material presence of the medium, introducing the word *materialist* to the form's title. Gidal and Le Grice saw structural/materialist film as challenging the passivity of the audience in narrative, commercial cinema: "The mental activation of the viewer is necessary for the procedure of the film's existence" (Gidal 1976: 2–3), similar to Sitney's emphasis on this active role for the viewer: "It is cinema of the mind rather than the eye" (Sitney 1974: 408). Through the minimal use of human protagonists, an attempt to be "non-illusionist" (Gidal 1976: 1), and the use of extended duration (Sitney 1974: 412), the viewer is provided with the time to look carefully, to see details and make connections and meaning that are often lost in the pace of narrative cinema. I have observed that in artists' film, spaces (rooms, landscape, cities) often constitute the filmed object but are frequently denied as subject. Rather, a space devoid of human protagonists is used to stand in as "nonsubject" and, as such, is filmed in order to produce work whose central concern is the self-referential material act of making and watching the film itself. This is particularly prevalent in structural films, in which this self-referentiality is frequently the aim, and these films are often called nonrepresentational (Gidal 1976: 1).

Architectural Representation and the Unbuilt Building

The notion of an active viewer constructing meaning while viewing a structural film resonates with the process of "reading" orthographic architectural drawings. Robin Evans (1989, 1995, 1997) and Alberto Pérez-Gómez and Louise Pelletier (1992, 1997) have written extensively about the role of representational practices within architecture, identifying the architect's primary medium as drawing, rather than the material from which their buildings are constructed. Evans explains that "projected information can be mobilized by the imagination of the observer" (Evans 1989: 19) and that in the reading of drawings a sense of the building is projected through such "activating imagination" (Evans 1989: 20). Sonit Bafna suggests that the architectural drawing can be used to stand in for the building, arguing that the drawing can be a work of architecture because "the experiential qualities of the building are invoked through the drawings" (Bafna 2008: 543), acknowledging that "the aesthetic experience of these drawings is . . . certainly nothing like the kind of experience derived from actually visiting a building" (Bafna 2008: 543–4). John Hejduk also asserts that "a drawing to me is a completed piece of architecture. . . . Each act is individually an act of architecture" (*Education of an Architect* 1993).

Evans, Pérez-Gómez, and Pelletier all refer to the impact that drawing and other forms of architectural representation have upon the making of architecture, with Juhani Pallasmaa (2012) noting that many qualities of the material world, experienced through the lived body, are not expressed through conventional, ocular-centric, orthographic, and perspectival architectural drawing. Jonathan Hill writes that architects could "look at drawings elsewhere, studying other disciplines that have developed articulate means to draw qualities relevant to architecture . . . to develop new ways to draw architectural qualities excluded from the architectural drawing" (2006: 56).

The Architectural Moving Drawing

> "Temporality is a fundamental aspect of architectural space. . . . Time-based drawings can be used to consider and communicate expressly temporal concerns through the embedding of duration in the media of representation . . . the change inherent within architecture and urban space can be drawn, making visible the processes by which supposedly fixed and frozen finished buildings emerge, and then begin to thaw." (Suess 2014: 244, 257)

Artists' film, particularly structural film, offers suitable precedent for the architectural moving drawing.

> The use in structural film of extended duration, limited human narrative, and tightly controlled structure, allows for a greater focus on architectural concerns . . . structural film shares with architectural drawing an explicit requirement for the viewer to be active in their reading of the work and in the construction of knowledge. (Suess 2014: 251)

Pallasmaa's (2012: 17) notions of peripheral and haptic vision relate to Walter Benjamin's (1992: 232–3) discussion of a distracted, incidental experience of architecture. Distraction implies that the experience occurs over time, not as a single, instantaneous view, but an accretion of subtle, almost unnoticed, peripheral aspects of the space; thus time-based architectural representation offers a new method for drawing such distracted experience.

Wavelength (1967)

Michael Snow's 1967 film *Wavelength* is a formative work within the history of structural film and has been influential in the subsequent evolution of artists' film practices (MacDonald 1985: 34). It employs predominantly "representational" footage, along with abstract elements such as flashes of screen-filled pure color, to construct an artwork whose intention is to express the form, structure, and media of the film artifact and highlight the processes of the viewer in watching the film. Snow had started with the idea of the zoom and the corresponding form of the cone of light from the projector (Snow, Mekas, and Sitney 1967: 41); the space of the room and the street beyond the windows were not the intended primary subject.

How might an *architectural* reading of *Wavelength* draw out the relationship between interior and exterior? Building upon previous detailed filmic analyses (Legge 2009, Wees 1981, Michelson 1971) and my own architectural interpretation (Suess 2014) of the film, I will show how the supposed "nonsubject" of space in many artists' film work can provide complex and rich content, demonstrating how a work of structural film may operate as a form of architectural moving drawing. Additionally, I will argue that the particular use of extended duration in the film produces a distracted, peripheral occupation of that room.

Figure 9.1

Wavelength—the zoom, start to finish. *Wavelength* © Michael Snow 1967 (photographs of projections).

The film is a continuous zoom which takes 45 minutes to go from its widest field to its smallest and final field. It was shot with a fixed camera from one end of an 80 foot loft, shooting the other end, a row of windows and the street . . . The room (and the zoom) are interrupted by 4 human events including a death. (Snow 1967: 40)

Snow refers to the film as "utilizing . . . prophecy and memory" (1967a: 40), looking back and forward simultaneously, implying a role for the viewer in actively constructing the whole out of these temporal fragments. The zoom invites the viewer to consider the space at an ever-increasing scale, with an accompanying narrowing of field of view (Figure 9.1). I suggest that through these processes of "prophecy and memory" the observer's "activating imagination" constructs the whole space (of the interior room and the exterior beyond) though these durationally dispersed scales. The row of windows at the far end of the room constitutes the primary architectural interface between interior and exterior, and from the first shot *Wavelength* addresses the relationship between the spaces on either side of these windows. Through both (limited) human and architectural narrative the film records the constantly changing connection between the interior room and the aural and spatial landscape beyond.

Figure 9.2

Wavelength—"4 human events." *Wavelength* © Michael Snow 1967 (photographs of projections).

Wavelength: 4 Human Events

For the majority of the film the loft room is devoid of human protagonists: Snow's "4 human events" are each very brief and interspersed across the full duration of the film (Figure 9.2). Snow acknowledges, "There is the implication of a story in the sense of human affairs" (Snow et al. 1967: 42), that the viewer may construct a "narrative" linking each of these events. However, Snow's intention is that "everything else is also an event, though of another kind" (Legge 2009: 5) and that there is not a hierarchy of the human and nonhuman events: "The image of the yellow chair has as much 'value' in its own world as the girl closing the window" (Snow et al. 1967: 44). The "empty" room is as important as the brief moments of human occupation: composer Steve Reich observed that in *Wavelength,* when "the people leave—the room is by itself. What does a room feel when no one is there?" (Yalkut 1968: 51).

The "human events" are the following: a woman and two men bring in and position a bookshelf; the woman and a friend return, listen to the Beatles' *Strawberry Fields for Ever* (1967)[3] on the radio, and close one window; it is night-time and sounds of someone breaking into the building and approaching footsteps precede a male "intruder" entering and collapsing, after which the camera zoom hides him from view; with a later return to night-time a third woman enters, sees the "dead" man on the floor, makes a phone call asking for help, and leaves.

The first human event takes place at the commencement of the film, and like the viewers of the film, these people have arrived from another place, the woman's coat and scarf implying they have entered from outside. These occupants confirm the scale of the room, the depth of the space is revealed as the foreshortened view is traversed, and the figures demonstrate the generosity of ceiling height. The women's gaze though the windows links interior to exterior, which is then severed by the window's closure and loss of the street's sound. The music apparently emanating from the radio is broadcast from a space beyond, and the song itself is created and recorded in yet another space and time. The intruder's initial incursion from the exterior is communicated through sound, and his "departure" occurs both through his apparent death and through his removal from view due to the camera's relentless zoom. However, the fourth event, which makes a connection "back in time and space" (Snow et al. 1967: 42), demonstrates that the intruder has not departed in body: the telephone call reminds the viewer of his presence and connects the room to the world beyond, a reversal of the earlier intrusion.

Each of these events changes the perceived "speed" of the space of the room by the presence and actions of the protagonists. The room is "slow" when it is devoid of human occupants: change within the space is largely imperceptible, beyond the continually stepping, hand-cranked camera zoom. Viewers begin to experience boredom (Fujiwara 2007: 242–3), shifting their focus to the glimpses of movement of flapping awnings, passing vehicles, and pedestrians in the faster space of the street. This boredom also encourages viewers to become more aware of their own position, of their body, their act of viewing, the space of the cinema and the mechanisms of the screening (Sobchack 1992: 180–1).[4] At these times, the attention of the viewers flows from the real, interior space of the cinema in which their own body is located, though the intermediate space of the depicted interior in the film, to the suggested space of the film's exterior. Despite their limited activity, the introduction of people to the film's interior space speeds it up through their acts of inhabitation and their linking of interior and exterior. Their movement through this space, and their interactions with each other and the room, are engaging. Time no longer feels drawn out, boredom is alleviated, and as such this (limited) human narrative causes viewers to lose the sense of their own position: the flow through the interior stops, with the viewers residing with the protagonists within the loft space.

Wavelength: Day and Night

The duration of the film is not equal to the duration of the filmed room; the 45 minutes of footage were shot over the period of a week, days and nights, allowing the film to communicate a variety of changing, spatiotemporal relationships. In particular, the alternating presence and absence of daylight impact the reading of the relationship between interior and exterior. The daylight in the room is always mediated by the external conditions: the movement of passing vehicles is echoed in the reflected light on the shiny surface of the tin ceiling, projecting an interior version of the movements of the street. The sunlight reflecting off the facade of the opposite building provides the room with much of its daylight; the artificial light struggles to expose the details of the room against this *contre-jour*. As the zoom tightens, the view outside of this brightly lit elevation is magnified and the building signage opposite becomes legible, drawing the viewer's attention to the exterior.

The shift from day to night (and back again) changes the spatial operation of the windows; during the day the glass is transparent, the moving outside world projected onto its panes, while at night the windows become opaque black rectangles, severing the connection between interior and exterior. At night the light within the room is brighter; the artificial illumination generates sharper shadows and cleaner colors and accentuates architectural details. This exposure of the interior through the change in light, coupled with the loss of the exterior world as a point of focus, shifts the viewer's attention, serving to intensify the interior, speeding it up.

Wavelength: The Space of the Viewer

A photograph of vast ocean waves (the wavelength metaphor made literal), which has occupied the center of the frame for the entirety of the film, now becomes central to the film's conclusion, acting as yet another "window" to an exterior space. The camera zooms inwards past the edges of the photograph, transforming it from a photographic artifact on a wall in a room to an image that fills the screen, transporting the viewer out of the space of the room into a different exterior world. However, the static image of this perpetually moving surface arrests time, and the multitude of spatial speeds presented in the film become fixed in this one moment. The zoom into this photograph of waves is the mechanism by which viewers exit the room and the film: their journey back to their own reality flowing though the timeless world of the frozen waves.

I argue that in the viewing of this film, and in the manner instructed by the artist (projected in a cinema), a propositional act of spatial construction takes place, that in the active reading of this architectural moving drawing, architecture is created in the mind of the viewer. But it is not the actual, original room, as filmed by Snow in 1966, that viewers (re)construct. *Wavelength* is not a simulation of a spatial experience of that room, at that point in time; it is a new space, in a new time, constituted as much by the space of the room on the audience's side of the picture plane as that flat image on the screen and the projected illusion of space beyond it. Just as with conventional architectural drawing, architecture also resides within this architectural moving drawing, and through a process of mental activation while "reading" the film, architecture is constructed by the viewer.

Additionally, "the theoretical or bored spectator" (Sobchack 1992: 181) has an awareness of the mechanism of the film's projection, the film provoking conscious reflection in its viewers of their own physical location and its relationship to that of the image on the screen (Fujiwara 2007: 242–3). In Snow's three-hour film *La Region Centrale* (1971), a similar process occurs: shortly after experiencing a recent theatrical screening of this film, I was struck by the clarity of its experiential nature (de Duve 1995). It was as if I, along with the entire audience, was encamped in a constructed place formed from the conjunction of the mountaintop in the film and the space of the cinema. Afterwards I felt as though I had emerged from this propositional place, having made a momentous journey.

As Snow himself states (Snow and Dompierre 1994), his work has always been concerned with the relationship of the viewer to the artwork, particularly in the active, reflective construction of meaning by that viewer. In a theatrical screening of *Wavelength*, the projected image on the screen, the pyramid of projected light, and the audience all constitute the work: "The space starts at the camera's (spectator's) eye, is in the air, then is on the screen, then is within the screen (the mind)" (Snow 1967a: 40). Snow asserts that only in such a theatrical screening is the artwork complete, that its being a film is integral to its meanings (Legge 2009); Snow has never released *Wavelength* on DVD.

I would assert that the relationship between interior and exterior in *Wavelength* includes the interior of the cinema (de Duve 1995: 34), the exterior space of the viewers' own journey to that cinema, and the interior and exterior spaces represented in Snow's 1966 loft room, all as communicated to viewers through their active reading of the film. The propositional construction of a new space occurs through these experiential acts, made anew at each screening of the film and in the experience of each individual viewer and then, ultimately, in the collective memory.

Notes

1. This is not to say that people are unimportant in architecture; quite the opposite, and artist's film practices can offer ways to consider issues of people's relationship to and interaction with architecture in a way beyond that of the mere "staffage" employed in most normative forms of architectural representation.

2. I use the word *film* to refer to moving image practices, regardless of media (i.e., film, video, digital film/video), although I recognize that the form of media is significant within many of these practices.

3. As the film was shot the year before the release of *Strawberry Fields*, this was added in the film's editing (Legge 2009: 24).

4. Fujiwara and Sobchack use the term *boredom* not as a criticism, but as a counterpoint to the nonreflective absorption the viewer experiences in fast-paced, narrative cinema.

References

Bafna, S. (2008), "How Architectural Drawings Work—and What That Implies for the Role of Representation in Architecture," *The Journal of Architecture*, 13 (9): 535–64.

Benjamin, W. (1992), "The Work of Art in the Age of Mechanical Reproduction," in W. Benjamin (ed.), *Illuminations*, 211–44, London: Fontana Press.

de Duve, T. (1995), "Michael Snow: The Deictics of Experience and Beyond," *Parachute*, 28: 28–41.

Deleuze, G. (1989), *Cinema 2: The Time Image*, London: Athlone.

Education of an Architect: Voices from the Cooper Union. (1993), [Film] Dir. K. Shkapich, USA: Michael Blackwood Productions.

Evans, R. (1989), "Architectural Projection," in E. Blau and E. Kaufman (eds.), *Architecture and Its Image*, Montreal: Centre Canadien d'Architecture.

Evans, R. (1995), *The Projective Cast: Architecture and Its Three Geometries*, Cambridge: MIT Press.

Evans, R. (1997), *Translations from Drawing to Building, AA Documents*, Cambridge: MIT Press.

Fujiwara, C. (2007), "Boredom, Spasmo, and the Italian System," in J. Sconce (ed.), *Sleaze Artists: Cinema at the Margins of Taste, Style, and Politics*, Durham: Duke University Press.

Gidal, P. (1976), "Theory and Definition of Structural/Materialist Film," in P. Gidal (ed.), *Structural Film Anthology*, 1–21, London: British Film Institute.

Hill, J. (2006), *Immaterial Architecture*, London: Routledge.

Lamster, M., ed. (2000), *Architecture and Film*, New York: Princeton Architectural Press.

Legge, E. M. (2009), *Michael Snow, Wavelength*, London: Afterall.

MacDonald, S. (1985), "Review: So Is This by Michael Snow," *Film Quarterly*, 39 (1): 34–37, doi: 10.2307/1212281.

Michelson, A. (1971), "Toward Snow, Part 1," *Artforum*, 9 (10): 30–37.

Pallasmaa, J. (2012), *The Eyes of the Skin: Architecture and the Senses*, Chichester: Wiley.

Pérez-Gómez, A., and L. Pelletier (1992), "Architectural Representation Beyond Perspectivism," *Perspecta*, 27: 21–39, doi: 10.2307/1567174.

Pérez Gómez, A., and L. Pelletier (1997), *Architectural Representation and the Perspective Hinge*, Cambridge: MIT Press.

Rees, A. L. (1999), *A History of Experimental Film and Video: From Canonical Avant-Garde to Contemporary British Practice*, London: BFI Publishing.

La Region Centrale (1971), [Artists' Film] Dir. Michael Snow, Canada.

Sitney, P. A. (1974), *Visionary Film: The American Avant-Garde*, New York: Oxford University Press.

Snow, M. (1967), "A Statement on 'Wavelength' for the Experimental Film Festival of Knokke-Le-Zoute," in M. Snow and L. Dompierre (eds.), *The Collected Writings of Michael Snow*, Waterloo: Wilfrid Laurier University Press.

Snow, M., and L. Dompierre, eds. (1994), *The Collected Writings of Michael Snow*, Waterloo: Wilfrid Laurier University Press.

Snow, M., J. Mekas, and P. A. Sitney (1967), "Conversation wih Michael Snow," in M. Snow and L. Dompierre (eds.), *The Collected Writings of Michael Snow*, Waterloo: Wilfrid Laurier University Press.

Sobchack, V. C. (1992), *The Address of the Eye: A Phenomenology of Film Experience*, Princeton: Princeton University Press.

Suess, E. (2014), "Doors Don't Slam: Time-Based Architectural Representation," in D. Maudlin and M. Vellinga (eds.), *Consuming Architecture: On the Occupation, Appropriation and Interpretation of Buildings*, 243–59, Abingdon: Routledge.

Suess, E. (2017), "Light Matter: The Transdisciplinary Practice of the Architectural Moving Drawing," in I. Troiani and H. Campbell (eds.), *Making Visible: Architecture Filmmaking*, Intellect.

Wavelength (1967), [Artists' Film] Dir. Michael Snow, Canada.

Wees, W. C. (1981), "Prophecy, Memory and the Zoom: Michael Snow's Wavelength Re-Viewed," *Ciné-tracts,* 14 (15): 78–83.

Yalkut, J. (1968), "Review: Wavelength by Michael Snow," *Film Quarterly*, 21 (4): 50–2, doi: 10.2307/1210605.

Chapter 10
The Indignant Beton

Elias Constantopoulos

Modernity and its aftermath, in a desire to reconnect humans' lost unity with the world, invented luring architectural schemes of crystalline transparencies and soft liquid forms. The vast repetitions of typical habitats of the modern metropolis and postmodern megalopolis expanded over land as densely packed homogeneous tapestries. Interiors are battlegrounds, lived and erased every day. Homes are palimpsests of apparent stability. Buildings are the benevolent shelters of such private worlds, cages of voluntary enclosure, simultaneously cozy, protected, and alienated. But life, private life in a box, however precious, erupts under pressure, spilling its indignant human contents outside. And there, in public space, people momentarily attempt to constitute society afresh, spatially redefining their borders and boundaries.

Palimpsests and Routines: Interior Lives and Solid Enclosures

Permanence and change are two aspects of what we consider a home: a place of homecoming that retains its character and identity despite the changes it undergoes over time. A study documenting changes in the spatial organization and the disposition of objects within a typical Athens apartment, over a period of 25 years, was presented at the Modern Interior Research Centre Conference (Constantopoulos 2010) (Figure 10.1). The study showed how this archaeology of interior lives, interweaving an inventory with an autobiography, uncovered a *palimpsest* of traces of past living alongside new arrangements of objects and spaces, betraying actions of destruction and creation, memory and rebirth, in this flux we call life.

If dwelling in an apartment is thus, on the one hand, considered as a process of continuous transformation, interiors can, on the other hand, also be seen as settings of repeated everyday actions, of conventional urban living. Dimitris Papaioannou's stage performance *Mesa* (*Inside*, Athens 2011) very forcefully illustrates this condition by reenacting monotonously, for six uninterrupted hours, the typical routine of living inside an Athenian apartment. The same stereotypical ritual (enter-undress-wash-eat-rest-sleep) is repeated over and over again by different actors, weaving a pattern of overlapping, more or less unchanging daily activities.

The two examples just mentioned (an apartment as palimpsest and the representation of an apartment as a theater of repetition) reveal a spatiotemporal paradox. While actions of everyday living are repeated in the same manner, seemingly unchanging in the short term, the transformations of interiors in the typical urban apartment simultaneously reveal significant changes over longer periods of time.

Figure 10.1 (over page)

Athens, view west toward the Acropolis. Photo Elias Constantopoulos 2015.

Athenian apartment blocks, normally comprising five to six stories, are the typical habitats of contemporary Greek cities (Constantopoulos 1999) (Figure 10.2). Built of a concrete loadbearing frame structure, materializing Le Corbusier's *Dom-ino*, these prosaic forms of enclosure are referred to as *match boxes*, or *cement-boxes* in Greek, signifying indifferent, anonymous building objects. Naming them *cement-boxes*, instead of plaster or brick boxes—a more accurate description of these enclosures— puts the blame on concrete, as if it is the material's fault for the poor conditions of modern urban living. These apartment blocks are not even boxes as such, but rather "frames-for-living-in," comprising floor slabs stacked above each other and with cantilevered balconies as expressions of their "horizontal ownership" status.

Figure 10.2

Apartment block, Paleo Phalero, Athens. Photo Elias Constantopoulos 2016.

In the collective Greek consciousness, these concrete boxes symbolize brutal, impersonal structures, enclosing lives in ways more reminiscent of a cell than a home, so repressed and impatient, ready to explode and break out. It is this unrelenting hardness of concrete that inspired Austrian author Thomas Bernhard to write the homonymous novel *Beton* (1982), a story that flows without interruptions, without conventional chapter or paragraph breaks. The relentless narrative comes abruptly to an end, describing the death of a man falling from a balcony, his head crashed on the *concrete* below and buried in a tall *concrete* grave bunker nearby. Making the title of the book horribly clear, concrete thus signifies the end because of its characteristic, unrelenting rigidity and hardness. Concrete stops the *flow* of life, as it also brings the *flowing* narration to an end. In an exemplary manner, Solidity is set against Fluidity, Disruption against Continuity, as Death against Life.

A problem hence arises as to how the negative perception of an epic modern material might be reconciled with modernity's attempt to open up and free space from past limitations.

Glass to Ground: From Transparency to Fluidity

If concrete was adopted for its ability to be formed into any shape, glass complemented it by bringing light to the interior and visually connecting it to the outside. From the *Bauhaus* to the *Seagram Building*, architectural modernity was captivated by the ideal of continuity, the uninterrupted *flow* of space between interior and exterior. Glass walls became the distinctive trait of modern architecture, as the clarity of physical as well as metaphorical transparency became the symbol of a brave new world, an open society that had nothing to hide.

Transparency in practice, however, proved to be far more complex, as argued by Rowe and Slutzky (1963, 1971), making a vital distinction between perceived and conceived visibility. Though glass still reigns today as a prime material for building enclosure, it has lost its unambiguous lucidity. Reflective, opaque, or screened, it now appears in many guises for different reasons (social, environmental, aesthetic), more translucent than transparent, more seductively suggestive of interior privacy than uncompromising publicity (Foucault [1977] 1980: 154).

Despite the rise and fall of glass as an agent expressive of modernity, the idea of *continuity* in architecture still persists, but through different means. A telling transformation may be witnessed in the architectural literature of the last twenty years, which has shifted its interest toward the flowing, skinlike forms of building enclosures. It seems that at the threshold of the twenty-first century the dominant architectural discourse has undergone a paradigm shift, courtesy of Deleuze's *Le Pli* (1988), in order to achieve continuity in space through both *liquidity* and *fluidity*.

In *Liquid Modernity* (2000), the Polish sociologist Zygmunt Bauman distinguishes between a *solid* and a *liquid modernity* so as to expose the contemporary condition of growing global social uncertainty. Citing the *Encyclopaedia Britannica*, he suggests that fluidity is the quality of liquids and gasses that distinguishes them from solids, because they "undergo a continuous change in shape when subjected to a stress force" (Bauman [2000] 2011: 1). Hence for Bauman fluidity or liquidity are "fitting metaphors when we wish to grasp the nature of the present, in many ways novel, phase in the history of modernity" (Bauman [2000] 2011: 2).

This concept of *liquid modernity* also seems appropriate in trying to understand dominant ideas in current architecture practices. Fluid forms are not new in Western architecture, and there are many examples that point to a recurring theme in its history, from the Baroque, to Art Nouveau, Expressionism, the futuristic Sixties, contemporary *Blobs* and *Folds*, and recent projects such as Foreign Office Architects' *International Passenger Terminal* (2002) in Yokohama.

This predilection for curvilinear shapes, flowing lines, and twisted planes, seemingly amorphous by classical standards, reveals a sustained interest in surface manipulation and continuity of space that make ground and landform a dominant architectural concept. Consider "*-scape*," a suffix akin to *shape* (Partridge 1958: 591), which is being abundantly used not only in defining *land-scapes* but also interior *domestic* and *office landscapes, city-scapes, ground-scapes, cloud-scapes*, and many more. Such neologisms, though they do not actually abolish physical boundaries, manifest a newfound desire for fluid configurations through the liquid *appearance* of form, complementing transparency and extending the scope of visual continuity. Examples of relevant literature since the late sixties are Frank Duffy's *Office Landscaping* (Duffy 1966), MoMA's exhibition catalogue *Italy: The New Domestic Landscape* (Ambasz 1972), *Scape—Asymptote Architecture* (Betsky A., Damdi Publ., 2004), *Groundscapes* (Ruby I. & A., GG 2006), and so on.

If *topography* refers to the morphology of a place (Greek *topos*), *topology* refers to the mathematical concept of the qualitative properties of spaces that remain invariant when they are transformed. It seems like a poetic coincidence, for an architecture that appears as *topography*, that *topology* also replaces Euclidean geometry, and the *Möbius strip* emerges as the paradigmatic image of an uninterrupted surface continuum in space, with neither an interior nor an exterior. The *Möbius House* in Het Gooi, Netherlands (1998), by UNStudio, was a first attempt at creating a *Möbius loop*, "the spatial quality of which means that it is present in both plan and section," enabling "the house to take in the extreme aspects of the landscape" and to convey "from the interior the idea of a walk in the countryside" (*Mobius House*, n.d.). However, since external, enclosing walls cannot be relinquished, the built concrete house lacks the continuity promised, as the architects themselves admit:

The mathematical model of Möbius is not literally transferred to the building, but is conceptualized or thematized and can be found in architectural ingredients, such as the light, the staircases, and the way in which people move through the house. So, while the Möbius diagram introduces aspects of duration and trajectory, the diagram is worked into the building *in a mutated way*. (*Mobius House*, n.d.)

The Dutch architects' subsequent efforts in realizing such a task are clearly reflected in their statement that "one of the most comprehensive concepts of our time is the single surface, which consists of planes mutating from floor into wall into ceiling" (UNStudio 2010: 149). This idea is reminiscent of F. Kiesler's experimental *Endless House* design of 1950, in which the fluid forms blur the distinction between floor, walls, and ceiling (*Endless House* 2015).

This craving of contemporary architecture for freedom from all constraints, spatial and constructional, can hardly be reconciled with the time-honored conception of architecture as the art and science of solidity. Modern architecture, in trying to liberate itself from old conventions that shaped it by following the laws of statics, employed formal elements such as the cantilevered slab and the corner window, which seemingly freed designs from gravity. Solidity, being the *sine qua non* condition of architecture, was already first challenged a century ago by the Futurists, in their glorification of the ephemeral and the transient. Since then, the ideas of lightness and flexibility pertaining to change have become commonplace, from Metabolism to Parametric architecture, with few significant exceptions, such as the works of Luis Barragan and Louis Kahn.

Modern humankind's longing for a reunion with its natural habitat, from which it has been cut off in the postindustrial era, is counteracted by the need to also seek protection, from both natural elements and adverse social situations. Not only architectural, but also philosophical, sociological, and psychoanalytic approaches, espoused by Simmel in *The Metropolis and Mental Life* of 1903, Freud's *Civilization and Its Discontents* of 1929, and Mumford's *The City in History* of 1961, have attempted to explain the state of division and ongoing crisis of modern urban life, in which humankind experiences inhabiting the world as an internalized, paradoxical schism. If, being at one with our environment calls for the abolishment of boundaries, the need for safety requires at the same time the establishment of new spatial boundaries that regulate social relations.

Though concepts of *transparency* and *fluidity* have dominated architectural thought as convincing metaphors for practice over the last one hundred years, spatial divisions have not been eliminated. This century-old quest of modernity for formal and visual continuity, which has only partially been fulfilled, can however be *physically* materialized in space that offers a real possibility of human interaction by establishing connections between neighboring regions and making them permeable along their borders.

Continuity, Literal and Phenomenal

Mies van der Rohe's Barcelona Pavilion of 1929 already provides us with an important precedent of actual spatial fluidity. Even though its rectilinear configuration betrays none of the *soft* forms of contemporary architecture, its composition is certainly one of the clearest expositions of flowing space. This pivotal building has been so exhaustively analyzed in architectural literature that there is no point in reiterating what is already known. Its design is based on the carefully calculated disposition of vertical surfaces (marble walls, glass panes, curtains), along with horizontal planes (roof slabs, water ponds, carpets), that demarcate different areas and encourage internal movement. What is important to note is that the Barcelona Pavilion's *fluidity* is not apparent in the *shapes* of the building elements, but in their *real spatial relationships*.

Figure 10.3

Apartment plan showing layers of changes, Paleo Phalero, Athens. Photo Elias Constantopoulos 2011.

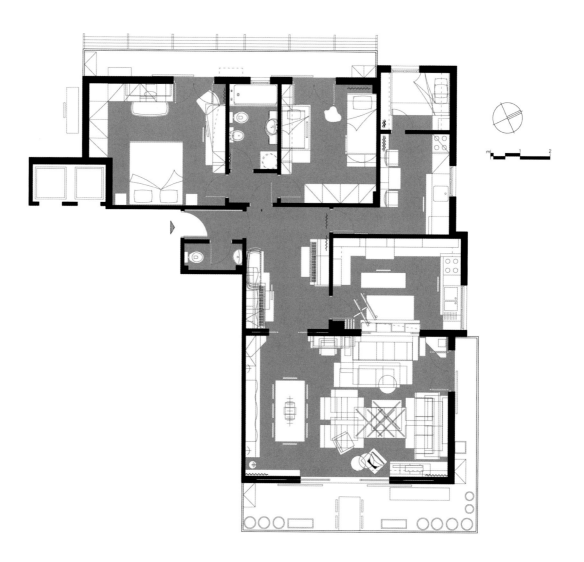

Spatial fluidity can easily be found also in structures of entirely different size and scope, such as in large-scale urban agglomerations. Athens, for example, is a city that has increased from tens of thousands to four million inhabitants during the last century. Alongside this population growth, numerous typical apartment blocks have spread over flatland and hills, climbing up to the surrounding mountains and down to the seashore, following the topography of the Attica Basin. Athens's compact municipal conurbations have grown into a large, ever-expanding cityscape, merging with the natural landscape, shaped into a wavy, undulating surface reminiscent of an *urban carpet* (Figure 10.3).

This contrasting relationship between the solid form of a concrete apartment block and the soft form of a city *tapestry* is analogous to sand, a granular material that displays overall qualities of an "incompressible flow," even though it comprises small solid particles. Sand, in its *local* form, consists of densely packed, discrete, solid grains, while in its *global* form it appears as a flowing, ever-changing formation of dunes. The analogy between dense intertwined urban formations, comprising discrete building structures, is reflected in their construction material, concrete, a solid substance made of compactly packed aggregates of sand solidified in cement.

The formal contrast between global and local scales, in a city like Athens, is made possible by the repetition of units within a grid following the contours of the land, adhering to the uneven *section* of the place. The wavelike flowing urban form is due to this varied section, to the outline of the topography, as the concrete dwellings follow Athens's hilly terrain.

Resetting Borders and Boundaries

If building blocks and sand grains grow as continuous surfaces giving the impression of fluidity, actual flow is observed more directly in the city, with the movements of the people forming the vibrant spatial identity of the community. Though we usually consider a space by its built material characteristics only, the presence of people within it is important in defining its identity as a place. The number of people occupying it, and their patterns of movement through it at different moments in time, alter its character, encouraging or discouraging certain behaviors in public, and contribute to defining its particular identity (or identities). *Syntagma* (Constitution) Square in Athens demonstrates the spatial, public *constitution* of the city in the different patterns formed by its inhabitants: as a meeting place and as a traffic hub, hosting the passage of pedestrians going to work or strolling at their leisure, gathering for a political party rally or union demonstration, and recently, assembling to protest angrily against austerity measures, as outraged as the Spanish *indignados* of the May 15, 2011, movement.

It is during these transmutations of the body public that, once outside their apartments, citizens appropriate the city square as another interior, a common *room*. This transitory transformation of contemporary urban areas redefines the bkoundaries between public and private domains. As people temporarily occupy the city square, declaring at such times that the city is their "home," they momentarily own it by defining the actions that take place within.

In such practices, which can be traced as far back as the Renaissance in Europe, the square does not stand as a symbol of social uprising; it actually makes it possible. The *indignant* citizens standing in front of the Parliament Building in *Syntagma* Square in Athens can only protest here, where the heart of the *demos* is, where it even demanded historically its first constitution. Such a social explosion must take place in public; it cannot be contained in the restricted confines of the private realm. The Austrian director Michael Haneke reenacts such an extreme example of an implosion within the confines of a home in his movie *The Seventh Continent* (1989), in which a family's reaction to the meaningless repetition of everyday routines gradually turns against itself through the systematic, self-destructive termination of life and property.

During city protests and demonstrations, the *indignant* citizens left their apartments in the *cement-boxes*, for concrete, as the *indignant* symbolic hard enclosure spews life out into the public space of the *square*. That is also the reason why in Athens the indignant citizens' impromptu movement was named after the place in which they gathered: it was called the *Plateia* (*City Square*), meaning that *wide* expanse of public space that they temporarily appropriated as a place of their own voice and presence.

Citizens, in their various roles and identities as workers, consumers, tourists, demonstrators, policemen, the homeless, and so on, amount, by their presence and their actions, to a physical spatiality. What happens in the interiors, in a controlled or private sphere, has its collateral in the open, common, public sphere. As Goffman (1959) observes, a connection exists between the kinds of "acts" that people put on in their daily lives and theatrical performances, and in social interactions there is an onstage area where individuals assume public roles and identities, as well as a backstage area where they can be themselves.

In an era of economic and social unrest, architecture, as a major human endeavor that shapes our environment, is again asked to take a stand. "Architecture or Revolution?" asked Le Corbusier in 1923, to which he responded, "Revolution can be avoided" (Le Corbusier [1923] 1989: 269). Social upheavals, nonetheless, require breaking boundaries and transgressing existing borders in order to construct new ones. In *The Public Realm* (2008), Richard Sennett makes a crucial distinction between "Borders and Boundaries," which signify different types of limits. Drawing a useful analogy from biology regarding the difference between cell walls and cell membranes, a boundary can be considered a closed limit that forbids access from one area to another, whereas a border is rather an in-between space that allows controlled crossing of limits, a zone of osmosis between two neighboring regions that fosters cross-fertilization.

Such distinctions today are of paramount architectural and social importance. The boiling pot of the twenty-first-century contemporary world has been transmuted in social and economic, as well as in spatial and architectural, terms. From industrial modernity's norms of homogenization and standardization, routine and repetition, and forms and processes, which were welcomed as efficient, socially controlling mechanisms, to post-post-modernity's chaotic practices, which maximize entropy in the quest for alternative kinds of order, the gap that needs to be bridged to achieve more just and humane structures and spaces to live in seems unfathomable.

Architects build walls, but they also build doors and windows in them to cater to this very simple but fundamental need to connect with each other. Architects and engineers divide up space and then build bridges over the divisions. Georg Simmel's essay "The Bridge and the Door" ([1909] 1997) constitutes a far-sighted understanding of human spatiality and ends with the words

> But just as the formless limitation takes on a shape, its limitedness finds its significance and dignity only in that which the mobility of the door illustrates: in the possibility at any moment of stepping out of this limitation into freedom. (Simmel [1909] 1997: 69)

If the new spatial paradigm of fluidity is something more than a stylistic *Glass Bead Game* (Hesse [1943] 1949), then its importance lies in responding to the Heraclitean flow of life, by weaving spatial continuums that foster social and cultural ties among different peoples.

Living in the ages of solid and liquid modernity, if we follow Bauman's scheme, the contemporary subject is experiencing a crisis of existence, which is nowhere more forcefully apparent than in space.

In symbolic as well as in physical terms, *transparency* and *fluidity* have been adopted as spatial agents that ameliorate separation and isolation, promoting continuity of space between interior and exterior. However, like every architectural concept, these dynamics acquire meaning when put to use in making apparent their social function. Then their ambiguity becomes clear.

An interior is a machine de répétition, and an interior is also a palimpsest documenting transformation.

A shelter is an enclosure of privacy, safety, and protection, and it is also a cell of containment, restriction, and alienation.

Flowing, spilling, liquidifying situations melt into chaos and entropy, but also transgress borders, occupy space, reclaim interior and exterior, and redefine public and private.

The anxiety of the modern subject may lead to withdrawal and passivity or to actions of involvement and participation. If Le Corbusier pits architecture against revolution, order against chaos, then Sennett and Simmel negate the absolute limit, exalting the inclusive and multidimensional. Spaces that permit osmosis and fermentation, crossovers and hybridity, encourage the freedom of choices and the possibility of reconsidering the political.

Constructing boundaries instead of borders, keeping life inside under a tight lid, forces containment into outburst. The cell of indignant Beton eventually explodes, as the house in Michelangelo Antonioni's *Zabriskie Point* (1970), asking for life to be released, to flow and reconfigure its place in space.

References

Ambasz, E. (1972), *Italy: The New Domestic Landscape*, New York: Museum of Modern Art.

Bauman, Z. ([2000] 2011), *Liquid Modernity*, 11th ed., Cambridge: Polity Press.

Bernhard, Th. (1982), *Beton,* Frankfurt/M.: Suhrkamp.

Betsky, A (2004) *Asymptote Architecture - Scape*, Seoul: Damdi Publishing Company.

Constantopoulos, E. (1999), "From City-Dwelling to Multi-Dwelling," in S. Condaratos and W. Wang (eds.), *Greece: Architecture of the 20th Century*, Munich: Prestel, DAM, HIA.

Constantopoulos, E. (2010), "Interior Lives as a Spatial Equivalent of Balzac's *Unknown Masterpiece*," paper presented at the *Interior Lives* conference, The Modern Interiors Research Centre, Kingston University, May 13–14.

Deleuze, G. (1988), *Le pli—Leibniz et le baroque*, Paris: Les éditions de Minuit.

Duffy, F. (1966), *Office Landscaping: A New Approach to Office Planning*, London: *Anbar.*

Endless House: Intersections of Art and Architecture (2015), New York: Museum of Modern Art. Available online: http://www.domusweb.it/en/architecture/2015/10/02/endless_house.html (accessed January 29, 2016).

Foucault, M. ([1977] 1980), "The Eye of Power," in C. Gordon (ed.), *Power/Knowledge: Selected Interviews and Other Writings 1972–1977*, New York: Pantheon Books.

Goffman, E. (1959), *The Presentation of Self in Everyday Life,* New York: Anchor Books.

Hesse H. ([1943] 1949), *Das Glasperlenspiel* (*The Glass Bead Game*), trans. M. Savill. New York: H. Holt [1949].

Le Corbusier ([1923] 1989), *Vers une Architecture* (*Towards a New Architecture*), trans. F. Etchells, London: Butterworth Architecture.

Mobius House (n.d.). Available online: http://architizer.com/projects/mobius-house/ (accessed January 29, 2016).

Papaioannou, D (2011), Inside, http://www.dimitrispapaioannou.com/en/recent/inside (accessed January 29, 2016).

Partridge, E. (1958), *Origins*, London: Routledge and Kegan Paul.

Rowe, C., and R. Slutzky (1963), "Transparency: Literal and Phenomenal," in Dobbins, J & M (eds) (1965) *Perspecta* 8. The Yale Architectural Journal, Cambridge: MIT Press.

Rowe, C., and R. Slutzky (1971), "Transparency: Literal and Phenomenal Part II," in Coombs, R (ed) (1965) *Perspecta* 13/14, The Yale Architectural Journal Cambridge: MIT Press.

Ruby, I & A (2006), *Groundscapes*, Barcelona: Gustavo Gili

Sennett, R. (2008), "Borders and Boundaries," in *The Public Realm*. Available online: http://www.richardsennett.com/site/senn/templates/general2.aspx?pageid=16&cc=gb (accessed January 29, 2016).

Simmel, G. ([1909] 1997), "Brücke und Tür" ("The Bridge and the Door"), in N. Leach (1997) (ed.), *Rethinking Architecture: A Reader in Cultural Theory,* London: Routledge.

UNStudio (2010), "The Fluidity of Living," in *Reflections/Small Stuff*, Amsterdam: Ideabooks.

Chapter 11

Republican Homes: Modern Flows in Domestic Architecture in Santa Fé de Bogotá, 1820–1900

Patricia Lara-Betancourt

The transformation of the bourgeois home in Santa Fé de Bogotá, the capital of the new Republic of Colombia in the nineteenth century, started with the inherited and traditional Hispanic type of dwelling, that of rooms surrounding an inner courtyard. It then witnessed the gradual introduction of changes to its façade and interiors, inspired by European trends and the adoption of new materials and building techniques, a process that culminated in a building boom in the last decades of the century, including the construction of large suburban villas surrounded by gated gardens.

Overall the basic floor plan did not change, yet new and remodeled dwellings displayed innovations that effectively shaped and produced a different kind of residence that called for a significantly different way of living and organizing space. The house of the first half of the century (inherited from the colonial era) was partially open to the elements and to the world outside, allowing an easy flow of people, animals, and goods. Nature and local life were integrated through its internal garden and patios, which accommodated plants, trees, and animals such as horses, pigs, birds, and pets. In contrast, the dwelling that materialized from the late 1840s onward gradually closed its doors, windows, and corridors to the outside while giving increasing preeminence to more refined indoor and interior living.

These changes reflected the general transformation of the country, the city, and the social elite. The enthusiastic adoption of current European material culture, together with notions of privacy, etiquette, social life, class, and gender, permeated domestic family spaces, interior furnishings, and decoration. The city and the nation moved away from a colonial system, which had been in place for the previous three hundred years, to a postindependence republican era (from 1810 onward), aiming to be defined as modern, capitalist, and democratic, one in which private property and owning a home acquired new meaning. The new home came to be seen as the defining marker of the elite republican citizen and the preeminent place for private life.

This chapter examines how the republican home gradually evolved to become more private, formal, sophisticated, and exclusive, changing forever the way its interiors related to the street and to the urban and natural landscape. This transformation went hand in hand with the modernization of the city and the emergence of new public spaces of sociability such as parks, boulevards, clubs, and theaters (Saldarriaga and Fonseca 1989: 185).

The Republican Home: Becoming Bourgeois

Spurred by Enlightenment ideas at the end of the eighteenth century, the city of Santa Fé de Bogotá, and indeed most cities and countries in Latin America, underwent a period of profound transformation that would take them through decades of independence wars (1800–1830), which were followed by the dismantling of a three-hundred-year-old colonial system and the establishment of a modern, liberal republic. In response to the industrializing world, and particularly from the 1860s onward, Colombia and the rest of Latin America became a major source of mostly mining and agricultural produce as raw material for European markets, in return developing a significant market for industrial imports. It was through this exchange of goods that the country integrated into the world economic system and was able to remain an independent country and safe from the threat of imperial rule.

As a result, by the end of the nineteenth century, Bogotá's population had increased fivefold to over 200,000 inhabitants, and the city had reacted to the new demographics by erecting new dwellings and refurbishing and repurposing old public and religious buildings. Gradually, the main streets were paved, a tramway system of public transport took shape, and various other urban infrastructure works emerged, all contributing to create a modern city with services such as running water, garbage collection, gas and electricity,[1] a telegraphic network, and a nascent police force. At the start of the twentieth century, the central part of the city exhibited the characteristics of a modern bourgeois metropolis (Mejía 1993).

A parallel and closely related process took place in domestic architecture. Many colonial houses belonging to the upper class were regarded as ugly and old-fashioned. Builders and architects responded to new notions of taste inspired by European models (Arango 1985: 69; Corradine 1989: 253) while still respecting the traditional layout. Buildings were refurbished by adopting new materials, building methods, and fashionable styles to modernize existing spatial layouts. The transformation was so thorough that it effectively conveyed a different type of dwelling that embraced novel aesthetic and cultural preferences. By the 1890s, some wealthy families started to commission new homes outside the city that completely left behind the colonial template, a trend that soon became the norm.

The Colonial Legacy

In the same way as all the other Hispanic cities, Santa Fé de Bogotá was laid out and built according to a preestablished plan and grid that extended from a central plaza surrounded by the main government, religious, and residential buildings. The dwellings of the nobility were traditionally located in the center of the city, on or as close as possible to the central plaza, an area called "La Catedral" (The Cathedral), where they remained until well into the twentieth century (Mejía 1993: 439–40, 444). The houses formed a continuous façade along the central plaza and main streets but had courtyard patios and gardens in their interior.

Figure 11.1

Zaguán and patio, Instituto Caro y Cuervo. Wikimedia Commons.

Figure 11.2

Colonial house. Birthplace
of poet Rufino José Cuervo.
Wikimedia Commons.

The traditional dwelling was structured by a hall called *zaguán* that led into an interior patio surrounded by open cloister corridors, with rooms opening directly onto the corridors and patio (Figure 11.1). In two-story houses the scheme was duplicated upstairs by adding a balcony to the façade. In larger houses the scheme was also repeated toward the back by adding more patios and ending with a large and walled open area called *solar* (Vawell 1978: 47).

The spatial organization of city dwellers' homes was a reflection of the social hierarchy, with the social position of each family being determined and expressed based on location such as proximity to important civil, religious, and commercial buildings, and on scale such as the preferred two-story dwelling. A hierarchy was also in place within the dwelling, with different places occupied by the paterfamilias, family members, and domestic servants. It was a domestic model well disseminated in Hispanic America (Lockhart 1990: 32), which embodied the two main sources of traditional power: land and family lineage. This hierarchical model was reflected in an architecture shaped by social, economic, and political forces rather than by the design of an individual architect.

The elite house in the first half of the nineteenth century was at the threshold of modernization, undergoing a profound process of change but still keeping features partly belonging to a disappearing world. As it had been traditionally, it was still a home in close relationship with the countryside, attentive to the rural world surrounding the city. Its interiors remained in constant and open communication with the outside, well integrated into the city rhythms and cycles, allowing through its doors, windows, patios, and gardens the easy circulation of family members, servants, visitors, goods, coaches, and beasts.

The building was large and spacious (Mollien 1978: 55), and access to it would be through the wide *zaguán*, which led to the patio. Its façade featured an enormous double door as gate and windows protected with iron grillwork and wooden jalousies, permitting dwellers, and particularly women, to look outside without being seen. Two-story dwellings included a first-floor balcony on the façade encompassing the length of the drawing room. Invariably the family would inhabit the rooms on the first floor because they were considered less damp and cold, while the ground-floor rooms were rented out as shops, storage, or living accommodation for artisans and travelers (Lara-Betancourt 1998a).

On the upper floor the most important rooms in the house faced the street, reflecting the family's spatial hierarchy (Figure 11.2). The large, well-lit, and ventilated drawing room opened onto the balcony (Martínez 1987: 212) and also led through a side door into the master bedroom (Gosselman 1981: 36). By contrast, domestic servants would inhabit the ground floor and the back of house areas surrounding the second or third patio, close to the kitchen and pantries.

The typology of the colonial dwelling was well suited to regions of hot weather, but in cooler Bogotá, people suffered from the cold and damp weather. There were no fireplaces or braziers in the formal and living areas of the house, as they were considered unhealthy. Rooms were made to feel warmer by the use of screens to prevent draughts, mats, carpets, curtains, and textile hangings (Gosselman 1981: 278; Le Moyne 1969: 113). Colored muslin and canvas covered the window frames to allow some light in, as a majority of windows lacked glass due to high costs; most balconies and windows were framed only by wooden or iron balusters (Le Moyne 1969: 118–19; Steuart 1990: 58). Describing the typical dwelling in Bogotá, a nineteenth-century American traveler, Isaac Holton, observed in the 1850s: "they have . . . small, few and barred windows, and women, like prisoners, spend their days looking out" (1981: 159). Indoors, most rooms were dark unless the door was open, as only the dining room had windows overlooking the patio. According to travelers' accounts, this arrangement compromised privacy, made the room colder, and exposed its inhabitants to the noise outside (Hettner 1990: 218; Díaz Castro 1985: 18). But to locals this was the normal way of living. Balconies and windows were used mostly by women, who never tired of observing the comings and goings of people outside without compromising their privacy. Balconies in particular were attractively decorated for religious processions such as Corpus Christi and Easter, when the whole family would come out to enjoy the spectacle (Le Moyne 1969: 138).

Houses were made with a compacted soil brick, *tapia pisada* (Holton 1981: 396), with walls up to 1 meter thick (Le Moyne 1969: 118). Interior walls were traditionally painted white or decorated with drawings and allegorical paintings, including flowers, vases, and wreaths. Gradually this type of ornamentation was replaced by wallpaper introduced from the late eighteenth century onward. The roof beams were visible (Mollien 1978: 55; Vergara 1931: 209–10), and in wealthy houses they were carved and the roof surface decorated with painted ornamental motifs.

Displaying a close contact with nature and the countryside, flowers, plants, trees, and animals populated domestic patios as an essential part of the dwelling in Santa Fé de Bogotá. Although originally patios were used for the dismounting and unloading of beasts, as time passed the first patio became more ornamental, displaying a well-cared-for garden. The corridors surrounding the patio were furnished with an abundance of flower pots (Hamilton[2] 1970: 64–5).The other patios could be orchards (with herbal and medicinal plants), corrals for the rearing of birds and pigs for family consumption (Ordóñez 1988: 98), and barns. The large *solar* at the end of the house could also be used as a playground for children (Carnegie-Williams 1990: 105; Hettner 1990: 217; Marroquín 1920: 15).

The Bourgeois Home: Decorative Care and Global Flows

From midcentury onward, in response to increasing demographic pressure and the need for more housing, some large colonial houses were demolished while other dwellings were remodeled or subdivided following modern building trends.[3] The result was a great transformation in the appearance and construction of the houses of the elite, which became more luxurious, elegant, and modern. Yet these changes also resulted in more formal and exclusive homes, restricting the previous relaxed ways of moving and circulating within and through rooms and spaces (Lara-Betancourt 1998a).

Thanks to the profits of the export economy, the government and Bogotá's inhabitants, particularly the elite, were able to indulge in expressing their recently acquired national identity and modern tastes. The emerging bourgeoisie was fiercely committed to following European models of modern living and consumption, particularly those coming from England and France (Lara-Betancourt 1998b). These conditions were a big boost for urban development and domestic architecture. Members of the elite traveled to Europe and the United States and sent their children abroad to get a professional education. Architectural expertise, books, journals, and magazines also came from abroad and disseminated quickly, advancing the aesthetic taste and preferences of the elite. In the second half of the century several foreign architects arrived in Bogotá, such as the Englishman Thomas Reed, the German Karl Schlecht (from 1858 to 1865), and the Italian Pietro Cantini (Téllez Castañeda 1989: 269).[4] Additionally, several local architects that had trained in Europe returned home (Marroquín 1967: 60).[5]

The city doubled its area, a response to the fivefold increase in its population, yet the number of houses built or refurbished increased 8.25 times (Mejía 1993: 517). From 1870 onward the central part of the city underwent a complete transformation. It became the place for banks, business agents, restaurants, hotels, and shops selling imported goods, while remaining the preferred residential area of the elite (Mejía 1993: 478, 480).

Overall the new and modernized dwellings displayed new spatial layouts and better construction methods, quality of materials, and finishes (Figure 11.3). Locals were now educated in stylish notions of taste, modern construction, and the use of color. These changes occurred simultaneously with the creation of new rooms and areas in the house designated for social life, which were adorned with fashionable furniture and furnishings (Lara-Betancourt 1998b). Decoration became increasingly important, as manifest also in the abundance and complexity of architectural features and details, the quality of materials, and the variety of color combinations, textures, and designs (Kastos 1972: 285–6; Samper 1925: 67).

Figure 11.3

Casa Republicana, Biblioteca Luis Angel Arango. Wikimedia Commons.

What was perceived as an avalanche of changes provoked a mixed response in the elite. Most felt proud of the progress they could see happening in front of their eyes, but some were also aware of what they were losing in return. As the writer Ricardo Silva put it: "Modern progress came and invaded everything taking away the distinctive character of our simple ways" (Silva 1973: 182; see also Kastos 1972: 284–5). As early as 1858 the writer Emiro Kastos (1823–1894) described the most prominent changes, referring to the austere and humble façades that gave way to elegant exteriors in keeping with equally impressive interiors (1972: 284–5). José María Vergara y Vergara also found the modern home wanting. He thought it was very small and had done away with its gardens and orchard, a common complaint (Vergara 1975: 40; Santander 1976: 481; Vergara 1969: 75). After the subdivision, houses with originally three and four patios were reduced to having just a small one. The writer Ricardo Silva wryly summed up the transformation of the new type of dwelling by describing the "modern small house":

> The merry elements typical of the modern home, the French home, well-furnished, tiny; with a salon measuring seven-meters high over a width of five. . . . Narrow apartments, their inhabitants say . . . blue sky [color] painted with indigo on the wall that surrounds the tiny patio of these narrow cages with absurd stairs, where the furniture can only go in with a pulley through the balcony, and which have replaced the old house of Bogotá, ample, well ventilated, comfortable, cheerful and smelling of "reseda" and "alhucema." (Silva 1973: 179–80)

In 1896 Miguel Samper summed up the main changes in the house: "Palatial façades . . . and narrow interiors" (Samper 1978: 101). The palatial façades would include the following features: smaller main door, elongated windows and more of them, symmetry in the distribution of balcony and windows, iron-grill work, glass panes, and artfully combined colors and shades for walls, plasterwork, and woodwork (Marroquín 1967: 59; Silva 1969: 162, 167).

Together, these innovations and reforms reveal a marked decorative intention reflecting a significant shift in aesthetic taste and in ways of inhabiting domestic space. The narrowed *zaguán* changed from being a functional passage into a highly decorated space with wallpaper, a fine mat, varnished frieze, and stuccoed ceiling. Beasts could no longer use this entrance as they had done for the previous three hundred years (Marroquín 1920: 19). Once kept open during the day, now the main and inner gates remained closed, signaling a home turning its back to the street and becoming more secluded. The *zaguán* and hence the home, traditionally linked to street life and the community, became a private, exclusive, and highly decorated domestic space, reflecting the emergence of interior living separated from the public sphere.

Internally, the main corridor, once open to the elements, turned into an alternate lounge closed in by wooden frames and glass-colored panes, functioning as a hall extension to the drawing room's area (Vergara 1975: 40; Rivera y Garrido 1968: 234). However, the main garden survived and was lavished with money and attention, welcoming statues, new types of plants, and attractive fountains (Lisboa 1990: 136–7; Carnegie-Williams 1990: 62).

The drawing room continued to occupy the same prominent place adjacent the balcony facing the street. Reflecting the increasingly active pursuit of social life and entertaining, a small reception room and the music room were added, with all spaces linked through connecting doors. In 1879, the writer Ricardo Silva mockingly identified these spaces with French names such as *boudoir*, *recevoir*, and *bureau* because they followed French fashions and with the predominant colors blue, grey, and yellow, used in their furnishings and decoration (Silva 1973: 179). Vergara also saw an excess in the decorative drive of these new interiors, pointing out that even the domestic servants' quarters had been wallpapered (Vergara 1975: 41). The drawing room and additional social spaces exhibited all the signs of this transformation: ornate ceilings with an abundance of plaster work, thin and straight brick walls, wallpaper, wooden floors, wood panelling, many large glass windows, and in some cases large frames to separate and connect the various social spaces: hall, corridor, reception room, drawing room, boudoir, and music room.

Progressive Flows

This chapter has shown the ways in which the elite house, which was inherited from the colonial past and survived until midcentury, transformed, leaving behind its traditional openness to nature and the outside through the *zaguán*, internal patios, corridors, and gardens. In responding to modern and fashionable ideas, in the second half of the century a new type of dwelling emerged due to the increasing flow of international capital and improving economic circumstances. Being completely open to the cultural and material influences from abroad, this home adopted a European ethic and aesthetic where privacy, interiority, and etiquette became paramount, thus distancing the house from the natural and built landscape while focusing on the newly acquired and created interior environment that displayed the riches of the modern, globalized world.

This transformation altered the flow and circulation of people and things: from an unimpeded physical, visual, and sensorial flow connecting the outside to the inside, to a more formal way of behaving and moving within and between spaces. Through a wide variety of new materials, textures, colors, forms, products, and ornamental objects, the interiors became rich, dense, and sophisticated, a world of their own, indulging people's imagination and newly acquired tastes that spoke to them of modernity, fashion, foreign lands, and progress. The transition from a colonial way of inhabiting ruled by convention to a fashionable and progressive one sacrificed the traditional flow between inside and outside and replaced it with a different kind: one of exciting industrial goods and European cultural influence.

Notes

1. The Bogotá Electric Light Company started to operate in 1890 and was followed by the Energía Eléctrica de Bogotá in 1900.

2. The English traveler Colonel Hamilton arrived in the country on January 20, 1824, and left on April 18, 1825.

3. Historian and architect Carlos Martínez explains that around the mid-nineteenth century "a consensus emerged disparaging the colonial heritage and as a result demolition work started" (1987: 216).

4. Thomas Reed (1810–1878) was born in Santa Cruz, a Caribbean island, at the time part of the Danish West Indies.

5. Mariano Sanz de Santamaría (1857–1915) graduated as architect from the Weimar Polytechnic in Germany in 1880. He worked in Colombia from 1883 to 1910.

References

Arango, S., ed. (1985), *La Arquitectura en Colombia*, Bogotá: Editorial Escala, Universidad Nacional y Universidad de los Andes.

Carnegie-Williams, R. (1990), *Un Año en los Andes o Aventuras de una Lady en Bogotá* [1881–2], Bogotá: Tercer Mundo Editores.

Corradine Angulo, A. (1989), *Historia de la Arquitectura Colombiana*, Bogotá: Escala.

Díaz Castro, E. (1985), *Novelas y Cuadros de Costumbres* [1858–64], vol. 2, Bogotá: Procultura.

Gosselman, C. A. (1981), *Viaje por Colombia 1825 y 1826*, Bogotá: Ediciones del Banco de la República.

Hamilton, J. P. (1970), "Del Magdalena a Bogotá" [1824–5], in AA.VV., *Viajeros Extranjeros en Colombia*, 47–90, Cali: Carvajal & Cía.

Hettner, A. (1990), "Viaje por los Andes Colombianos (1882–1884)," in M. G. Romero (ed.), *Bogotá en los Viajeros Extranjeros del Siglo XIX*, Bogotá: Villegas Editores.

Holton, I. (1981), *La Nueva Granada: Veinte Meses en los Andes* [1852–4], Bogotá: Banco de la República.

Kastos, E. (Juan de Dios Restrepo) (1972), "Bogotá Después de Algunos Años de Ausencia" [1858], in E. Kastos, *Artículos Escogidos*, 282–7, Bogotá: Banco Popular.

Lara-Betancourt, P. (1998a), "La Sala Domestica en Santa Fé de Bogotá, Siglo XIX. Arquitectura Domestica: Lenguajes Colonial y Republicano" (The Drawing Room in Santa Fe de Bogotá, Nineteenth Century: Colonial and Republican Domestic Architecture), *Memoria y Sociedad*, 3 (1): 53–75.

Lara-Betancourt, P. (1998b), "La Sala Domestica en Santa Fé de Bogotá, Siglo XIX. El Decorado de la Sala Romántica: Gusto Europeo y Esnobismo" (The Romantic Salon: European Taste and Snobbism in the Drawing Room in Santa Fe de Bogotá, Nineteenth Century), *Anuario Colombiano de Historia Social y de la Cultura*, 25: 109–34.

Le Moyne, A. (1969), *Viaje y Estancia en la Nueva Granada* [1828–39], Bogotá: Biblioteca Schering Corporation USA.

Lisboa, M. M. (1990), "Relación de un Viaje a Venezuela, Nueva Granada y Ecuador" [1853], in M. G. Romero (ed.), *Bogotá en los Viajeros Extranjeros del Siglo XIX*, 123–54, Bogotá: Villegas Editores.

Lockhart, J. (1990), "Organización y Cambio Social," in *Historia de América Latina,* Barcelona: Crítica.

Marroquín, J. M. (1920), "El lujo: II. Mis Nuevas Confidencias" [1879], in J. M. Marroquín, *Artículos Literarios*, vol. 1, 13–34, Bogotá: Librería Santa Fe.

Marroquín, J. M. (1967), "El Cuarto de los Trastos" [c. 1870], in AA.VV., *Cuadros de Costumbres*, Bogotá: Biblioteca Schering.

Martínez, C. (1987), *Santafé Capital del Nuevo Reino de Granada*, Bogotá: Editorial Presencia, Banco Popular.

Mejía, G. (1993), "Los Años del Cambio: Espacio Urbano y Urbanización en Bogotá 1819–1910," PhD diss., University of Miami.

Mollien, G. T. (1978), "1823," in C. Martínez (ed.), *Bogotá Reseñada por Cronistas y Viajeros Ilustres: 1572–1948*, Bogotá: Escala.

Ordóñez, M. (1988), *Soledad Acosta de Samper: Una Nueva Lectura*, Bogotá: Ediciones Fondo Cultural Cafetero.

Rivera y Garrido, L. (1968), *Impresiones y Recuerdos* [1860s], Cali: Carvajal & Cía.

Saldarriaga, R., and L. Alberto y Fonseca (1989), *Un Siglo de Arquitectura Colombiana*, in AA.VV. *Nueva Historia de Colombia*, vol. VI, Bogotá: Editorial Planeta.

Samper, M. (1925), "Retrospecto," in *Escritos Político-Económicos*, vol. 1, 67, Bogotá: Editorial Cromos.

Samper, M. (1978), "1896," in C. Martínez (ed.), *Bogotá Reseñada por Cronistas y Viajeros Ilustres*, 101, Bogotá: Escala.

Santander, R. E. (1976), "Los Artesanos" [c. 1860], in E. L. Muñoz (ed.), *Narradores Colombianos del Siglo XIX*, 470–85, Bogotá: Colcultura.

Silva, R. (1969), "Un Remiendito" [c. 1880], in AA.VV. *Cuadros de Costumbres*, 156–69, Cali: Carvajal & Cía. Article written most probably at the end of the 1870s.

Silva, R. (1973), "Las Llavecitas" [1879], in R. Silva, *Artículos de Costumbres*, 179–91, Bogotá: Banco Popular.

Steuart, J. (1990), "Narración de una Expedición a la Capital de la Nueva Granada y Residencia allí de Once Meses, 1836–1837," in M. G. Romero (ed.), *Bogotá en los Viajeros Extranjeros del Siglo XIX*, 57–120, Bogotá: Villegas Editores.

Téllez Castañeda, G. (1989), "La Arquitectura y el Urbanismo en la Época Republicana, 1830–40 / 1930–35," in J. Jaramillo Uribe (ed.), *Nueva Historia de Colombia*, 251–96, Bogotá: Planeta Editorial.

Vawell, R. (1978), "1819," in C. Martínez (ed.), *Bogotá Reseñada por Cronistas y Viajeros Ilustres: 1572–1948*, Bogotá: Escala. This chapter is taken from Vawell´s book *Campaigns and Cruises in Venezuela and New Granada and the Pacific Ocean, from 1817 to 1830*.

Vergara y Vergara, J. M. (1931), "Un Par de Viejos" [1868], in J. M. Vergara y Vergara, *Cuadros de Costumbres*, 207–22, Bogotá: Editorial Minerva. Article written in 1868 but referring to 1848.

Vergara y Vergara, J. M. (1969), "Las Tres Tazas" [1860s], in AA.VV., *Cuadros de Costumbres*, 72–101, Cali: Carvajal & Cía.

Vergara y Vergara, J. M. (1975), "El Lenguaje de las Casas" [1865], in M. G. Romero (ed.), *Enciclopedia de Colombia*, vol. 5, Barcelona: Editorial Nueva Granada.

Chapter 12

A Place Out of the Archive: Reprise under [the Condition of] Flow

Gini Lee and Dolly Daou

This project, "A place out of the archive," seeks other practices of representation to convey shifting aspirations and occupation in the lives of buildings. To enable this we reprised respected works from the architectural past in order to examine or test their transformed contemporary condition. These works are drawn from the architectural archive as the primary source for nominating once grand and/or experimental interiors, recently revisited. We note how the currency of the present inflicts itself on the past. The interior landscape is remade according to other narratives, such as efficiency beyond attraction; everyday event beyond unique experience; and the shattering of expectations from an arguably more elegant time. We record the passing of the original alongside the altered conditions brought to bear on these places under the flow of "modernizing" cultures and economies.

These photographic works document the interiors of well-loved buildings in the city of Adelaide, Australia, and are held in the University of South Australia Architecture Archive. They include the 1940s public school, the nineteenth-century station, the 1920s public hospital, the once fashionable tearooms (now a low-cost garment store), and the repurposed first stock exchange, all of which still exist in various forms. When walking through these places, we noticed and apprehended everyday material conditions as if on an interior treasure hunt. Mindful of the austere archival records that brought us to these places, we first attempted to faithfully capture the interiors in sharp relief and through considered photographic framing. We then reduced these images to black and white as if to recall the past methods of the original untouched photograph. We encountered both the public and hidden spaces and annotated their condition through image fragments that seek out the original aspirations of the buildings' makers. Most often, these fragments revealed only ghosting remnants of a detail, pattern, or material past. Following this process we prepared captions by extracting the words of the original architects, builders, politicians, and developers with wry amusement regarding the scenes that met us in the next century.

In the second stage of the project, we retraced our initial steps and made new interior recordings, in which we experimented with capturing moments by tracing the trajectory of our eye and the camera as we looked around and about, up, down, and over. Using the sensibility of our peripheral vision, we appropriated the photographer Uta Barth's regard for the blur as "an inherent optical condition that functions in the human eye as it does in the camera lens" (Barth 1997). However, everyday perception negotiates constant eye movement to reduce the blur of the outside world and to attain our customary equilibrium. To regard the scene in front of us as a coherent whole, we processed numerous sequences of out-of-focus and moving imagery. Our roving camera captures multiple scenes, resulting in color fields of merging objects, forms, surfaces, and bodies. These color montages of the reprised interior revealed a contemporary, hyper-real condition beyond merely abstract color works. Between the original and its facsimile, real and imagined histories challenge the archival gaze through applying an atmospheric lens to the seemingly static interior. These momentary grabs reactivate interiors subject to temporary inhabitation and uncertain futures to infer possibilities yet to come; if you blur your eyes, you may recall or begin to imagine ghostly reminders of the past made present.

Reference

Uta Barth. In conversation with Sheryl Conkelton, *Journal of Contemporary Art 8,* no. 1 (summer).

Chapter 12.1–12.5

Public school, public hospital,
railway station, tearooms, first
stock exchange

"The school must be a welcoming place of light and color combining strength with lightness and color and sufficiently monumental to be worthy of an important public building." Adelaide High School

"The outbreak of the Second World War in 1939 no doubt had some influence on this project, and the additional accommodation provided in this new building made the Royal Adelaide Hospital the biggest single hospital unit in Australia." Royal Adelaide Hospital

"Of particular note was the enormous domed marble hall that served as a grand and dignified main waiting room." Adelaide Railway Station

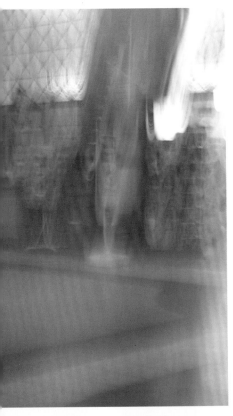

"Our cake shop in Rundle Street enjoys the reputation of being
the busiest cake shop in the Southern Hemisphere." Balfours Cake Shop

"In several places there were silver fittings, while Boyle ventilators and Tobin tubes ensured a constant supply of fresh air, adjudged to be of great advantage in the event of a sudden market slump." Adelaide Stock Exchange

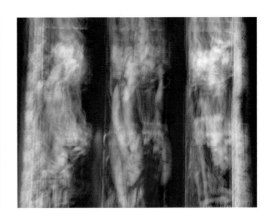

Chapter 13

Projective Views

Eleanor Suess

The chapter "Light Events" examines relationships between interior and exterior space, positing that techniques found in artists' film practice are particularly suitable for communicating the expressly temporal aspects of the constantly shifting spatial relationships between interior and exterior. It also builds upon notions of the active imagination of the viewer in both structural film (Gidal 1976: 2–3) and architectural representation (Evans 1989: 19), claiming that in the relationship between film, screening room, and active viewer a new spatial condition is formed. The practice-based work presented in this visual essay expands this thesis to present a series of connected spatiotemporal artworks, commencing with the Projective Views installation designed for the Wunderlich Gallery, Melbourne, for the FLOW2 conference in 2012.

Figure 13.1

Six windows, three countries. © Eleanor Suess 2016.

The Wunderlich installation comprised several film projections showing a series of views through windows from a number of international locations (Figure 13.1). The locations, in London, northern Italy, Perth, and New South Wales, are homes of friends and family. These are places where I regularly dwell; the views through these windows are familiar to me. The footage was projected onto the gallery panels positioned in front of the room's long row of windows and on the opposite wall, thus transposing new virtual "windows" onto these other, distant exterior spaces (Figures 13.2–13.4). The projected window together with the interior space of the gallery, and the real window with a view to the local exterior of the gallery building, collectively formed a new spatial condition for the duration of the projection (Le Grice 2001). The resulting piece is therefore both observational (through its use of recordings of existing conditions) and propositional, through the creation of a new hybrid experiential space formed of both projected and material space.

Figure 13.2–13.4

Projective Views, installation in the Wunderlich Galley, Melbourne. © Eleanor Suess 2016. Photographers Andrew Cerchez and Gini Lee.

Unable to attend the Melbourne exhibition in person, my only access to the completed work was via photographic documentation. As a development of the now dismantled installation, I undertook a "reconstruction" of the piece through the creation of a physical architectural model of the gallery, using a miniature data projector to project the filmed windows. This reconstruction was based on photographs (supplied by others)[1] of the space before and during the exhibition and the CAD drawings of the gallery. The model was constructed from paper and card, at a scale of 1:33,[2] sufficient to obtain the necessary amount of detail and to be able to accommodate the data projector. As the model was constructed and photographed in my London studio, the "real" exterior seen through the window[3] is different from that of the actual gallery in Melbourne, but as the reconstruction is an easily transported model, this "exterior" can change, unlike that of the original exhibition and gallery. From this reconstruction a series of "documentary" photographs were produced (Figures 13.5–13.10), constituting secondary documentation of the original installation but also resulting in a new piece of work. The reconstruction also enabled recordings of the installation at different diurnal conditions, particularly the shift from day to night, when the "real" (model) window becomes a black pane rather than an aperture into another space. The reconstructed installation was also filmed, thereby generating the time-based footage missing from the original installation documentation. This will support the production of a third work, an artists' film that can explore the temporal qualities of the installation.

Figure 13.5–13.10

Projective Views, model photograph. © Eleanor Suess 2016.

This development of the original Projective Views installation into new work is a continuation of my artists' film and architectural installation practice. Elsewhere I have outlined the trajectory of my practice (Suess 2014), which, from my grounding in both art and architectural practice, resides in a "third space" (Grosz 2001: xv) between the disciplines of artists' film and architectural representation. This transdisciplinary[4] practice has consistently dealt with architectural issues, and as both artist and architect I work from within the subject of architecture, acknowledging Jane Rendell's positioning of architecture as subject as well as discipline (Rendell 2004: 143).

One aspect of my practice is focused on the creation of digital films using architectural models, particularly reconstructions of architectural installations. As Buskirk, Jones, and Jones (2013) explain, the terms *reconstruct, recreate,* and *refabricate* imply a connection to an original work of art, but also involve a process of translation and creation of new work. The original installations are normally ephemeral, no longer existing[5] except through the photographic and textual documentation—echoes of the original artwork. The reconstruction "remakes" the space, and unlike a digital reconstruction, it is a physical space, albeit at a reduced scale. This new space can be "experienced" through a primary interaction with the model itself, and through the secondary experience of viewing photographs and films taken from within the model. Photographic and filmed imagery allows a view from inside the model, as the body of the camera can be accommodated in these compressed spaces.

Figure 13.5–13.10

Projective Views, model photograph. © Eleanor Suess 2016.

As the models are made to be photographed and filmed, rather than exhibited, only I, as the artist, have access to the primary experience of the model. Because of its reduced scale, my body cannot enter the space itself, only peer in through cut-away walls and ceilings. Film theorist Vivian Sobchack (1992) introduces the notion of the "film's body," which she asserts spans from camera to projector and screen, giving the film a holistic material and spatial presence. This "body" has separate relationships with the filmmaker behind the camera, the spectator[6] in front of the screen, and the material world that all inhabit. For the filming of architectural models, using a miniature camera, Sobchack's assertion of the relationship between filmmaker, camera, and material world takes a different turn. As the filmmaker cannot inhabit the same space as the camera, Sobchack's "embodiment relation" (1992: 183) between the body of the filmmaker and the body of the camera is diluted. In the space of the model the camera has a scale similar to that of a human body, and it is therefore the camera's body alone that occupies the scaled-down space of the model. If the camera has the facility to show its view on a separate screen (such as on a smartphone, tablet, or computer), then the filmmaker's relationship to the image, as it is filmed, is closer to that of Sobchack's spectator than as filmmaker.

Filming allows a new form of "experience" of the "original" artwork where no time-based documentation of that original exists. Architectural installations are designed to be experienced by a living, moving body, over a period of time; a film of a scaled model reconstruction of the installation, while not simulating the actual bodily experience of that original space, generates a parallel, analogous experience in the active viewer of the film. The making of a film of the scaled model reconstruction also constitutes the production of new work.

These multiple versions of the Projective Views installation question where the artwork and/or architecture resides. Is it in the experience of the space and time of the original installation in Melbourne, in the photographs of the original installation, in the artifact of the scaled model reconstruction with its miniature projection, in the photographs and film of the reconstruction, or in the experience of viewing the new film? Or is it in the critical dialogue that surrounds the work, such as in this chapter, of the same name? Perhaps both artwork and architecture reside in all of these.

Notes

1. At no point was I able to visit the space of the installation, and therefore this space was always, for me, only ever constructed within my imagination. The gallery space has since been demolished, with a new gallery in a new building in its place.

2. 1:33 is not a standard architectural scale, but the nearest architectural scales would have been too large to construct in the space available, or too small to allow enough detail. 1:33 is a scale commonly used for model aircraft, and it fitted the miniature projector perfectly.

3. Unlike the exterior in the original installation documentation, the model's "exterior" is only hinted at, consisting merely of blurred images of Australian trees and shrubs planted within a London garden.

4. Bremner and Rodgers define interdisciplinary practice as that which has a primary, as well as a secondary, discipline, as opposed to transdisciplinarity, in which no single discipline is primary, enabling practitioners to "work in and contribute to both [disciplines] and generate unique conceptions and artifacts as a result of an emergent transdisciplinary perspective" (Bremner and Rodgers 2013: 11).

5. For the Wunderlich piece, the space of the site itself has also been "unmade."

6. *Spectator* is the term Sobchack uses, but it is a term that I find too passive for the very active role of the viewer. It also implies that spectators are witnessing a spectacle, which in films about the everyday, they are not.

References

Bremner, C., and P. Rodgers. (2013), "Design Without Discipline," *Design Issues*, 29 (3): 4–13, doi:10.1162/DESI_a_00217.

Buskirk, M., A. Jones, and C. A. Jones (2013), "The Year in 'Re-,'" *Artforum International*, 52 (4): 127.

Evans, R. (1989), "Architectural Projection," in E. Blau and E. Kaufman (eds.), *Architecture and Its Image*, Montreal: Centre Canadien d'Architecture.

Gidal, P. (1976), "Theory and Definition of Structural/Materialist Film," in P. Gidal (ed.), *Structural Film Anthology*, 1–21, London: British Film Institute.

Grosz, E. (2001), *Architecture from the Outside: Essays on Virtual and Real Space*, Cambridge: MIT Press.

Le Grice, M. (2001), "Real TIME/SPACE [1972]," in *Experimental Cinema in the Digital Age*, 155–63, London: British Film Institute.

Rendell, J. (2004), "Architectural Research and Disciplinarity," *arq: Architectural Research Quarterly*, 8 (2): 141–7, doi:doi:10.1017/S135913550400017X.

Sobchack, V. C. (1992), *The Address of the Eye: A Phenomenology of Film Experience*, Princeton: Princeton University Press.

Suess, E. (2014), "Doors Don't Slam: Time-Based Architectural Representation," in D. Maudlin and M. Vellinga (eds.), *Consuming Architecture: On the Occupation, Appropriation and Interpretation of Buildings*, 243–59, Abingdon: Routledge.

3

Part 3
Continuum

Introduction

Pat Brown

Continuum is the given fluid context of FLOW within which interior and landscape practice performs. Continuum has both depth and breadth, across ranges of scales, within and beyond horizons; it embraces physical and material layers of that which exists and that which might be proposed. It is both spatial and temporal, recognizing everyday and seasonal change that is continuous, cyclical, and fluctuating. The idea of continuum does not register a clear distinction between inside and out, but rather sequential conditions of occupation, experience, and perception. It is inclusive of former conditions and their traces, as well as trajectories of change and aspiration.

Themes of connection and continuity are focused and expansive, from the immediate personal experience to collective experiences of occupation, cultivation, and projection through time. The continuum of FLOW includes journeys, consumptions and outputs, and their individual and shared impact on quality of life. FLOW depends on conditions of ownership and access, familiarity and understanding, and the quality, agency, and attraction of environments within which we live, work, and play. The health and quality of interior and exterior environments are enhanced by discerning practices of heating and cooling, harnessing of microclimatic conditions and responses to macroclimatic shifts, and material selection. The reuse of buildings and land, which propel social and spatial regeneration, are each part of a continuum of change, just as are food production, harvest, distribution, and diet.

In the continuum of spatial and material practice, there is an ongoing trajectory of making, testing, and measuring on the ground and in the field, and projective testing through modeling and mapping. The potentials for shared ecologies of practice, reflection, and action, between disciplines and geographies, scales and programs, are alluded to in the chapters that follow, from the individual and domestic, to the local, neighborhood, urban, regional, and cross-border experience of place.

The case studies are reflective and contemporary, moving from the nineteenth century to the present and across continental geographies. They range from representation of the domestic artifact, to thresholds of the individual dwelling and relationships with the public realm beyond. They include local neighborhood experience and the continuum of FLOW of cities, overlapping programs of urban forest and high-rise living. Themes embrace individual expression and perception, health and well-being, social cohesion, and green infrastructures. Specifically, continuum includes the inner worlds of reflection, observation, and focus.

In his essay, "The Interiority of Landscape: Gate, Journey, Horizon," Jeff Malpas, philosopher and Distinguished Professor, University of Tasmania, examines the dynamics and interiority of landscape. The essay engages with the experience and perception of landscape, and specifically of *place*, through marker elements of *gate*, *journey*, and *horizon*, replacing the idea of landscape as scenic backdrop. This foregrounding of the experience of *being within* recognizes specifics of the micro and macro landscape. Malpas draws on the work of the New Zealand painter Colin McCahon and the ideas of Georg Simmel and Martin Heidegger, and he reveals landscape as fundamental in asserting an understanding of *place*. These ideas embrace an inclusive, big picture as well as a microcosmic and nuanced view of the key relationships between interior and exterior place. In nurturing explorations of scope and potentials of fresh thresholds, and connections of private and public, there can be a reappraisal of the edge and its creative occupation. Significantly, in studies of nature and ecology, it is at the periphery or transitions of habitats, rather than the center, that biodiversity is at its richest. Transference of these ideas across conditions of scale and time suggests fresh interpretations, which are included in the chapters that follow.

At the domestic and local scale, from the Yucatán Peninsula in Mexico, the chapter "Transitional Spaces in Late-Nineteenth-Century Domestic Architecture in Mérida, Yucatán" is presented by Gladys Arana López, Universidad Autonoma de Yucatan, and Catherine Ettinger, Universidad Michoacana de San Nicolas de Hidalgo, Mexico. These spaces are described in the context of houses built by hacienda owners in the Yucatán Peninsula. The examples are specific to the last decade of the nineteenth century and the first decade of the twentieth century. They reflect improved urban conditions, increasing affluence, new European spatial models, and changes to the placing of houses on lots. New edge conditions between public and private, made for fresh transitions between inside and out, planted screens, front courtyards, windows replacing shutters, and porches as thresholds between interior foyer and garden. This rearticulation of the immediate gate, journey, and horizon of domestic daily life in Merida redefined the modulation of privacy and transparency and provided for the accommodation of expanded activity and choreography of new arrival experiences with fresh social, spatial, and material potentials.

Similar potentials are explored, at the scale of the local community, in the chapter "A Continuous Landscape? Neighborhood Planning and the New 'Local' in Postwar Bristol," by Fiona Fisher, Kingston University, and Rebecca Preston, Royal Holloway, University of London. The focus of the study is the new "local" or public house (pub) that opened in 1958 at the heart of the postwar development of Lockleaze, on former agricultural land on the periphery of Bristol. From the naming and signage of the *Blue Boy* public house, which immediately references Gainsborough's portrait and eighteenth-century picturesque landscape painting, and in the street names of Lockleaze, the setting and the significance of the pub are explored. Here the continuum of FLOW makes reference to an earlier ideal and is place- and time-specific in its intentions for the new community and in the literal flows of occupation and servicing within the pub and its immediate setting.

The materials of construction of the *Blue Boy* and its exterior topography and activities are locally referenced and choreographed on Gainsborough Gardens within the new network of public places, with site-specific attention to detail and prioritizing of the opportunities for social interaction for all, inside and out. The local brewery funding, and engagement with local ambitions for the new community, aligned with wider UK postwar neighborhood planning aspirations for inclusive social, spatial, educational, and commercial identity of place. They reflected national planning and, specifically, New Town agendas.

In the chapter that follows, identity of place, at scales from the domestic to the city, continues the theme in "Like Vessels: Giorgio Morandi and the Porticoes of Bologna" by Vicky Falconer, Visual Artist, London. Falconer discusses the specificity of place within the artist's work and engages with its continuing contemporary experiential legacy in the context of the city. This is a reflective review of the still life paintings of Morandi: his careful assemblages of ceramic pieces, pots, and bottles, salvaged everyday domestic objects of the city, displayed with careful attention to light within, and glimpsed views from his studio to the Bologna porticoes and city beyond. Falconer went to Bologna, initially to visit the two Morandi museums, and found herself drawn to the unique experience of walking the porticoes of the city, which themselves represent an extraordinary continuum of boundary and mediating interior, within and through the city (since the seventeenth century). Falconer understood that she was tracing routes of Morandi's daily walks over more than forty years, through the city, and experiencing similar qualities of color, shifting light, and shadows. Falconer suggests that Morandi's work and representation of the found and displayed domestic artifacts represent an appreciation of the nuanced outlines observed, from the scale of the small domestic pieces to the city porticoes and their spatial and material qualities. The 37-km matrix of Bologna porticoes forms an inhabited boundary and evocative seam of reflection. The porticoes have continued to evolve, modulating glimpses of what lies beyond and holding the unique experiences of the interior–exterior continuum within this city.

Moving to the consideration of the domestic continuum on the west coast of the USA, "Rethinking Flow and the Relationship between Indoors and Out: California, c. 1945–c. 1965" is presented by Pat Kirkham of Kingston University, London. Through studies of the literature of the period and, in particular, architectural drawings and contemporary photographic records, Kirkham traces the continuity, or otherwise, of FLOW between inside and out, including horizontal surfaces and coverings, materiality, planting, and furniture. She charts the likely routes and arrangements for a journey such as from kitchen to barbecue and back. Kirkham finds that California living between inside and out was far from seamless and responded to climatic and pragmatic priorities. Her studies include the review of seasonal use and arrangement of houses with reference to significant California case study houses, including those of Charles and Ray Eames, Eero Saarinen, and John Entenza, John Lautner's *Carling House*, and Frank Lloyd Wright's *Walker House*, and their expression of modern living in their specific California settings and climate. In particular, Kirkham identifies evidence of the appreciation of feelings of security, comfort, and enclosure of the inside condition, as she notes seating that specifically faces inward, in the *Walker House*, away from the view of the Pacific Ocean. Kirkham draws attention to the particular demands for maintenance between inside and out at the Loewy *House to Swim In* by architect Albert Frey with Raymond Loewy (1946–7). She recommends an expansive rather than literal view in recognizing the continuum of FLOW at the immediate interface between the inside and out in the context of California modern living.

This expansive view is extended to the scale of the city in "Green Interiors: Transitional Spaces in Multilevel Buildings." Elisa Bernardi of the Politecnico di Milano, Italy, charts the realization of planted terraces and green roofs of individual apartments, and the accumulation of interest and potential for a continuum between multilayered planting at all levels of the building and between buildings, extending the capacity for green infrastructure in cities. Bernardi makes reference to a lineage of aspiration including Le Corbusier, *Immeuble-Villas* apartments (1922), James Wines's SITE with Emilio Ambasz, a proposal for a theoretical project, *High Rise Homes* (1982), each unit with a plot of land, and others, including D. Denison's *Culver House* in Chicago (2008). Bernardi also describes the Stefano Boeri project—the vertical forest, *Bosco Verticale*, in Milan (Boeri Studio, 2014). This project with its two towers has become emblematic of the scope of green infrastructure in relation to the measure of capacity, agency, and benefit: where the two towers of 76 and 110 meters physically support planting equivalent to a hectare of forest. The project's ambition has been to reduce the energy consumption of the buildings, improve air quality, absorb carbon dioxide, reduce sound pollution, and increase biodiversity. The projects cited are seen to engage with health benefits from the planted filtering membrane between inside and out; the increasing permeability of the urban surface; and opportunities to develop multilevel private places and communal gardens that respond to aspect and seasons as they grow, bringing together nature and culture and making effective contributions to the planted and social continuum of the city.

With the visual essay "Between Concentration and Distraction," Sarah Breen Lovett, University of Sydney, Australia, explores experience and perception through video installations, including the *Skewed Screen*, *Dome Detail*, and *Window Detail*. Breen Lovett references individual experiences of perception and the states of concentration and distraction described by Walter Benjamin, and she considers concentration and absorption, which might inform perception of the stimuli of art and architecture, with a third state between the two, described by Duttlinger as "threshold." The author's work explores and tests perceptions in the context of visual imagery that removes us from the predictable vantage point or view. It serves to disorient perception of a known sense of place to propel new experiences of "being within" or "moving through" a place, disorienting and distorting the perception of boundary and horizon and overlaying and inverting, sometimes subverting, expectations. This provokes a closer attention to spontaneous feelings rather than an analytical assimilation of detail, material, space, and time. As such the work triggers a valuable respite and stimulates an immersive dreamlike quality of reflection. Seeing the world projected on the oblique soffit as *Skewed Screen* seems to suggest views glimpsed from within the Bologna Porticoes; the forest seen from crawling through it, or inverted, helps conjure something of the many and varied experiential dreams of the *Bosco Verticale,* Milan. The slow pace is important too. The superimposed *Dome Detail* from within provides interest and fluid perceptions of edge, boundary, light, and shade and relates directly to movement between inside and out, where the sky becomes ceiling, the topographies of site and ground morph, and water, wind, people, and birds leave fluid traces through the changing light and sound of a day. The *Window Detail* and its fragmented perception capture a continuum of FLOW as filter, reflector, and portal of light and exchange. The frame of the window may define a sample of what lies beyond. Specific characteristics of openings and frames are discussed in Part 4.

Chapter 14

The Interiority of Landscape: Gate, Journey, Horizon

Jeff Malpas

There is a gap there you can look through into infinity (McCahon, 1979, speaking of the paintings of Braque [Brown 1984: 54]).

Figure 14.1

Colin McCahon, *French Bay*, 1957, Chartwell Collection, Auckland Art Gallery Toi o Tamaki. © Courtesy of the Colin McCahon Trust.

I.

It is commonplace to talk of the increasing fluidity and virtuality of contemporary spatial environments. Yet what is the real content of such talk? Is the "virtual" anything other than another mode of engagement, one specifically mediated by technology, within the already existent materiality of the world? (Malpas 2009).

What would it mean for there to be an increase of or alteration in any such mode of engagement? What is fluidity? Is its use here metaphorical, and if so what is the nature of the metaphor? Is it only *space* that is properly at issue here, or (assuming their distinction) is place also implicated? Are the virtuality and fluidity in question actually a reflection of the more basic dynamism of place itself, a dynamism in which flow appears in the open emergence of the boundless within the realm of the bounded—flow as appearing in the taking place of place? In this brief essay, my aim is to undertake a partial exploration of flow through an understanding of the dynamics of *landscape* as given in gate, journey, and horizon. This means that what is attempted is essentially a rethinking of flow *from the perspective of place*, a rethinking of flow even as it might be construed as also a fluidity in and of space. It is also, of course, a rethinking of landscape and its structure, a rethinking of its own *interiority* (Malpas 2015: 77–85).

II.

How do we enter into landscape? The very question may seem strange. Surely landscape is that which we find ourselves already "in" as the background to our movement through and across it; it is just "there." Yet we are never entirely "in" landscape as if it were already completely given before us; not only can we move between landscapes as we can move between places, but even in being "in" a landscape, the landscape itself is never simply open to us. The experience of being "in" landscape, if we attend to it, is more akin to the experience of a constant opening of the landscape, and so a constant moving into it. Without a sense of entry "into," a landscape becomes merely an uninterrupted stretch of territory that we traverse, a spatial region the boundaries of which are more or less arbitrary and that is given its primary representation, in an objective sense, in the form of the map. One may even go further and say that without a sense of entry, and of entry into, without the sense of movement *across a threshold* (namely, a *limen*, which is also a *limes*, a boundary) which that brings with it, there can be no sense of landscape *as landscape*, no sense of orientation such that landscape can even appear. The idea of *entry into* is itself connected with the sense of landscape as that *within which* we find ourselves; the sense of the "within" requires a sense of the "without," and so also the sense of connection of these and the possibility of movement between them (Malpas 2015).

The sense of "within" that belongs to landscape derives from the understanding of landscape as a mode *of place*, and it is in this sense that landscape must be understood as possessing an essential *interiority* that is also, as in every interiority, an *opening up*.

III.

Interiority surely belongs first *to the room*, although what the room is, and what counts as exemplary of the room, should not be taken for granted. The room is that which *gives room*, which gives *space* (the connection here being stronger in the German, in which *Raum* means both "space" and "room" in a way only partially recalled in some uses of the English word *room*). The way in which the room gives room, however, is also tied to the character of the room as enclosed. It is in being enclosed that the room is indeed constituted *as a room*, and so as that in which room is made. The giving of room thus occurs through the enclosing of space, and this enclosing can also be said to give rise to interiority, the latter being the "within" of the enclosed. If interiority belongs to the room, as it surely does, then "room" is just that which names the space of interiority, no matter how it is instantiated, whether in the interiority given by the spaces of the ordinary house or the interiority that belongs to any and every place, as that which allows a mode of being-in that is also a being-there, including the interiority of landscape.

IV.

Every "room" has its "door" (where "door" is understood "functionally" rather than merely "conventionally"). The door—and, along with the door, the *gate* (or any such "portal")—allows both entry and departure (it allows *movement*, whereas the window, as window, allows *communication*). The door is thus the marker of a certain limitation or bound, and yet it is also that by means of which that limitation or bound is, even if never completely, surpassed. Georg Simmel writes,

> The enclosure of his or her being by the door means, to be sure, that they have separated out a piece of natural being. But just as formless limitation takes on a shape, its limitedness finds its significance and dignity only in that which the mobility of the door illustrates: in the possibility at any moment of stepping out of limitation into freedom. (Simmel 1997: 170)

In Simmel's terms, the "movement through" that the door allows constitutes a "stepping out" into the free, but it is also a movement into or from *an interiority* as well as into or from that which is *exterior*. The door, or the gate, allows both entry and departure, and both of these constitute a "stepping out" into the free, as well as a movement into or from *an interiority* and also into or from that which is *exterior*. Here the free is not to be understood as identical with the unbounded. Just as the room "has" room by virtue of its walls, so only with bounds does freedom or boundlessness genuinely open up; thus one might say that the infinite opens up as infinite only *within the finite*. The door or gate, as the point of entry or departure, partly establishes that into which it opens or from which it closes. Similarly, the entry into landscape is what establishes that landscape and so also marks its bounds. Interiority is just the sense of openness within bounds into which one can enter or from which one can depart.

Figure 14.2

The Grotto at Bowood House, Wiltshire, England. View from the grotto back toward Bowood House. © Copyright Linda Bailey, image used under Creative Commons Licence—original available at http://www.geograph.org.uk/photo/108020.

V.

Door and gate stand in an essential relation to horizon or boundary. The door and gate afford entry, and it is only with the entry into the field of appearance constituted by the horizon that the horizon becomes effective *as* horizon, only with the entry into the field of appearance that the boundary functions to *bound* (and "to bound," it should be noted, is not the same as, nor is it even etymologically connected with, "to bind"). Movement, *or flow*, occurs both *into and out of*, but also *between and within*, within the space opened up by the horizon and so between places opened up within the landscape (as well as between other landscapes, other places, and so within the larger horizon of world). Moreover, in its character as boundary, the horizon is itself active, shifting, indeterminate, altering as the movement and activity within it also alter. Boundaries, and horizons, are thus not mere lines (and no mere line suffices as a horizon or as boundary proper), just as what lies within the horizon is not just some delimited area of extended space. Horizon and boundary establish a region, and thus they function to allow separation, but they do so in a way that also connects; it is thus that movement or flow is indeed always and only a movement—across, between, into, and out of—that operates precisely in relation to the boundary. Entry and departure belong to the boundary as they do also to the horizon. It is through movement *across* the boundary, through entry and departure, that we are oriented in landscape in such a way that we can then move *within* the landscape (though every movement has its own threshold, its own character as a movement *across*, even when it is also a movement *within*). Landscape opens up within its horizon, is oriented in relation to entry and departure into and from it, and is shaped by and through the journeys that are possible within it.

VI.

A common claim in contemporary discussions, especially in those that thematize "virtuality" and "fluidity," is that "there is no such thing as a boundary" (Thrift 2006: 140). Yet this can be no more than hyperbole at best, since in the absence of the boundary there can be no gate, no horizon, no journey, no landscape, no place, no flow, no connection, nothing "virtual" nor "real," nothing to speak of whatsoever. Heidegger draws attention to the underlying point at issue here in the course of a discussion of the connection between boundary and space in a way that also resonates with what was said previously concerning the connection between boundary and *room*:

> A space is something that has been made room for, something that is cleared and free, namely within a boundary [*Grenze*], Greek *peras*. A boundary is not that at which something stops but, as the Greeks recognized, the boundary is that from which something begins its presencing. That is why the concept is that of *horismos*, that is, the horizon, the boundary. (Heidegger 1971b: 152)

Figure 14.3

Leigh Woolley—Hobart from across the Derwent.
© Copyright Leigh Woolley, used by permission.

The boundary does not simply *restrict*, but properly understood, the boundary is precisely that which *produces*. Indeed, without the boundary no thing can come to presence, no thing can appear. The rejection of the boundary is often coupled, in

contemporary discussions (including that exemplified by Thrift), with a contrasting emphasis on the idea of flow itself, understood as an unbounded relationality. There is a fundamental misconception at work here, however, since the idea of boundary does not stand in contrast to that of relation, but is rather intimately tied to it. The boundary may separate, but in its separating it also connects; there is no separation that is not also a connecting, and no connection that is not also a separating (a point made especially clear in Heidegger 2002). The idea of an unbounded relationality of the sort supposedly at issue in the idea of pure "flow" is simply a confusion; inasmuch as it involves the dissolution of bounds, it involves the dissolution of anything to be related, the removal of the difference on which the very possibility of flow depends (for a discussion that is more specific to the position exemplified by Thrift, see Malpas 2012b). Without boundary there is no flow. The boundedness of landscape is itself directly tied to the relationality or connectivity that makes for the structure of landscape and that is expressed in the form of journey and movement, even though it is also a boundedness that opens into the unbounded. Only within a horizon can a journey be undertaken; only within bounds can there be a between; only within bounds can there be an infinity, can the unbounded open up. To repeat Simmel: "the mobility of the door illustrates . . . the possibility at any moment of stepping out of limitation into freedom." Here the connection between boundary, or limit, and the unbounded is affirmed. The door or gate stands both within and between places, and so at their boundary, marking the boundedness of one place as well as enabling entry into the openness of another. As that which allows entry, the door or gate does indeed have an essential mobility, as Simmel puts it, and is thus also the marker of the relationality of the boundary. The door and gate themselves stand in a close relation to the bridge, that which enables the passage over and across, and which, through the connecting of that which is separated, also makes salient that very separation. In the form of the bridge, connectedness itself brings forth boundedness.

Figure 14.4

Leigh Woolley—Tasman Bridge, Hobart. © Copyright Leigh Woolley, used by permission.

VII.

The bridge functions both to connect and to separate; it opens up a between, and in doing so establishes distinct places. As Heidegger writes, in an especially significant passage:

> The bridge swings over the stream with case and power. It does not just connect banks that are already there. The banks emerge as banks only as the bridge crosses the stream. The bridge designedly causes them to lie across from each other. . . . With the banks, the bridge brings to the stream the one and the other expanse of the landscape lying behind them. It brings stream and bank and land into each other's neighbourhood. (Heidegger 1971b: 150)

In fact, the character of the bridge in this respect already appears in Simmel, for whom it is directly related to the character of the human being:

Because the human being is the connecting creature who must always separate and cannot connect without separating—that is why we must first conceive intellectually of the merely indifferent existence of two river banks as something separated in order to connect them by means of a bridge. And the human being is likewise the bordering creature who has no border. (Simmel 1997: 170)

Simmel's final comment here is also echoed by Heidegger. The human being, he says, "is [the one] who walks the boundary of the boundless" (1971a: 41). The connecting/ separating that the bridge exemplifies indicates the character of the bridge as itself functioning in direct relation to the boundary, indicating, in turn, the way such connecting/separating is part of the structure of place as well as operating between places. The productive character of the boundary, including its role in relation to bridge, door, and gate, does not differ between different polities, societies, cultures, institutions, social formations; it is a fundamental *ontological* structure that may be obscured, but not obliterated. The very possibility of appearance begins *at and with the boundary* and not with that which appears within it. It is thus that one might be led to affirm that the boundary is more powerful than the center. As Ed Casey puts it of the particular form of boundary that he terms the "edge": "*The power is in the edge* . . . the endemic Western metaphysical privileging of centrist models of power and force here falls short—indeed, falls flat . . . the edges of landscape contain an unsuspected power . . . *Every edge has power*" (Casey 2012: 101). Every edge bounds, and so every edge opens up; it is "at the edge" that space, "room," and landscape first appear.

VIII.

In the work of the seminal twentieth-century New Zealand painter Colin McCahon, the issues of entry, journey, and horizon develop as key elements in his approach to landscape or, as one might also say, to place, and place is certainly at issue at the very heart of McCahon's work. For McCahon, the question of entry is first a question of how to enter into landscape as it is given in the painting, how to enter into the open realm of the landscape through the flat painted surface. Indeed, this is a question *for* painting as well as for landscape *in* painting. His solution is to employ differing views, movement, and contrasting panels. These, like the paintings themselves, are both his *gates* and his *journeys* (hence the title of one of his most important and major retrospectives; see Gifkins 1988). The landscape that appears in McCahon's works is itself understood in terms of its essential relationality, a relationality that moves out in all directions as part of the horizontal opening of and to the landscape. It is this relationality, and the openness that belongs to it, that is space. McCahon writes, "Space is no longer tied to the Renaissance heresy of lines running back from the picture frame but is freed from these ties to reach out in all directions from the painted surface of the picture" (McCahon 1954: 69). As McCahon's work developed over the course of his career, it moved, in the words of the catalogue for McCahon's 1961 *Gate* exhibition, toward "an even more 'abstract' style in paintings whose forms, with their forceful antithesis of black and white, 'earth' and 'sky', often remain, in

Figure 14.5

Colin McCahon, "Northland Triptych," 1959, Hocken Collections, Uare Taoka o Hakena, University of Otago. © Courtesy of the Colin McCahon Trust.

some mysterious fashion, 'landscapes'" (Gifkins 1988: 34). McCahon's landscapes are, however, like those to which Geoffrey Hill also refers, landscapes that are "like revelation" (Hill 1985: 185, Malpas 2012a). They are, moreover, landscapes that draw attention to their own character *as revelatory*. Indeed, what is brought to appearance here is the revelation—the opening—of space, of landscape, of place.

IX.

The rhetoric of fluidity and virtuality that is nowadays so commonplace is a rhetoric largely driven by the supposed effects of contemporary technology. It is this same technology that supposedly breaks down boundaries, erases distinctions between places, and transforms everything into elements within a single interconnected network. It is thus that technology is taken radically to alter the character of contemporary space and place, and so also to alter the character of contemporary landscape. Yet place does not come after technology, but the other way around: technology is itself always placed, operating in and through place, always subject to the determinations of place. It is thus the structure of place, and so of landscape too, that shapes contemporary technology. Even forms of fluidity and virtuality appear only in relation to specific places and forms of place. If it is common to suppose otherwise, then this is partly because the *hubris* of technology itself leads to the misconstrual of that which is effective *upon* technology as an effect produced *by* technology. Technology does not change place in any radical or fundamental fashion, and the phenomena of fluidity and virtuality do not themselves constitute genuine alterations in the constitution of place or landscape. Technology itself changes, as do modes of action and interaction of the sort that might be associated with the fluidity and virtuality, but place is changed only in terms of the manner in which it is now represented and understood, and so, perhaps, in its very *visibility*. The assumption that place and landscape are indeed radically changed by contemporary technologies is itself part of the mode of self-presentation of those technologies, a mode of self-presentation that is directly tied to the way in which they are intermeshed with structures of commodification, consumption, and corporate capitalism. The structure of landscape and place, and the understanding of fluidity as itself tied to the dynamic character of place, imply an essential finitude and boundedness (even though they also give rise to the unbounded). The fluid and the virtual, as well as spatiality itself, arise only within those same bounds. Those bounds are what ground the very possibility of appearance, the very opening of landscape, and of place, into world. It is this toward which both Heidegger and Simmel direct our attention, and which McCahon lays bare in the illumination of canvas and of paint.

References

Brown, G. H. (1984), *Colin McCahon: Artist*, Wellington: A. H. and A. W. Reed.

Casey, E. S. (2012), "The Edge(s) of Landscape: A Study in Liminology," in J. Malpas (ed.), *The Place of Landscape: Concepts, Contexts, Studies*, 91–110, Cambridge: MIT Press.

Gifkins, M., ed. (1988), *Colin McCahon: Gates and Journeys*, Auckland: Auckland City Art Gallery.

Heidegger, M. (1971a), *On the Way to Language*, trans. P. D. Hertz, New York: Harper & Row.

Heidegger, M. (1971b), *Poetry, Language, Thought*, ed. and trans. A. Hofstadter, New York: Harper & Row.

Heidegger, M. (2002), *Identity and Difference*, trans. J. Stambaugh, Chicago: University of Chicago Press.

Hill, G. (1985), *Collected Poems*, Harmondsworth: Penguin.

McCahon, C. (1954), "Louise Henderson," *Home and Building*, 16 (10): 40–41, 69.

McCahon. (1979), "Colin McCahon in Interview with Gordon Brown," March 14, unpublished typescript (based on three cassette tapes), deposited with the Alexander Turnbull Library, Wellington, NZ.

Malpas, J. (2009), "The Nonautonomy of the Virtual," *Convergence: The International Journal of Research into New Media Technologies*, 15: 135–9.

Malpas, J. (2012a), "The Problem of Landscape," in J. Malpas (ed.), *The Place of Landscape: Concepts, Contexts, Studies*, 3–27, Cambridge: MIT Press.

Malpas, J. (2012b), "Putting Space in Place: Relational Geography and Philosophical Topography," *Planning and Environment D: Space and Society*, 30: 226–42.

Malpas, J. (2015), "Place and Singularity," in J. Malpas (ed.), *The Intelligence of Place*, 65–92, London: Bloomsbury.

Simmel, G. (1997), "Bridge and Door," in D. Frisby and M. Featherstone (eds.), *Simmel on Culture*, 170–4, London: Sage.

Thrift, N. (2006), "Space," *Theory, Culture and Society,* 23: 139–46.

Chapter 15

Transitional Spaces in Late-Nineteenth-Century Domestic Architecture in Mérida, Yucatán

Gladys Arana López and Catherine Ettinger

Introduction

During the late nineteenth and early twentieth centuries, Mexican domestic architecture underwent a great transformation. The colonial courtyard house, in which daily activities were cloistered and life was carried out behind thick walls (Ancona 1987: 39), was replaced by a new scheme, a house set in a garden. A series of transitional spaces were introduced to articulate a new relationship between interior and exterior space as well as between the house and the street. These changes are particularly manifest in houses in the city of Mérida on the Yucatán Peninsula, where the tropical climate and family customs required filters between indoor and outdoor space.

This transformation took place during the government and dictatorship of Porfirio Díaz (1876–1911), a period of relative peace, stability, and modernization that included the development of railroads and other modern infrastructure through foreign investment. The presence of European entrepreneurs and professionals and the circulation of books and magazines led to the vogue for all things European, particularly French. Mexico's elite traveled to Europe and brought back fashionable clothing, furniture, and other novelties; they studied French customs and manners and sought to imitate them. Serving French dishes was considered sophisticated, and, of course, French, Italian, and European architecture in general was greatly admired. Although traditional historiography marks a clear rupture between the Porfirian period and that of the Mexican Revolution (1911–1921) and the Post–Revolution (after 1921), in architecture, particularly domestic architecture of the elite, there are many continuities between these periods.

Traditionally, Yucatán was a region of difficult territorial conditions for growing produce, and there was nothing of much worth to be exported. To make matters worse, its ports did not have a big enough draft and were too far from the capital city. However, the demand for agave fiber (known as henequen) for rope making during the second half of the nineteenth century transformed things. Due to a rise in rope price and demand for henequen, the period was one of great economic growth for the Yucatán Peninsula and connected it to international commerce. The new export turned Yucatán, from one of the poorest states, into the second wealthiest in the country, and Mérida became the city with the highest per capita income. The *hacendados*, or large landowners who grew agave, enjoyed tremendous wealth, and the city of Mérida, capital of Yucatán, became the showplace of fashion and architecture for the region. Large houses built in new areas of town, specifically on the spectacular Paseo de Montejo, presented foreign grandeur to passersby and articulated a new lifestyle. These houses are singular examples of the Porfirian age in Mexico.

This chapter examines these houses and the way in which transitional spaces served as a bridge between the colonial patio house and the modern house that would follow by establishing a distinct relationship between interior and exterior and forging a new pattern for domestic architecture in the region. It relies on sources such as newspaper articles and period photographs, as well as on the study of houses still standing, in order to establish the link between the changes in house form and in daily life and customs.

The Porfirian House

The last quarter of the nineteenth century witnessed the transformation of Mexican cities (Martínez 2006: 11). Mérida, which enjoyed an economic boom (Lapointe 2008: 33–65), is a good example of the process of modernization that included the introduction of new infrastructure as well as the building of schools, hospitals, and prisons. Streets were paved, public lighting was installed, and the cloistered colonial aspect of the city slowly receded as avenues and houses opened up. Modernity was everywhere, not as an illusion but as a quantifiable and tangible reality. Everything was stimulating: the electric lights of the houses that illuminated the street, the European food that challenged the palate, advertisements that encouraged consumption, the disappearance of the urban miasma, new vehicles that invited one to go on outings, the telephone that simultaneously strengthened bonds and allowed its users to avoid contact, and running water for general use and bodily hygiene. Society participated in the modernizing process both as a critic of the decisions of its governors and as an agent in this renovation through the remodeling of homes or the building of new ones in areas of urban growth (Ramírez 1994: 34–9).

The house was a family matter, particularly for the bourgeoisie; it was a meeting place that represented the ambition and success of a couple and their offspring. In Porfirian society, having a new house was a social requirement, and its location and architectural embellishments were decisions to be carefully considered. From the street the most notable changes in the city were the large houses built for the families of the elite. They looked different from earlier houses because of their volumetric, spatial, and formal composition. They were also inhabited differently (Figure 15.1).

The newly built houses of the bourgeoisie changed the traditional architectural patterns in order to materialize a comfortable private space with a subtle functional rationalism and a marked aristocratic nostalgia. The domestic typology of the courtyard house or simple row of rooms, such as the "Casa de Montejo" built in the late sixteenth century, was substituted by a new house built away from the street, set in a garden away from property lines, and raised above the ground (Chico 1999: 339). The separation of interior and exterior space, and the redefinition of the public and the private spheres, required the support of material elements such as iron grilles and gates, frontal gardens, windows, loggias, and terraces. Most of these houses were built on the Paseo de Montejo, a new, wide tree-lined avenue, or in the nearby old quarter of the city.

Figure 15.1

Residence at the end of Paseo de Montejo, 1906. Photograph Gladys Arana López, 2010.

The Gate to the Street: Spatial Control and Visual Continuity

Because of the new disposition of the house in the center of the lot, the grille work fence served a dual purpose, providing both spatial control and visual continuity. The grille, as an element of security, was moved to the front limits of the property; the metal bars and wooden shutters typical of the colonial house came off the windows and were, in a sense, repositioned to separate the street from the garden. Fences and gates allowed visual continuity in both directions and compensated for the small lots by giving the house a large context. From inside its rooms, the family could observe urban happenings without being part of them. The ironwork fences were robust and imposing, and they reflected a taste for American, French, and English models. Ornamental motifs such as scrolls, volutes, and knots referenced nature as the only true inspiration for art and were concentrated on the stone base for the grille (Islas 1966: 12). The life of the street permeated the boundaries of the lots; its sounds wandered through the gardens and entered the service areas. The artistic detailing marked and emphasized property limits, revealing the beauty of the garden (Figure 15.2).

The Front Garden: Filter of Intimacy

The garden, as its etymology reminds us, limits and protects the house from the exterior. Its multiple variations attempt to recover the quality of the past and to imitate the conditions of country life (Alberti 1944: 571–3). The gardens and their plants are a discreet reflection of human capabilities in domesticating nature, of an attempt to control the seasons and establish a link with outdoor space (Fariello 2004: 9–12). They are a reflection of the character, culture, and specific taste not only of their creators, but also of those who use them, enjoy them, and care for and maintain them. The making of a garden, from design to construction, implies both technical and aesthetic knowledge related to the social exigencies of the moment (Fariello 2004: 9–10).

Figure 15.2

Quinta "El Recuerdo," 1900, located within the brand new "Colony" known as "Chuminopolis," outside Mérida. View of the gardens and house from the main gate. Photograph Gladys Arana López, 2010.

The garden, depending on its complexity and aesthetic composition, was understood by some as a work of art and by others as a space for reconciliation with nature and the exterior world (Fariello 2004; McDonald 2012; Waymark 2005). Trips taken by Yucatecans to Europe—in which they visited country estates, acquired books on gardening, and met landscape architects—inspired many gardens of the period. The gardens varied according to size. Most commonly, the front garden, which separated the house from the street, had a depth of between 3 and 12 meters and was divided by a path that led to the front steps and the entrance to the house, such as in the Montes Molina house. Larger houses might boast magnificent front gardens of more than 40 meters in depth with pedestrian and vehicular entrances flanked by fruit and palm trees and surrounded by an expanse of lawn, such as at the Berzunza residence. In most cases, though, small front gardens shielded the house from contact with the street and were planted with roses and other floral plants. Birdbaths, benches, and wrought or cast iron embellishments, as fountains and sculptures, were also common (Hijuelos 1942: 153).

All of these gardens could be seen from the street through the grille work fence. They helped to shield the house from the hustle and bustle of the street and to distract the eyes of curious onlookers. The gardens also fulfilled other purposes, such as hygiene, by allowing for greater ventilation and recreation as understood in positivistic thought. Porfirio Díaz and his cabinet, whose members were known as "the scientists," embraced Positivism. This philosophy was based on the notion of order, and hygiene was fundamental to it. Dwellings therefore were expected to be well ventilated and clean, requiring appropriate water and drainage systems.

Windows and Balconies: The Eyes of the House

With the appearance of paved streets and gardens, the elements of environmental control changed. Doors and windows were no longer monolithic barriers and became more transparent, allowing the observation and enjoyment of a docile and domesticated nature from within. The openings of the windows were placed rhythmically along the facades. Although they continued to be vertical, with a proportion of one to two or two and a half, the increase in the percentage of openings with respect to total surface was notable. When the windows on the ground floor went to ground level, it was common to find physical barriers, such as balustrades or elaborate grille work. However, on the upper floors, distant from the street, they had beautiful balconies perched on the facades, bordered with moldings and varied ornamental details. These elements served to emphasize the verticality of the openings and to balance the horizontal tendency of the volume.

The windows and balconies of the upper floors were favorite places for women, who could see what was happening in the city without being seen. In the afternoons, hidden by the curtains, they could peek out onto the street, feel the cool breeze, and chat about daily affairs. The use of glass had the dual effect of strengthening the visual proximity of the outdoors through transparency and reducing the direct link between interior and exterior.

Loggias, Terraces, and Porches

Beginning with the large ironwork railings that established limits between the public and the private, the paths that linked street and house marked directionality and an axis for composition while at the same time framing the focal point, the house itself. The placement of the path helped to define the first impression of the property and the symbolic importance of the house. It was common for Porfirian houses to be raised off the ground, which implied steps leading to the entrance. This stairway was flanked by marble banisters with elegant ornaments shaped like cups or flowerpots that made them pleasant and imposing at the same time. Simple designs were used for the stairways, and their length varied, although they tended to be wider at the base in order to receive visitors and narrower at the top upon entrance to the loggia or foyer. However, the width always allowed for the passage of two people at once. Some beautiful examples of these stairways exist today in the residencies that belonged to the families Montes Molina, Peón de Regil, and Molina Vales.

At the top of the stairway was a porch that emphasized the transition between interior and exterior. With grand proportions, the entrance loggia functionally linked three spaces: the stairway, the interior vestibule, and, to the side, the terrace or loggia. This was usually framed by columns, with textured surfaces and ornate capitals; at the center it was common to place a family monogram, which emphasized the relationship between wealth and social status in Porfirian society.

The front loggias were rich in formal and spatial expression; they provided spaces for a variety of leisure activities, such as resting while sitting in the shade, often in bentwood rockers (Arnold and Tabor 1909: 72) or rattan furniture, but these spaces served also as halls for receiving visitors and for small gatherings. They marked the transition between indoor and outdoor space, opening a window to social areas. The terraces were a complement to the garden and, at the same time, an extension of rooms in the house. Often the master bedroom, the dining room, or the salon were linked to these transitional spaces, allowing for their expansion to the outside. This space reinforced the link between the interior and the exterior, opening visual continuity toward the garden. The volume of the house, viewed from the garden, was partially hidden from sight through the use of trees, vines, porches, terraces, and balustrades.

Figure 15.3

"Villa Beatriz", Montes Molina Residence 1906, located in Paseo de Montejo. Interior view from the main door toward the backyard. Photograph Gladys Arana López, 2010.

Another nonexplicit limit appeared between the loggia and the vestibule. The vestibule or entrance hall was an intermediate space that linked the inside and the outside like an orderly transept that articulated the relations between intimate, public, and service areas. It also tended to emphasize the compositional axis of the house and, due to its central locations, marked the circulation of servants, inhabitants, and visitors as well as conditioning the viewpoint of the spectator (Figure 15.3).

Conclusions

During the late nineteenth and early twentieth centuries, the Mexican elite in general, and the Yucatecan in particular, lived in an atmosphere that was both materialistic and romantic. This elite accepted technological innovation, adapted to new circumstances, and at the same time preserved a refined life in which idealism prevailed over reality.

Obsessed with appearances and afraid of the lower classes, the Yucatecan elite consolidated the materialization of modernity, both functionally and symbolically, through their houses, where space responded to a particular rationality, order, and intention that produced a long-lasting spatial and formal conception. This new architectural model, a hybrid that revealed the aspirations of Porfirian society in tropical Yucatán, melding European decorative embellishments with a plan that included transitional spaces responding to both custom and climate, became part of the regional collective imaginary, embedded in local memory.

The house became the site where private life, the deepest part of being, had to be protected, and so houses had to produce a new *sui generis* relation to the outside. Distance was placed between city and home through grilles and gardens that limited property and the sphere of the individual. The concept of distance-limit was thereby consolidated; although the street and house apparently lost their direct relation, the link between the interior and exterior had never been so balanced. Symbolic elements were used to express order, protection, and representation as new social practices were introduced.

With the passage of time, these novel spatial ideas were strengthened in the languages used in the homes of the Yucatecan elite beyond the period that followed the Mexican Revolution, in which case the transitional spaces were essential to the introduction and development of a new housing model. The house at the turn of the century was the foundation for the modern Yucatecan house as it consolidated its attributes and spatial relations while transmuting formal expressions.

References

Alberti, M. (1944), "La Casa Conquista al Jardín—El Jardín Conquista la Casa," *Revista de Arquitectura*, 20 (288): 571–3.

Ancona, R. (1987), "Arquitectura Civil en Mérida Colonial," *Cuadernos de Arquitectura de Yucatán*, 1: 30–42.

Arnold, C., and F. Tabor (1909), *The American Egypt: A Record of Travel in Yucatan*, New York: Doubleday.

Chico, P. (1999), "Sitio y Arquitectura Coloniales," in A. García and P. Chico (eds.), *Atlas de Procesos Territoriales de Yucatán*, Mérida: UADY.

Fariello, F. (2004), *La Arquitectura de los Jardines: De la Antigüedad al Siglo XX*, Madrid: Mairea/Celeste.

Hijuelos, F. (1942), *Mérida, Monografía*, México City: SEP.

Islas, L. (1966), "El Arte del Hierro Forjado," *Artes de México*, 8: 12–16.

Lapointe, M. (2008), *Historia de Yucatán, Siglos XIX y XXI*, Mérida: UADY.

Martínez, L. (2006), *El Porfiriato*, México City: UAM-AZC.

McDonald, E. (2012), *A Garden Makes a House a Home*, New York: Monacelli Press.

Ramírez, L. (1994), *Secretos de Familia: Libaneses y Elites Empresariales en Yucatán*, México City: CONACULTA.

Waymark, J. (2005), *Modern Garden Design: Innovation Since 1900*, London: Thames & Hudson.

Chapter 16

A Continuous Landscape? Neighborhood Planning and the New "Local" in Postwar Bristol

Fiona Fisher and Rebecca Preston

In 1941, the author of *Reconstruction and the Public House* foresaw the importance of the postwar social landscape to the pub of the future. It will be, he said, "the surroundings which will determine the character of the public house. Everything must be appropriate, intelligent, civilised. A tide of determined idealism is sweeping the country" (Atkins 1941: 7).

Postwar planning encouraged the building of communities with civic, social, and shopping centers, industry, and green belts, combining the best of town and country with provision for further development; the ultimate expression was in the New Towns designated from 1946 onward, but policy also shaped smaller settlements, which were designed to create greater cohesion between architecture and landscape and between people and place. Architects and planners charged with housing the population after the Second World War gave, as this study will show, close consideration to the place of the pub within the new communities. The immediate postwar years were also ones in which the relationship between "the pub and the people" (Mass Observation 1943) was expressed through the use of new terminology. The idea of "The Local," the title of a book on the London pub by Maurice Gorham (1939), republished in 1949 as *Back to the Local*, gained currency with breweries and their architects to express the ideals of the pubs planned in new neighborhoods, many of them for families displaced by bombing and slum clearance. Designed to meet the needs of local men, women, and children, these new "locals" were not only understood as public amenities but were also intended to create and cement social relations by giving new housing estates and their residents a sense of place.

Focusing on the design of one 1940s housing estate and its brewery-owned pub, the Blue Boy at Lockleaze, in Bristol, this chapter examines the aesthetic and social ideals that informed neighborhood planning and public-house design in postwar England. Key to understanding building in this period, David Matless argues, is "the way in which the architecture of modern Englishness in reconstruction sought to define itself as combining tradition and modernity, whether in city or country" (1998: 212). Socially and architecturally, this characterizes both the planning of Lockleaze and postwar public-house design. What follows considers the various agents at work in the planning and design process and how these ideas found expression in the pub's landscape setting, architecture, and interiors. Consideration is given to the influence of the past upon modern estate planning and design, as the Picturesque (in the form of Georgian landscape arts) and the medieval village green were reinterpreted for a new society. Attention is then paid to the ways in which the design and materials of the Blue Boy and its sociospatial and commercial flows might have been viewed by those involved as forming a continuous landscape, expressed in the visual, material, spatial, and intellectual associations brought into play through the pub's setting, design, and name. The example of the Blue Boy is indicative of the wider context of the planning and design of the new "locals" and the new communities they served in 1950s England, as well as the collaboration of breweries and planners in the creation of these new environments.

The City, Postwar Housing, and the Plan for Lockleaze

Bristol was the fifth most heavily bombed British city of the Second World War. Masterminded by the city architect, John Nelson Meredith, and the city engineer, H. Marston Webb, the Reconstruction Plan for Bristol began in the early 1940s and covered the rebuilding of the city center and new outlying settlements. The Blue Boy public house at Lockleaze was opened by the Bristol Brewery, Georges & Co. Ltd., on December 1, 1958, and was situated in Gainsborough Gardens (later Square), which formed the heart of the new housing estate.

Laid out from 1944 onward on 416 acres of agricultural land, Lockleaze grew to house a population of around 6,760 by 1952 ("Lay-out of New Estate" 1944: 3; *City and County of Bristol* 1952: 24). Typical of Bristol's housing policy and in keeping with government guidance, it was located at the city boundary and planned on "neighbourhood unit" lines ("Post-War Municipal Development in Bristol" 1950: 258). Leading planners, including Sir Patrick Abercrombie in his *County of London Plan* (Forshaw and Abercrombie 1943) and *Greater London Plan* (1945), promoted the neighborhood unit as a means of creating distinct communities within a greater urban whole—the unit representing the smallest convenient cluster of people together with everything necessary for their daily needs. The neighborhood plan was then designed to create distinct "villages" that would together constitute a greater Bristol ("Neighbourhood Planning" 1946: 3). Each neighborhood was to have a "focal point, a definite centre for public and semi-public buildings" (*City and County of Bristol* 1952: 15).

If the neighborhood was in many respects socially innovative, it was also, as indicated in the *Plan for Plymouth*, backward-looking, being "a development of the mediaeval community around the village green" (Watson and Abercrombie 1943: 85). Thus conceived, it was to provide "not only for the material requirements of the citizens by the economical grouping of shops, taverns, and places of amusement . . . around the secluded green, but also for . . . social, physical and educational life" (Watson and Abercrombie 1943: 85). In Bristol, too, it was thought that "happy communities" would be achieved on the "principle of the close or village green," in which each group of 100 to 300 houses would contain families of similar backgrounds

Flow

and interests ("Neighbourhood Planning" 1946: 1). The pubs followed the people, and the breweries sought "to provide the infant communities in the suburbs with new houses where they could meet and have a drink in an informal and friendly atmosphere" ("Golden Cockerel" 1961–2: 7).

Figure 16.1

Detail of Town Map for Bristol, showing Lockleaze. Gainsborough Square lies towards the center of the image, at the intersection of the grid lines. The Blue Boy is on the north side of the Square. *City and County of Bristol. Town and Country Planning Act, 1947. Development Plan* (1952). © The British Library Board Maps 36.e.6.

As indicated in Figure 16.1, Lockleaze was envisaged as a community centered around a "village green," with "a group of shops next to a public house and a garden site, swimming baths, a library, a community centre, health centre, Corporation offices and a car park" ("Design for the Future," 1947: 5). A Co-operative Store, police station, and churches joined the other amenities. Although not everything promised materialized, Lockleaze exemplified the early postwar planned community in which the pub nestled with the architecture of the welfare state around a village green.

Alongside the concept of neighborhood and the new village green, the adaptation of Picturesque principles to planning and landscape design—or "Townscape," on the premise that it was equivalent to the art of the eighteenth-century estate improver—was also prevalent in contemporary planning, and both informed the design of postwar New Towns and estates. The Picturesque revival had roots in the prewar period, as articulated by artists and architects in the architectural press, especially the *Architectural Review* (Darling 2007: 30). Taken up by Nikolaus Pevsner and others, the interweaving of the Picturesque with Modernism carried through into the 1950s (Powers 2002: 73). Historians note a broader revival of eighteenth-century art and design at midcentury (McKellar 2004), "Georgian" emerging as a "term particularly favoured by art and architectural historians to demonstrate the subtle links between the material manifestation of buildings, works of art . . . and the growth of modern Britain" (Greig and Riello 2007: 275–6). It had, as Barry Curtis indicates, a "long deployment in the terms of a negotiated British modernism" (1985–6: 1)—particularly in the landscape design of urban areas, where the Picturesque was reinvented for a new social landscape, being especially associated with New Towns. As David Matless notes, Pevsner's 1955 Reith Lectures, and his book, *The Englishness of English Art*, concluded with photographs hailing New Towns as the latest examples of "Picturesque principles applied to urban conditions" (1998: 205).

Harriet Atkinson argues that wartime and postwar planning were characterized by a search for a "revived" or "new Picturesque," and since the main commissioners of new buildings and landscapes were public authorities, the aesthetic and social impact was considerable (2008). This was, she says, a "practical aesthetic for reconstructing places predominantly in public ownership" (2008: 24). The new Picturesque was manifest at Lockleaze and elsewhere in open planning and the informal clustering of cottage-scale houses with gardens and amenity buildings within an enveloping parklike landscape. As *Rebuilding Britain* put it, a new neighborhood should "certainly have a park, and [. . . if] planned with skill it might in itself be almost a park, with the buildings set in it in groups" (RIBA 1943: 33).

Figure 16.2

The Blue Boy, Gainsborough Square, Lockleaze, c. 1958. © Courage Archive, Bristol (Heineken, UK).

Taking heed of the mistakes of the interwar years, in which vast housing estates were built without public houses, Bristol Corporation began to favor the creation of smaller neighborhoods and gave greater thought to, and permission for, the location and building of pubs by private enterprise within them. In 1952 the Conservative Government's "Licensed Premises in New Towns" Bill halted plans to bring the liquor trade under state management in New Towns, compromising the collectivist ideals of planners and signaling a more liberal attitude to licensing and the place of the pub within postwar life. Thus, Bristol's breweries were able to build new pubs on land leased from the Corporation, while the Corporation retained control over their number, size, and location and the City Architect's Department over their design.

Under the direction of the sociologist John Madge, ARIBA, Bristol Corporation's Planning and Reconstruction Committee was responsible for allocating social amenities to the new estates. In 1947, reflecting a national trend for building smaller outlying or suburban pubs than had been typical before the war, it was decided that, "On Bristol's future housing estates the smaller 'inn' type public house" would be preferred over "large multi-barred premises" ("Your Local Will Be Smaller" 1947: 5). In general, building controls prevented the opening of new permanent pubs until late 1954, however, and when the Blue Boy opened in 1958, it was only the eighth pub to be completed by Georges & Co. since 1939 (Figure 16.2).

Revived interest in the eighteenth-century landscape permeated the naming of Lockleaze, its roads, and its pub, as well as the planning. This conformed to Bristol's postwar road-naming policy of creating "new associations to be recorded in the annals of the City and honour[ing] ancient ones" (Harris 1968: v). The pastoral name of Lockleaze was considered favorably in the Bristol press, since it had precedents locally and, it was said, called to mind the opening lines of Thomas Gray's poem *Elegy*; it also avoided the stigmatizing title "council estate" ("What's in a Name?" 1944: 3). Meanwhile, all the streets were named for artists, and, in keeping with the Picturesque theme, the roads—the most important being Gainsborough Square—were named for British landscape painters, including those of the early-nineteenth-century Bristol School, whose work promoted Bristol as a city of landscape.

This echoed a wider investment in English landscape painting in the period, which was mobilized for patriotic reasons during the war and reconstruction through, for example, touring exhibitions of Georgian landscape painting. In 1943 Bristol Museum and Art Gallery, in association with the Council for the Encouragement of Music and the Arts, showed a "remarkable collection of landscapes . . . by such famous painters as Gainsborough, Constable and Crome" ("Landscapes of 18th Century" 1943: 3).

An article in Georges & Co.'s in-house magazine claimed that the name of the Blue Boy, one of Gainsborough's best-known paintings, was selected

> to establish some sort of cultural connection (admittedly tenuous) in an otherwise typical housing-estate. From the names of the roads hereabout, the Corporation of Bristol decided to use the names of the great English painters. There is, for instance, Landseer Avenue, Constable Road, Hogarth Walk and Turner Gardens. ("Blue Boy, Lockleaze" 1959: 22)

Landscape painting was evidently believed to have a heritage worthy of local commemoration, and, despite the brewery's scepticism, the pub name followed the road naming in reflecting a Reithian spirit of public education. As one resident recalled,

> Once farmland and meadow, it was now wide roads and new houses. On my way up to the post office I often made a detour along Landseer Avenue. All the roads around there were named after famous English painters—although, truth to tell, it was the first time in our lives we'd ever heard of such people as Chrome, Bonnington or Hogarth. The shopping area was romantically named Gainsborough Square, and outside the pub the sign that swung and creaked in the wind depicted Gainsborough's "Blue Boy." (Storey 2004: 356–7)

The Blue Boy

As the principal public house for Lockleaze, the Blue Boy was located in the main shopping center, shown in dark blue to the west and north of Gainsborough Square in Figure 16.1. The remaining plots (shown in red) were reserved for "civic, cultural or other special uses" and, in addition to the houses, were surrounded by public and private open space (green or hatched). The pub was, therefore, conceived as part of an integrated neighborhood setting—aesthetically, socially, and commercially.

Two principal designs of pubs were favored for Bristol's fringe settlements: cottage or chalet style, with steeply pitched roofs, dormers, and gables, and "new-style" two-story pubs with shallow pitched roofs, such as the Blue Boy. Under N. G. Brice, Georges & Co.'s chief surveyor, the design of Bristol's 1950s estate pubs reflected a growing interest among architects in creating buildings that harmonized with local topography. Regarding a new pub for a contemporary housing estate to the northwest of the city, the brewery considered that "the soft mellow tone of Cotswold stone was . . . the ideal material to contrast with the leafy green back-cloth provided by a group of tall plane trees" ("Penpole Inn" 1957–8: 8). While local stone was frequently used for cottage-style pubs, those in the "new style" often included a variety of materials; at the Blue Boy, Ibstock facing bricks were combined with natural Bath stone and a rough-cut plinth of blue Pennant sandstone, the stone quarried locally.

Varied topography also had practical uses, and the pub's architect worked with natural gradients to facilitate the flow of products and empty bottles and barrels to and from the site, a "considerable fall" from east to west, allowing the creation of an unloading deck for lorries with direct access to the cellar ("Blue Boy, Lockleaze" 1959: 22). The pub's exterior design expressed its function in other ways, an aspect of its modernity to which the brewery drew attention: "By preserving the simplicity of line of the upper structure, it was intended to divert interest to the lower and more functional part of the building, which, incidentally, shows a variation in outline indicative of the types of service to be found within." At the front of the building, "a large projecting bay with cantilevered roof, and a recessed Off-Sales shop" drew the eye and potential customers to the building ("Blue Boy, Lockleaze" 1959: 23).

In his book *The Renaissance of the English Public House* (1947), architect Basil Oliver set out certain principles of public-house design, among which was the idea of continuous service from room to room. Although no plan has been found, the central location of the Blue Boy's off-sales department appears consistent with that aim. Within the wider civic and commercial setting of Gainsborough Square, it mediated the semipublic space of the pub and surrounding public and private spaces. Prominently located to the front of the building, finished in contrasting materials, and with an independent entrance and a window display, it appeared from the Square as a clearly articulated retail space.

Signage was another means through which Georges & Co. related the pub to its setting. The brewery introduced a new approach to external signage after the war, not only using local artists, but also introducing new forms, such as decorative plaques, alongside more traditional free-standing signs, reflecting the incorporation of art within architecture in British postwar design more broadly. As the brewery explained, above the door to the lounge bar was

> a hand-painted reproduction on glazed frost-proof tiles of Gainsborough's painting of Master Buttall, better known as "The Blue Boy." It is framed in painted hardwood which effectively separates it from the surrounding brickwork, giving it the appearance from street-level of a large pendant miniature. ("Blue Boy, Lockleaze" 1959: 23)

By referencing the famous portrait, the plaque—and by extension the pub—sought to create a sense of place and, perhaps, to engender a sense of community cohesion in a new social space. Gainsborough's painting had popular cultural resonance during the twentieth century (Daniels 2007), and the brewery and its design team may have imagined the Blue Boy as a familiar figure, standing, like its namesake, amidst sweeping parkland but in the modern setting of a council estate.

The Blue Boy theme continued inside, where the use of color was said to have been of particular interest to the brewery's chief surveyor in creating "a distinctive 'atmosphere.'" The two bars were decorated in blue, and the lounge incorporated a "frieze of stylized Blue-Boys in silhouette, white against blue—a charming feature which adds greatly to the attractiveness of the room" ("Blue Boy, Lockleaze" 1959: 24). In the lounge, a large bow window faced onto Gainsborough Square (Figure 16.3). While the brewery's description of the interior emphasized its brightness, photographs show net curtains at the window, lending it a homely feel that, while perhaps compromising its designers' social and architectural intentions, chimed with the brewery's aim to create "a 'local' which will be meeting-place, rendezvous and home-from-home" ("Blue Boy, Lockleaze" 1959: 24). Conceivably echoing the public architecture of Georgian Bristol, as well as postwar ideals, the pub had an Assembly Room, with a kitchen, which was "intended to be the centre of much of the community life" ("Blue Boy, Lockleaze" 1959: 24).

Figure 16.3

The Blue Boy, Lounge, c. 1958. © Courage Archive, Bristol (Heineken, UK).

The Blue Boy's two-bar plan was typical of those built by Georges & Co. for Bristol's new estates in the late 1950s and early 1960s. On the ground floor, the off-sales shop was placed between the lounge to one side and the public bar leading to a skittle alley to the other, retaining, albeit in less complex form, a socially hierarchical approach to public-house design that began to break down in the following decade. The "experimental" skittle alley tapered at the delivery-end, which was wider "to allow for the congestion of players around the bar" and narrower at the skittle-end "to assist concentration on the pins" ("Blue Boy, Lockleaze" 1959: 24).

Skittles, a popular outdoor game in the West Country, moved into enclosed spaces, often in public houses, in the nineteenth century. Skittle alleys remained an important feature of Bristol's postwar pubs, and their inclusion produced distinctive ground plans. Between the wars, Bristol's licensing magistrates had regarded them as public amenities and had preferred that people be free to enter and play in them without obligation to buy alcoholic refreshments (Fisher and Preston 2015). In this way, they emerged as intermediate spaces between the public house and the local community. The postwar emphasis on spatial flexibility in the planning of public-house interiors began to alter that relationship; new alleys were more often directly connected to a central service space and in some newly built pubs were designed with folding screens to allow them to double as function rooms.

Like the skittle alley, the garden was often planned in line with the idea of continuous service. In contrast to suburban pubs of the 1930s, those built for Bristol's postwar estates had quite modest gardens. While open fronts with views of greens adhered to the aesthetic side of planning, drive-through forecourts and car parking (which reduced the space for gardens at the rear) conformed to planning legislation and architectural guidance on practical public-house design ("Car Parks and Replanning" 1941: 3; Yorke 1949: 46). Paved drinking areas were more in evidence than formerly, and a correlation can be drawn between this aspect of pub design and the courtyards and patios that featured in the domestic work of British architects after the war. Several of Georges & Co.'s postwar pubs had outdoor "lounge courts" in "Cotswold stone and crazy paving" ("Penpole Inn" 1957–8: 8) and were carefully considered in relation to family needs. In common with those of its contemporaries, the customers of the Blue Boy could enjoy "garden-service, from a special bar which commands a wide view of playground and garden through plate-glass doors. The garden itself contains a large shelter and a special toilet for children" ("Blue Boy, Lockleaze" 1959: 24). In sum, as one local paper put it, "Inside and outside The Blue Boy is typical of the modern Georges' pub. Contemporary is the operative word" ("Blue Boy" 1958: 1).

Surveying "pubs today" in 1959, and looking to New Town pubs as examples, architect E. B. Musman observed that the architect "must combine traditional qualities which have become part of the ordinary-man-in-the-street's idea of a pub, with the change which has taken place in the whole approach to drinking and the use of the pub." Smaller and fewer rooms, "broken up so as to give a sense of intimacy and comfort," was the first principal change; the second was the growth of catering and availability of nonalcoholic drinks such as Coca Cola; finally, he noted the "growing importance attached to outdoor drinking," including "the use of the forecourt and the effect of flowers and the provision of terraces and garden"—all of which changes, Musman said, would profoundly affect the type of plan provided for the successful new pub (1959: 300).

Conclusion

From its name and setting in a council estate, to its roads named for English landscape painters and its signage and interior design, the two-bar Blue Boy on the new village green responded to the present and the past, to national planning ideals and to the geography of Bristol. Placed at the heart of this new community, the pub's architecture complemented the landscape design of the estate, which, in turn, coalesced with the commercial ideals of the brewery: with a continuous service ideal expressed in the flowing spaces of the interior and exterior, with the commercial movement of goods and people between bars, assembly hall, skittle alley, and garden, and with the wider relationship between the pub and the community in which it was situated. These related both to commercial and functional ideals and to a newly imagined social relationship between the pub and the people. To the brewers, this new social landscape presented increased commercial opportunities. The design of the new "locals," and the work of the architects and planners involved, are a measure of how far-reaching were the ideals born from reconstruction, flowing even into commercial buildings in the new neighborhoods.

In 2010 the Blue Boy closed and has since suffered years of neglect. Now bricked up and graffitied, it stands abandoned within a major regeneration project that promises to transform the public realm of Gainsborough Square. A glimmer of hope is on the horizon, however, as there are local calls for Bristol City Council to save it by compulsory purchase to retain it for community use ("End in Sight for Derelict Lockleaze Pub?" 2015).

Acknowledgment

This research expands on work commissioned by Historic England in 2014, published in 2015 as *The Nineteenth- and Twentieth-Century Public House in Bristol*. We would like to thank Nicola Beech (The British Library), Emily Cole (Historic England), Stephen Daniels (University of Nottingham), Dawn Dyer (Bristol Central Library), Ry George, and Kenneth Thomas (Heineken, UK) for their assistance with our chapter.

References

Abercrombie, P. (1945), *Greater London Plan 1944*, London: HMSO.

Atkins, J. B. (1941), *Reconstruction and the Public House*, London: Monthly Bulletin.

Atkinson, H. (2008), "A 'New Picturesque'? The Aesthetics of British Reconstruction after World War Two," *Edinburgh Architecture Research*, 31: 24–35.

"Blue Boy" (1958), *Bristol Evening World*, December 2: 1.

"Blue Boy, Lockleaze" (1959), *What's Brewing*, Summer: 22–24.

City and County of Bristol Town and Country Planning Act, 1947: Development Plan: Report of the Survey and Written Analysis (1952), Bristol: City Council.

"Car Parks and Replanning" (1941), *Western Daily Press*, October 20: 3.

Curtis, B. (1985–6), "One Continuous Interwoven Story: The Festival of Britain," *Block*, 11: 48–52.

Daniels, S. (2007), "A Study in Denim," *Tate Etc.*, 10 (Summer). Available online: http://www.tate.org.uk/context-comment/articles/study-denim (accessed January 28, 2017).

Darling, E. (2007), *Re-forming Britain: Narratives of Modernity Before Reconstruction*, Abingdon: Routledge.

"Design for the Future" (1947), *Western Daily* Press, April 22: 5.

"End in Sight for Derelict Lockleaze Pub?" (2015). Available online: http://www.bristol247.com/channel/news-comment/daily/news-wire/end-in-sight-for-derelict-lockleaze-pub (accessed April 29, 2016).

Fisher, F., and R. Preston (2015), *The Nineteenth- and Twentieth-Century Public House in Bristol*, Historic England. Available online: https://historicengland.org.uk/images-books/publications/nineteenth-and-twentieth-century-pubs-bristol/.

Forshaw, J. H., and P. Abercrombie (1943), *County of London Plan*, London: Macmillan.

"Golden Cockerel" (1961–2), *What's Brewing*, Winter: 7.

Gorham, M. (1939), *The Local*, London: Cassell & Company.

Gorham, M. (1949), *Back to the Local*, London: Percival Marshall.

Greig, H., and G. Riello (2007), "Eighteenth-Century Interiors—Redesigning the Georgian," *Journal of Design History,* 20 (4): 273–89.

Harris, H. C. W. (1968), *Housing Nomenclature in Bristol, 1919–1967*, Bristol: Bristol Corporation.

"Landscapes of 18th Century" (1943), *Western Daily Press*, April 2: 3.

"Lay-out of New Estate at Lockleaze" (1944), *Western Daily Press*, May 9: 3.

Mass Observation (1943), *The Pub and the People: A Worktown Study by Mass Observation*, London: Gollancz.

Matless, D. (1998), *Landscape and Englishness*, London: Reaktion.

McKellar, E. (2004), "Popularism Versus Professionalism: John Summerson and the 20th-Century Creation of the 'Georgian,'" in B. Arciszewska and E. McKellar (eds.), *Articulating British Classicism: New Approaches in Eighteenth-Century Architecture,* 35–56, Aldershot: Ashgate.

Musman, E. B. (1959), "Pubs Today," *Architect and Buildings News*, October 14: 300.

"Neighbourhood Planning" (1946), *Western Daily* Press, January 11: 3.

Oliver, B. (1947), *The Renaissance of the English Public House,* London: Faber and Faber.

"Penpole Inn" (1957–8), *What's Brewing*, Winter: 8–11, 15.

"Post-War Municipal Development in Bristol" (1950), *RIBA Journal*, May: 257–65.

Powers, A. (2002), "Landscape in Britain," in M. Treib (ed.), *The Architecture of Landscape, 1940–1960*, 56–81, Philadelphia: University of Pennsylvania Press.

RIBA (1943), *Rebuilding Britain*, London: Lund Humphries.

Storey, J. (2004), *The House in South Road: An Autobiography*, ed. Pat Thorne, London: Virago.

Watson, J. P., and P. Abercrombie (1943), *Plan for Plymouth*, Plymouth: Underhill.

"What's in a Name?" (1944), *Western Daily Press*, May 19: 3.

Yorke, F. W. B. (1949), *The Planning and Equipment of Public Houses*, London: Architectural Press.

"Your Local Will Be Smaller" (1947), *Western Daily Press*, April 25: 5.

Chapter 17

Like Vessels: Giorgio Morandi and the Porticoes of Bologna[1]

Vicky Falconer

I.

In thinking of twentieth-century artists that could be associated with some kind of interior perspective, Giorgio Morandi might surely be one of the first to come to mind. Morandi's primary subject matter, from around 1920 right up until his death in 1964, was a collection of bottles, vases, and containers—quotidian objects salvaged at home or picked up in markets, and set up in carefully articulated arrangements. For most of each year, Morandi worked from a modest apartment on Bologna's Via Fondazza, the same family home that he had lived in as a student and which, after the death of his parents, he shared with his two sisters. Giorgio occupied a modest studio-bedroom at the back of the apartment. It was sparsely furnished, with bare plaster walls, and his stored bottles were stacked up, huddled together on the tiled floor or on shelves and tables, and coated in a filmy patina of dust.

Within this interiorized setting, the exterior remained very much within sight and mind. The southeasterly light coming into the room from the shuttered window was an integral element of Morandi's work. Each arrangement of objects was set up on one of three deliberately situated surfaces: a small table just adjacent to the window, and two cantilevered, adjustable platforms facing the window from the other side of the room. Just beyond the balcony, the backs of the upper floors of neighboring apartments were visible, and Morandi would make regular recordings of the view— variegated, when seen together today, by the amount of foliage on the trees or the vantage point selected. But most particularly the city itself, outside the apartment's immediate environs, was ever-present in the depiction of these ostensibly domestic objects. Architectonic constructions as much as still-life studies, their umber volumes and tower-like forms are suffused with the very atmosphere and appearance of Bologna. The resemblance is commented on in almost every text on Morandi, and indeed, over the years, the artist and the city have become increasingly synonymous.

The most striking and defining feature of the cityscape by far, however, is the fantastic and seemingly endless porticoed streets, or *portici*. They seam together, in an astonishing 37-kilometer matrix, palazzi, civic architecture, ecclesiastical buildings, nineteenth-century urban vernacular, and even postwar office blocks. Exactly how the porticoes became so ubiquitous in Bologna is still a matter of some speculation,

Figure 17.1

Max Hutzel, *Strada Maggiore*, 1960–1990. Digital image courtesy of the Getty's Open Content Program.

which perhaps adds to their charged, almost surrealistic appeal today. The first wooden porticoes were twelfth- and thirteenth-century additions to extant buildings; by supporting outward extension of the first floor level, they provided a practical solution to the pressure on living space that had resulted from the influx of students to the university (Miller 1989: 36–9). Gradually, porticoes were incorporated into the standard lexicon of building design and urban planning, an embracing of form that conceivably may have owed much to the continuing of tradition and a sense of civic identity. Perhaps it was also in acknowledgment of the benefits afforded by combining the functions of housing, leisure, business, and trade in one contiguous urban space. And so it remains in modern Bologna, where the porticoes are, as cinema critic and longtime commentator on the city, Renzo Renzi, writes, "the architectural conjunction that binds together the usually contradicting characters of public and private life" (Packard 1983: 20, 29).

Figure 17.2

Luigi Ghirri, *Bologna, Studio Giorgio Morandi*, 1989–1990. © Estate of Luigi Ghirri, Courtesy Matthew Marks Gallery.

Like Morandi's work, then, even on an immediate level, the porticoes participate in a distinct dialogue between interior and exterior. Visiting Bologna for the first time to see the two Morandi museums, and without any prior knowledge of the city, I was fascinated and captivated by its totally unique topography: these ongoing, but always changing "inside" spaces, through which one could walk and walk, from one unfamiliar area to another. And, having sensed quite strongly that exploring the city in this way would tell me as much about Morandi's work as a visit to the museums alone, I was curious to find, later, that so little has been written about Morandi in the specific context of the porticoes. Karen Wilkin, in her *Works, Writings and Interviews* monograph, provides the most in-depth discussion I've found. "Is it far-fetched to assume," she asks, "that the almost daily activity of walking through the rose-red arcaded streets of Bologna, an experience replicated for over 40 years, somehow finds itself into Morandi's work?" (2007: 124).

Likewise, after having been compelled to follow up my first experience of Bologna with further research, it seemed appropriate that this same activity of walking and observing should frame my thoughts on a second visit. In addition to considering my own responses, I wanted to consider the way in which Morandi might have experienced the city—throughout the year, every year, both observed and recollected.

II.

When thinking further about an interior/exterior duality, it seemed to me that within the Bologna cityscape's reconfiguration of this dynamic, interior is often privileged over exterior. With individual buildings incorporated into a whole and continuous entity, for instance, the porticoes render a traditional hierarchy of architecture (with the facade as one of its signifiers) redundant. For instance, a magnificent palazzo might have its main entrance relegated to a narrow side street, or a baroque church might lie behind just one of many similarly unprepossessing doors along a walkway. Often one can glimpse, behind a door left open, porticoed loggias and inner courtyards that replicate, in more intimate scale, the very same features of the street from which they lead (Miller 1989: 33). The interiors that lie somewhere behind these unsuggestive and layered exteriors really are *within*, and all the more appealing to the imagination of a passer-by, to envisage opulent, ornate, or decadently faded spaces of which the outside appearance reveals little clue.

Chapter 18

Rethinking Flow and the Relationship between Indoors and Out: California, c. 1945–c. 1965

Pat Kirkham

"We believe in California . . . homes complete with patio, pool and poodle . . . indoor-outdoor living." (*Californian* 1947)

Introduction

This chapter challenges a postwar Modernist mantra, namely, the seamless integration of, and flow between, indoors and out by highlighting some of the visual and material disruptions to any such integration, particularly at the points of transition, and seeks to offer a broader understanding of the relationships between indoors and out. My point is not to deny indoor-outdoor living, but rather to add to the historical lenses through which we view this phenomenon in the two decades after World War II. As a case study, it focuses on "California Modern" dwellings because they are thought to epitomize the seamless integration of indoors and out in the postwar period (Olsberg 2011: 120). If the analysis need expanding for these types of houses, then they do also for many others.

"California Modern" is used here as an umbrella term for a type of architecture that was closely associated with several magazines, institutions, and architects across California, including *Arts & Architecture*'s Case Study House initiative, ranch-style houses designed by Cliff May and others, and the eleven thousand homes built by real estate developer Joseph Eichler between 1949 and 1966, all of which paid attention to indoor-outdoor living (Kaplan 2011: 46). Conventional narratives about supposedly seamlessly integrated indoor-outdoor living in postwar California focus on a benign climate, more informal ways of living, and single-story, single-family homes with plate glass doors leading onto outdoor spaces, usually with patios and/or pools.

In terms of sources, period architects' drawings suggest a greater seamlessness than period photographs of furnished homes that reveal a variety of visual and material barriers to, and disruptions of, a seamless flow, even when the photographs were staged by the architect, photographer, homeowner, or all three and taken shortly after the houses were first inhabited. In a drawing of the house and garden for the Ladera Peninsula Housing Association (1947, Garrett Eckbo, John Funk, Joseph Stein), for example, there is no furniture close to either side of the glass windows and sliding doors that divide indoors from out (Olsberg 2011: 133). Photographs of contemporary houses, however, almost invariably show furniture, other objects, and plants close to the demarcation between the two spaces; indeed, the very differences between the objects and the ground coverings on either side of the divide indicate the continuation of some prewar conventions about how indoor and outdoor living areas should look and highlight a greater formality inside than out, as does the use in some homes of transitional spaces between the main living area and outdoors, including terraces and canopied walkways (Weisskamp 1964; Kirkham 2011: 151).

Weather and Flow

A symbol of affluent living in the 1930s, indoor-outdoor living was a feature of middle-class life in postwar California, where people flocked in search of jobs, better weather, and healthier, more informal, lifestyles. Any flow between living indoors and out, is dependent, in part at least, upon the weather, and at temperature extremes the weather itself serves as a barrier to seamless flow between inside and out. The Mediterranean-style climate of southern California did not guarantee year-round enjoyment of indoor-outdoor living, nor did the rain and fog encountered in northern California. In southern California, parts of autumn and winter could be cool and sometimes wet and cold, and the designers Charles and Ray Eames regretted not having a fireplace in their house in Pacific Palisades, especially on chilly mornings (Kirkham 1995: 119), while a home-furnishings critic who moved to the Los Angeles area discovered that it was "generally too cold in the evenings to sit out on the spacious patios" ("Design on the West Coast" 1957: 51). Nor did the blisteringly hot summer weeks in southern California favor indoor-outdoor living at a time when few middle-class homes had air conditioning. Hot weather slowed down, and to a degree reversed the flow from inside to out, as people stayed or moved indoors seeking respite from the heat. *Sunset* magazine advised potential house purchasers to pay particular attention to the orientation of the living room vis-à-vis the heat of the afternoon sun ("A Critical Look at the Changing Western House" 1956: 74). Large expanses of glass produced considerable solar heat. Before air conditioning, curtains served as heat-reducing barriers. When drawn, they interrupted flow from inside to out, both visually and materially. When selecting images of houses with large expanses of glass, pro-Modernist accounts rarely choose exterior photographs taken with curtains closed during daylight because they do not show the glass to advantage. Yet some of the images taken by photographer Julius Shulman of now iconic houses in the Case Study House Program (Julius Shulman photography archive, Getty Research Institute, The

Getty, Los Angeles) include exterior shots with curtains drawn inside, either wholly or open only sufficiently for access through a small area where the sliding glass doors had been opened. For John Entenza, editor of *Arts & Architecture* and initiator of the program, it was not just a case of blocking out the heat at his own home (Entenza House, 1945–9, Case Study House #9, Charles Eames and Eero Saarinen). He was not keen on sunlight per se, yet it flooded into the house (McCoy 1998: 13; McCoy 1977), and that may have been one of several contributing factors to his selling the house in 1955. Inside hung two different types of curtains: lightweight ones that helped filter the sunlight and plain, more tightly-woven, thicker ones that were capable of blocking out more light and heat (see Figure 18.1).

Figure 18.1

Entenza House, Case Study House #9 (1945–49, Charles Eames and Eero Saarinen). Photograph: Julius Shulman. © J. Paul. Getty Trust. Getty Research Institute, Los Angeles (2004.R.10: 752–8).

Weather permitting, outdoor cooking was easier if the necessary equipment was located near the kitchen. Barbeques were popular, and most of the equipment used for outdoor cooking differed from that used indoors, as did the types of food (Moss 2010). Some homes, including many Eichler ones, had sliding glass doors from the kitchen to patios and other outdoor spaces, thus helping the flow of food and of those cooking or preparing it from indoors to out (Adamson and Arbunich 2002). Many kitchens did not open directly onto the outdoors, however, and thus the more complicated movement of food, china, utensils, and people in and out mitigated the seamless flow.

Enclosure

Despite, and perhaps as a result of, a greater emphasis on outdoor living, there was a strong desire for enclosure in the postwar years. This was a period of Cold War anxieties as well as an age of affluence, and, to a degree, the concern for security and enclosure stood at odds with indoor-outdoor living. Postwar Californian interiors with a strong sense of enclosure include the long, low cavelike interiors at John Lautner's Carling House (1947–9) and at his Berger House (1953), which in many ways epitomized a blurring of the boundaries between inside and out. The low cozy corners in architect Howard Morgridge's 1959 house provide another example (Weisskamp 1964: 136–9; Olsberg 2011: 131–5). Frank Lloyd Wright, with whom Lautner and several others working in postwar California trained, understood the importance of psychological markers of "home." At his Walker House (1954), the huge twenty-seater built-in sofa in the "dusky cave" living area "turned its back" on the stunning view of the Pacific Ocean, suggesting that there was no simple flow from inside to out (Weisskamp 1964: 43). Charles and Ray Eames likened their home to an "old cave," and the Entenza House had a windowless, soundproof "womb-like" study, while Eero Saarinen's sculptural lounge chair (1946–8; see Figure 18.1), designed for comfort and relaxation, was known as the "Womb Chair" (Kirkham 1995: 126, 189; Kirkham 2011: 152). Thus, from chairs to cavelike interiors, this contemporary appreciation of enclosure and womblike comfort tempered the turn to, and flow of, indoor-outdoor living.

Material Markers of Transition

Those emphasizing seamless transition often cite the same materials being used indoors and out, particularly ground coverings, but rarely did the materials used outdoors exactly match those within (Weisskamp 1964; Olsberg 2011). In the richest state of the richest country in the world at a time of high consumption, many California Modern interiors were far more densely and luxuriously furnished than generally acknowledged. J. R. Davidson's aim of linking inside to out at Case Study House #1 (1945) by using tile for the living room, entrance space, and patio is held up as an example (Stern and Hess 2008; Olsberg 2011: 133). But tile was only one of several materials used outside, and therefore the visual and material effect between inside and out was not unified. Similarly, at the Cannon House in Palm Springs (1961),

William Cody extended tile from the space near the sliding door to the outdoors, but there it joined four other materials—concrete, pebble, pebbled concrete, and grass—none of which was present indoors (Stern and Hess 2008: 124–7). At the Bass House in Altadena (1957–8, Case Study House #20, Buff, Straub & Hensman), quarry tile moved from indoors to out, where it joined other materials, including pebbled concrete and grass, as a partial integration of the ground materials ("Case Study House #20" 1958: 18–22, 31).

For her own home, designer Greta Grossman used a shiny dark-grey terrazzo for flooring in the main living area directly up to the sliding doors, creating a strong contrast with the uneven, natural-colored pebbled slabs on the patio (Weisskamp 1964: 121–3). In photographs the terrazzo has a similar effect to a fitted carpet. Soft wool carpeting increasingly became a marker of comfort and luxury in many postwar homes, and in the Entenza House it was sufficiently soft to serve as seating when covering steps in the main living area (see Figure 18.1). It flowed to the sliding-glass doors, where, abruptly, it met the cold, hard slabs of the patio. The popularity of both soft, thick, pale carpeting and indoor-outdoor living raises the issue of dirt carried indoors from out by the traffic of adults, children, pets, food, and drinks and suggests that, in this instance, contemporary furnishing desires were somewhat at odds with indoor-outdoor living.

Figure 18.2

Loewy House (1946–47, Albert Frey with Raymond Loewy). Living area meets pool area. © *Time*/Getty Images.

The pale, thick-pile, off-white carpet at the Loewy House in Palm Springs (1946–7, Albert Frey with Raymond Loewy), adding to the Hollywood-style elegance of interiors (Figure 18.2), was particularly luxurious ("House to Swim In" 1947: 113, 116). The Loewys had a live-in maid, and keeping it clean must have been time-consuming. The stylish interiors featured sixteenth-century Mexican antiques alongside sleek modern pieces and handwoven draperies by Dorothy Liebes ("They're Swimming in the Parlor" 1947: 46; Stern and Hess 2008: 57). Given the high quality of the interior furnishings, the join between the soft carpet and the hard concrete of the pool area was crude (Stern and Hess 2008: 57–8) and disrupted what presumably was intended as a smooth transition. The bold frame of the glass door and a light white curtain that was sometimes pulled across to filter the hot sun also disrupted the visual flow, along with the large bowl of fruit standing sentinel at the entry to the living area, as if warning people not to enter the space if wet from the pool (see Figure 18.2). The most talked-about feature of the Loewy House was the small section of the pool that intruded into the living space. In Figure 18.2, Raymond Loewy, the flamboyant industrial designer with a background in window display and fashion illustration who codesigned the house, stands to the left. In many ways, the blurring of boundaries was a token gesture. Reputedly, when film star William Powell fell into the waist-high pool, he managed to hold his cocktail glass upright throughout (Faust 2011). Because of the danger of guests falling into the water, the Loewys erected a metal safety barrier when entertaining more than a few people ("House to Swim In" 1947: 116). Given that the barrier marked the boundary point, its very presence flagged the lack of a seamless flow between inside and out.

Furniture, Furnishings, and Flow

Transitions from indoors to out were further complicated by the differences between the various objects on either side of the divide. Hung on the inside but visible from both sides, curtains, as already noted, visually, and sometimes physically, disrupted the flow from indoors to out and vice versa. It was rare for the same or similar pieces of furniture to appear inside and out. Despite the best intentions of some designers and the claims of manufacturers about pieces suitable for use both indoors and out, few homemakers elected to use the same pieces inside and out. Most consumers were not prepared to pay as much for outdoor furniture as for indoor pieces, and therefore there was next to no visually or materially consistent flow from inside to out in terms of furniture (Kirkham 1995: 240–9; Kirkham 2011: 149–51). The prewar conventions about appropriate furnishings for indoors and out continued to be influential, and the increased interest in outdoor living led to the production of an increasing amount of specialized outdoor furniture that was more durable and weather resistant than that used indoors, and often lighter too. Metal furniture was popular for outdoor use, and some was treated with rust-proofing finishes for greater durability. Metal retains heat, and thus wood, cord, or upholstered seats were often added. Such furniture, however, was rarely used indoors, partly because of conventions and partly because of the growing desire for Scandinavian or Scandinavian-style wood furniture (Kirkham

2011: 165). Even when metal furniture was designed specifically for use both indoors and out, it was rarely used for both purposes. In the early 1950s, for example, Pacific Iron Products of Los Angeles commissioned several local designers to create such furniture. The amount of upholstery used in Paul Laszlo's "Americana" metal frame suite, however, made it more appropriate for a covered terrace than full outdoor use, while the general lack of acceptance of metal-framed furniture for indoor use mitigated against this use. Milo Baughman's "The Californian" low side chair with a metal frame in the same line was so well upholstered that it is difficult to imagine it being left outdoors for long (Kirkham 2011: 151). The Eames' Aluminum Group (1958) began as indoor-outdoor furniture, but, largely because it was high budget, it was bought mainly for use in high-end domestic interiors and offices (Kirkham 1995: 165). Lightweight metal-framed loungers with strung cord were popular for patios and pool areas, and a prewar design by Hendrick Van Keppel and Taylor Green using tubular steel and maritime cord proved popular with architects and designers, as did a 1948 version by the Brown Jordan company that used more durable vinyl cord (Weisskamp 1964; Kirkham 2011: 149–51). Such metal and cord pieces were mainly used outdoors.

Although woven rattan (cane) or reed furniture was used indoors during the interwar years, usually in sun rooms and conservatories, such transitional spaces between indoors and out fell out of fashion, and this lightweight, durable, and relatively cheap furniture that withstood humidity well and was easily cleaned was mostly used outside in the postwar years. At the Loewy House, for example, the sophisticated furniture featured in the interior stood in direct contrast to the more informal rattan chairs and floor cushions used outside ("House to Swim In" 1947: 115–16; "They're Swimming in the Parlor" 1947: 46–7).

The chair that most effectively "flowed" across the cultural and material boundaries between indoors and out in the postwar years was the BKF Chair (1938, named after its architect designers, the Catalan Antoni Bonet and Argentinians Jorge Ferarri-Hardoy and Juan Kurchan). This was popularly known as the "Butterfly Chair" (Figure 18.3). It was originally designed with a leather cover, but canvas versions became enormously popular in the United States in the 1950s; low-cost imitation pieces with canvas covers in a variety of bright colors sold from as little as six or seven dollars (Kirkham 2011). These light, bright, cheap but elegant chairs with an amoeba-like seat form reminiscent of the art of Jean Arp and others were also easy to fold and move. Extremely popular for outdoor use, they were sometimes also used indoors, especially by younger and less wealthy homemakers.

In the image of the Bailey House (1947–8, Figure 18.3), a yellow-canvas Butterfly Chair stands immediately outside the full-length windows and sliding-glass doors that demarcated the lounge area from the outdoors. In contrast, a heavily upholstered lounge chair, designed by the Finnish architect and designer Alvar Aalto in 1931–2, stands on the other side of the divide. Sometimes known as the "Tank Chair," this much more substantial item, with a molded plywood frame and deep upholstery covered in rust wool, again suggests that the visual flow between inside and out was far from integrated. Further contrasts are evident between the outdoor metal-framed dining table and chairs and the wooden dining table and chairs indoors. The metal suite stands on a patio, in an outdoor "room": a small domesticated space within a tree-filled landscape. Inside, the fitted grey/brown carpeting runs directly to the sliding-glass doors, contrasting with the trees, grass, and pale slabs on the other side, the combination creating an abrupt transition from indoors to out.

One can imagine adults moving from the carpeted living space directly to the outdoors and back, but when serving outdoor meals they probably accessed the patio directly from the kitchen. The small child riding his tricycle on the patio raises the question of whether or not the Bailey children were allowed a seamless flow of movement from outdoors to in via the adjacent living area—probably not, especially if dusty or dirty from playing in the surrounding meadow and trees. The pristine interior (almost certainly more so than usual because of the photoshoot) suggests that the children probably moved between outdoors and in, elsewhere.

Figure 18.3

Bailey House, Case Study House #20 (1947–48, Richard Neutra), living area and outside patio. Photograph: Julius Shulman. © J. Paul Getty Trust. Getty Research Institute, Los Angeles (2004.R.10: 350-27K).

Plants

Plants selected for use inside tended to differ from those outside, thus further inhibiting seamless visual and material flow. For example, rubber plants and philodendrons were among those that marked postwar interior spaces as modern. They were used mainly indoors and further inhibited seamless visual and material flow. Where the same plants featured on either side of a glass division, they helped highlight the visual flow, but in Figure 18.3, the four isolated rubber plants placed at each corner of the patio at the Bailey House serve more to highlight the exterior "room" than facilitate a seamless transtion. Containers for both indoor and outdoor plants were designed by companies such as Architectural Pottery, a California company established in 1950, and, for the most part, they differed from one another, albeit subtly. In the early 1950s, Architectural Pottery advertised its white ceramic containers (Figure 18.4) as helping to make outdoor patios and terraces look more like living rooms, an effect seen also at the Bailey House (discussed previously, Figure 18.3). In about 1957, however, the company introduced wooden stands to make them appropriate for indoor use, for "the softened, elegant, carpeted living-dining-entry room décor," but the very act of designing special stands speaks to differences as well as similarities between indoor and outdoor spaces (Kirkham 2011: 149) (see Figure 18.4). Some homemakers used the containers indoors without wooden stands, thus providing a direct continuity between inside and out, but others used them outdoors with metal stands akin to the wooden ones, thus subtly flagging both similarity and difference between inside and out (Weisskamp 1964; Stern and Hess 2008; Julius Shulman Photography Archive, Getty Research Institute, The Getty, Los Angeles).

From plants, plant containers, and stands, to furniture, curtains, carpets, and ground coverings, as well as the effects of weather, the examples cited in this chapter provide sufficient evidence for historians to think more expansively about the complexities of visual and material flow, especially that between the main living areas and the outside spaces that were on either side of plate-glass windows and sliding-glass doors, and to ask whether or not, to what degree, and in what circumstances, there was a seamless integration of, or blurring of boundaries between, inside and out.

Figure 18.4

Earthenware planter and walnut stand (La Gardo Tackett and John Follis) for Architectural Pottery c. 1957. La Gardo Tackett Estate, Architectural Pottery, Vessel ® USA Inc. All rights reserved. LACMA M.2009.137a–b. (c. 1957).

Acknowledgment

This chapter grew out of a research project that led to the *Living in a Modern Way: California Design 1930–1965* exhibition curated by Wendy Kaplan and Bobbye Tigerman. I am grateful to the curators for involving me in that project, and to Staci Steinberger, Kate Fox, Elizabeth St. George, and Craig Lee for research assistance.

References

Adamson, P., and M. Arbunich (2002), *Eichler: Modernism Rebuilds the American Dream*, Layton, UT: Gibbs Smith.

"Case Study House #20: By Buff, Straub and Hensman, Architects, in Association with Saul Bass" (1958), *Arts & Architecture*, November: 12–22.

"A Critical Look at the Changing Western House" (1956), *Sunset*, May: 74.

"Design on the West Coast" (1957), special issue *Industrial Design*, October (4): 50–1.

Faust, C. M. (2011), "Loewy House by Albert Frey—1946 Classic Desert Modern Home." Available online: https://spfaust.wordpress.com/2011/12/12/loewy-house-by-albert-frey-1946-classic-desert-modern-home/ (accessed December 12, 2012). NB: The date for the house is usually given as 1947.

"House to Swim in Is a Paradise for Raymond Loewy and His Friends" (1947), *Life*, March 24: 113–15.

Kaplan, W., ed. (2011), *Living in a Modern Way: California Design 1930–1965*, Cambridge: MIT Press/ LACMA.

Kirkham, P. (1995), *Charles and Ray Eames: Designers of the Twentieth Century*, Cambridge: MIT Press.

Kirkham, P. (2011), "At Home with California Modern, 1945–1965," in W. Kaplan (ed.), *Living in a Modern Way: California Design 1930–1965*, 147–78, Cambridge: MIT Press.

McCoy, E. (1977), *Case Study Houses: 1945–1962*, Los Angeles: Hennessey & Ingalls.

McCoy, E. (1998), "Remembering John Entenza," in B. Goldstein (ed.), *Arts and Architecture: The Entenza Years*, 13, Santa Monica: Hennessy and Ingalls.

Moss, R. F. (2010), *Barbecue: The History of an American Institution*, Tuscaloosa: University of Alabama Press.

Olsberg, N. (2011), "Open World: California Architects and the Modern Home," in W. Kaplan (ed.), *Living in a Modern Way: California Design 1930–1965*, 117–45, Cambridge: MIT Press.

Olsberg, N., ed. (2008), *Between Earth and Heaven: The Architecture of John Lautner*, New York: Rizzoli.

Stern, M., and A. Hess (2008), *Julius Shulman: Palm Springs*, New York: Rizzoli/Palm Springs Art Museum.

"They're Swimming in the Parlor" (1947), *Californian*, June: 46–7.

Weisskamp, H. (1964), *Beautiful Homes and Gardens in California*, New York: Harry N. Abrams.

Chapter 19

Green Interiors: Transitional Spaces in Multilevel Building

Elisa Bernardi

By the end of the nineteenth century, inhabiting a fixed dwelling had increasingly become a desired condition of well-being, and the city was considered the most civilized place for human society to inhabit (Berrini and Colonnetti 2010). The city has for long been considered an incredibly flexible, efficient, and effective model for human society, a place where most of the world's population lives today (Kollhoff 1997). However, the amount of work needed to maintain and renovate cities often disrupts the urban environment as well as human activity. Humans transform cities to improve their living conditions, but this has led to a separation between humans and the natural environment, while intensive urbanization has restricted the availability of space for gardens, parks, and other green places.

The industrial age has been defined as an age of consumption "with no conscience" (Fornari 1972). Humanity stopped living in nature and began to exploit it, becoming in the process both builder and destroyer, and failing to grasp the consequences of these actions. A harmonious landscape between society and nature can be seen as a place where sensory experiences can emerge and where nature is far more than a mere human product. Only by becoming aware of our capacity to work with the natural environment in high-density cities can we aspire to return to a more balanced relationship with nature.

Such a shift of perspective is discussed here by investigating the evolution in the use of green spaces in multilevel buildings and how these transitional spaces, including balconies, windows, terraces, bow windows, and roof gardens, allow novel solutions in architecture and landscape design to connect exterior and interior spaces through green thresholds and intermediate borders. Particular focus is given to the architects proposing transitional spaces as a solution to the way dwellings connect with nature, including Le Corbusier, James Wines and SITE, Yositika Utida, Shu-Koh-Sha Architectural and Urban Design Studio, Dirk Denison, and Studio Boeri.

The term *inhabiting* is used here to denote the organization of domestic space, as well as the contemporary transformation of housing culture. The term *dwelling* is understood in its broader meaning of "feeling at home on earth," with the notion of "residence" being part of it. According to this perspective, interiors are not only the indoor spaces (a room, for instance), but also the artificial environment of urban spaces, such as squares and other outdoor gathering places. Interiors are the expressive environments of our collective and private lives and include open spaces as well as private, semiprivate, and public areas. If we consider how a building relates to nature, streets, and other architecture, and consider grass as the floor and "sky as the ceiling" (Ottolini 1996), we can define this urban green exterior as an interior or a continuum of adjacent interior spaces, and we can achieve the dual benefit of designing green spaces with as much detail as interiors and of pursuing improvements in inhabitants' sensations.

In his book, *Greater Perfections: The Practice of Garden Theory*, the English landscape historian John Dixon Hunt focuses attention on the relationship between human beings and vegetation, and he provides the definition of the "Three Natures" (Dixon Hunt 2000). For Dixon Hunt, the "First Nature" is a wild and unmediated environment, while the Second Nature includes the agriculture and infrastructure necessary for human beings. The "Third Nature" includes the first two natures but goes beyond and is characterized as a combination of nature and culture. In particular, Dixon Hunt argues, the garden is considered an artifact on the basis of which we can interpret each society's unique culture (Figure 19.1). As the human interest in roof gardens spans the ages, from the Hanging Gardens of Babylon through to the contemporary age, the use of vegetation in dwelling areas has evolved beyond its symbolic, aesthetic, and ornamental functions to reflect societal features and needs. From the theoretical and, to some extent, utopian concepts of former private gardens connected to dwellings, developed with the beginning of intense urbanization, the presence of green spaces in multilevel buildings has become fundamental today in real projects as an answer to the demand for green spaces in high-density cities.

Figure 19.1

Frontispiece, Curiositez de la Nature et de l'Art by l'Abbé de Vallemont, 1705. Note the well-distinguished First Nature (in the background), the Second Nature (in the middle ground), and the Third Nature (in the foreground).

The Private and the Collective in Le Corbusier's *Immeuble-Villas*

Since Modernism, there has been great attention paid to the idea of architecture as a mechanism for improving the health of the mind and the body (Wilk 2006). As early as 1922, Le Corbusier proposed the *Immeuble-Villas* project. His purpose was to achieve a healthy and comfortable modern way of life for a society increasingly concerned with industrial mass production. The industrialized city and its growing population inspired Le Corbusier to make several attempts to rationalize and modernize cities to make them safer and healthier.

What seems to have been a major inspiration for Le Corbusier's urban project was the visit he paid to the Galluzzo Charterhouse in Ema, Florence (c. 1910), after which he started developing his ideas about the private life of modern man. In this monastery, three sides of the central cloister were bounded by small monks' cells. Each of these cells was equipped with a small garden, providing a view of the Tuscan countryside through the windows and the wall enclosing the garden. Protected by the monastery walls, the monks could study, meditate, and garden in perfect isolation. While the communal facilities were located on the west side of the cloister, the cloister itself served as a public garden. This systematic organization of daily life into two basic types, the private and the collective, would be of great relevance through the entire career of Le Corbusier, far beyond his first proposals for the *Immeuble-Villas*.

The *Immeuble-Villas* ideally aimed to provide a new model for the bourgeois house in order to allow it to survive in the industrial age (Figure 19.2). In fact, Le Corbusier never meant to declare the bourgeois house obsolete; rather, he believed it should be improved upon according to the evolving economic and urban context. In the Villas' design, every apartment occupied two levels and was equipped with all the facilities appropriate to someone's daily life, with the space organized around a two-story terrace and a living room. Two grids of six cells, one above the other, faced each other along two sides of a central courtyard.

The *Immeuble-Villas* apartments aimed to offer their inhabitants the essential joys of air and sun, together with collective facilities and amenities situated on the other two sides of the project, on the courtyard level. Each apartment featured a terrace garden that provided a filter to the outside world. The garden was physically separated from the inner bedrooms through a patio-type opening at every level. The result was an empty space that separated some rooms of the house from the terrace while maintaining a direct connection through the living room and providing a source of fresh air for the house. The industrially produced furniture on the terrace (mobile and fixed) added another room to the house with a different function from those in indoor rooms.

Figure 19.2

Sketch view of the garden terrace from the apartment of the *Immeuble-Villas* by Le Corbusier, 1922. Fondation Le Corbusier. © FLC/ADAGP, 2017.

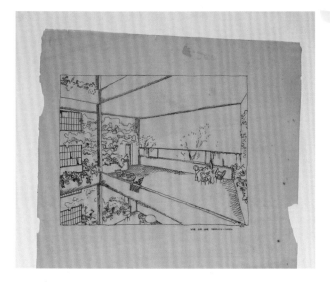

High-Rise Green Architecture

In the 1970s, a form of architecture that was strictly integrated with the environment provided the basis of the green architecture movement that was developed by James Wines and Emilio Ambasz. In 1981, with his group SITE, Wines proposed a provocative theoretical project named *Highrise of Homes* (SITE 1982) (Figure 19.3). It consisted of a vertical structure featuring different styles of apartments and houses, each with its own private garden.

SITE's aim was to develop a design that represented an alternative to the generic, mass-produced, urban high-rise apartment building. The ten- to fifteen-story-high residential complex could either be newly built or constructed using the steel and concrete framework of existing factory buildings. Each level of this complex would consist of plots of land with streets, upon which individual houses would be custom-built according to the preferences of the owner. The houses were to be built around a rectangular core to ensure that all the plots received natural light. The *Highrise of Homes* was to combine the conveniences of urban living with a sense of individuality not typically found in a large city.

Figure 19.3

View of the project *Highrise of Homes* by SITE, 1981. MoMA Archive.

Roof Gardens in Contemporary Cities

In recent decades, the traditional trade-off between private and collective spaces has been revised in light of the need to improve the quality of human life in contemporary cities. The integration of vegetation with constructed spaces must keep pace with the demand for energy efficiency in buildings, the creation of natural lighting and ventilation to apartments, the reduction of climate warming, a rebalancing of local microclimates, a decrease in acoustic and electromagnetic pollution, and the protection of biodiversity by the creation of new habitats (Boeri 2007).

Next 21 by Osaka Gas with SHU-KP-SHA (Jong-Jin, Brouwer, and Kearney 2002; Osaka Gas Experimental Housing 1995, 2009) gives an example of this idea of a contemporary residential building and vertical landscape. This was an experimental residential complex demonstrating new concepts of multifamily housing units that incorporate sustainable design methods and advanced technologies. The design of this building was conceived to solve issues relating to high-density urban housing and resource conservation, taking into consideration highly individualized lifestyles. The building project was initiated to test new models for reducing energy consumption and preserving the environment through waste processing and composting, while at the same time creating apartments adapted to individual residents' needs and lifestyles. The creation of a green inner-city oasis for humans, as well as for wild birds and insects, was reinforced by the construction of an open, elevated street. One of the objectives of the project was the integration of nature in the design of collective housing. Grass and trees were planted on the roof, and small atria were created on the balconies. In addition, the elevated street and a courtyard located on the ground level were stocked with plants to attract wildlife. This infusion of nature into the building enabled occupants to experience nature through the building and give them a better perception of seasonal changes in an urban setting.

Another example of the contemporary interpretation of green roofs is D. Denison's *Culver House* (2008), a Chicago-based project in an urban context conceived to provide space for living and working. The main goal of *Culver House* was to promote the envelope of green design strategies in a private mixed-use project. The façades optimized the benefits of their orientation by the implementation of thermal mass walls, while both interior- and exterior-planted spaces served to buffer the interior from Chicago's cold winters and hot, humid summers. These green spaces also worked as buffer zones by allowing for the expansion and contraction of the double-skinned façade at critical points along its length. The planted places worked as winter gardens that could be fully opened to the favorable outside weather or fully closed to create a tempered space in less desirable weather. In addition to these dynamic spaces, exterior terraces provided shade as well as a direct connection to the exterior and to the project's park beyond.

Similarly, the *Bosco Verticale* in Milan (Boeri Studio, 2014) was designed to be a residential high-density building consisting of two towers of respectively 76 metres (18 floors) and 110 metres (26 floors), which together held 480 large- and medium-sized trees, 250 small trees, 11,000 groundcover plants, and 5,000 shrubs, or the equivalent of a hectare of forest. Every apartment had one or more terraced, covered gardens connected to the interior by a sliding French window. One of the main objectives of the *Bosco Verticale* project was to decrease the expected energy consumption of the buildings by around 30 percent. This was made possible by climate optimization from the shielding offered by the planted façade to reduce the energy costs of air conditioning the interior. Further goals were the improvement of air quality by the reduction of air pollutants, a significant production of oxygen, the absorption of around 20 tons of carbon dioxide per year, protection against noise pollution, an increase in biodiversity, and the creation of an environment for the preservation of animal and plant species.

Tomorrow's Challenge and the Role of Roof Gardens

The previous examples illustrate a variety of approaches to green spaces in multilevel buildings in contemporary cities. Ultimately, green interiors enable architecture and landscape design to meet evolving social needs and human behavior in a close, intimate connection.

When a residential block is directed outward by a succession of private or semiprivate outdoor spaces, it works as a filtering membrane between a dwelling's interior and the environmental conditions. This intermediate area between the public and the private may take on the features of a loggia, a winter garden, or a terrace shadow—all elements of social aggregation for a building's inhabitants, who may be engaged in direct and personal care of the area's planting. Virtually all residents in such a building would have a terrace, in which a garden is a representation of their dreams. People have the opportunity to look after a garden, and the whole family can participate in its creation. The verdant planting becomes a tangible part of the everyday lives of the building's residents. An important factor in the success of this type of environment is the ability to apply knowledge and experience in plant biology in order to manage the soil where the plants grow. Furthermore, to observe a plant growing is an educational and social experience.

A terrace may create a sense of privacy by allowing one to retreat a little from the outside world by stepping back from the window. At the same time, windows that look onto a garden where one has planted and grown flowers bring the garden into the apartment. The terrace can encourage contact between people. Apart from their aesthetic features, living green spaces may form a link between people and the environment. In this sense, such spaces allow people who live in "liquid modernity" (Bauman 2000) to discover a solid space, a quiet area where they may relax, think, or meet other people.

There is another goal for green terraces that will take many years to be realized: the inhabitants themselves will transform buildings, and therefore the city, through the things that they plant. The relationship between adjoining and elevated spaces, with a specific focus on the role of green terraces across two or more building levels, allowing the creation of visual and perceptible connections between living spaces and natural environments, would become a key element in contemporary society. In providing inhabitants with the impression of living in the countryside or in a garden, vertical green architecture constitutes a versatile system offering potential throughout a city.

Keen attention to energy performance has spurred the development of unique spaces within buildings that transcend their seemingly functional nature and become real amenities for residents by creating three-dimensional landscapes linking interior and exterior spaces. Green roofs used on an urban scale may have morphological and functional implications and can be a landscape system that establishes a series of naturally beneficial processes if extended over a portion of the city large enough to have a measurable impact on microclimate and energy flows. This application would contribute to the realization of fresh urban ecological infrastructure.

Imagine the widespread use of green roofs in terms of the eco-environmental benefits to an urban setting, as well as the possibility of an ecological recovery of our cities through a modification of the concept of functional and aesthetic building facades. This would transform the city through the morphological and chromatic reconfiguration of the buildings' exteriors. There would be a change, therefore, in the traditional planting of the city developed over the centuries, the inclusion in the urban structure of specific and/or linear plant elements (trees and vines), the definition and the preservation of widespread green spaces (parks and gardens), and the formation of residual spaces that are more or less vegetated (flowerbeds, areas for production, brownfield sites).

We are therefore faced with the exciting possibility of a new trend in the interaction between landscape and architecture that reverses the normal canons of intervention in urban landscape. This turnaround would be from a physical standpoint, since the shell would become operational and the degree of intervention would not be restricted to street level, but also on the buildings. At the same time, this would generate a conceptual subversion of the growth pattern of the city according to a new sustainable vision. The roofs and buildings would cease to be prodigious consumers of energy and resources but would contribute to environmental enrichment.

A symbol of modernity, the roof garden is creating today a new spatial ideology and definition. It can expand the interior room and offers a yet unknown perspective to the larger natural and constructed environment. This is particularly true in urban areas, where roofs constitute a large fraction of the overall surface area, considering also that from now on the metropolis is expected to grow together with the pursuit of an enhanced quality of life.

References

Bauman, Z. (2000), *Liquid Modernity,* London: Polity Press.

Berrini, M., and A. Colonnetti (2010), *Green Life: Costruire Città Sostenibili*, Bologna: Editrice Compositori.

Boeri, S. (2007), *Manifesto per il Bosco Verticale*, personal communication.

Dixon Hunt, J. (2000), *Greater Perfections: The Practice of Garden Theory*, Philadelphia: University of Pennsylvania Press.

Fornari, F. (1972), "L'individuo e la simbolizzazione dell'ambiente," in V. Mathieu (ed.), *Individuo e Ambiente: Seminari Interdisciplinari di Venezia*, Bologna: Il Mulino.

Jong-Jin, K., R. Brouwer, and J. Kearney (2002), *NEXT 21: A Prototype Multi-Family Housing Complex*, Ann Arbor: University of Michigan Press.

Kollhoff, H. (1997), "Costruzione Urbana contro Alloggio," *Lotus International*, 94: 100–2.

Ottolini, G. (1996), *Forma e Significato in Architettura*, Roma: Laterza.

Osaka Gas Experimental Housing (1995), "NEXT 21," *The Japan Architect*, 17.

Osaka Gas Experimental Housing (2009), "NEXT 21," *The Japan Architect*, 73.

SITE (1982), *Highrise of Homes*. New York: Rizzoli.

Wilk, C. (2006), "The Healthy Body Culture," in *Modernism, 1914–1939: Designing a New World*, 248–67, London: V&A Publications.

Chapter 20

Between Concentration and Distraction

Sarah Breen Lovett

There can be a dualism falsely perceived in the famous essay by Walter Benjamin, which indicates that we experience art in a state of concentration and architecture in a state of distraction (Benjamin 1936). However, as Benjamin explains, instead of seeing distraction as a state of nonconcentration, one can see it as another way to experience, a habituated and haptic way of absorbing multiple stimuli simultaneously. Therefore, both concentration and absorption can be thought to inform our reception of art and architecture. Further, as, Carolin Duttlinger points out, Benjamin also referred to being caught between the two states as being in a third state: at the *threshold* (Duttlinger 2007). The creative works within this visual essay aim to explore such simultaneous experiences of the states of concentration and distraction. One can experience this threshold state by becoming so absorbed by a state of distraction that a new form of awareness is generated, or so absorbed by the state of concentration that the stimuli are all-consuming, and the mind switches off and subconscious absorption takes over. This notion will be discussed by briefly touching upon three creative work installations made as part of my doctoral research called *Expanded Architectural Awareness: Through the Intersection of Architecture and Expanded Cinema*.

The first work that will be discussed is *Skewed Screen* (Figure 20.1), which was created to concentrate on the distracted spatial perception we have with oblique architectures. The oblique is between the vertical and horizontal. The habituated body, normally traversing horizontal planes while surrounded by vertical planes, encounters the oblique with an adjusted positionality. The body positions itself in order to feel stable in relation to an oblique surface.

To explore this relationship with the oblique in a moving image installation, it became evident that the imagery used would have to be that of which the body has a kinesthetic relational awareness. Therefore, imagery of moving horizontally through a forest was filmed because the haptic body has a relational perspective with trees. When one looks at the image of trees, there are visual clues to which way is up and which way is down. The image of the trees was projected on the soffit and made to rotate vertically, so at times the imagery was the right way up, and at other times it was upside down. This aimed to increase awareness of the oblique soffit being between the vertical and horizontal. At the same time, the slow speed of the projection allowed space for the mind to wander, becoming emptied by the turning image.

Figure 20.1

Skewed Screen (2010),
Archetype Gallery, Chauvel
Cinema, Paddington, Sydney.
Photograph by the author.

The second installation is Dome Detail (Figure 20.2), which explores the visually distracted, fragmented way domes can be perceived. Within a dome we are surrounded, enclosed by an omnipresent structure. Unable to see the whole dome, we experience it in fragments, yet it extends to our peripheral vision. In a dome the usual parameters of horizontal ceiling meeting a vertical wall are erased. The ceiling in a dome morphs and becomes the wall without the delineation of a corner. This creates a space where our normal senses of boundaries are challenged and our peripheral vision is given space to expand.

In the installation, films of Islamic domes and details were projected over the geodesic dome, creating a perceptual tension by which the materially rich architectural imagery sliding over the light, ethereal fabric dome inverted the boundaries between the filmic projected imagery and the *real* architectural dome. Because of the movement of this imagery, at times the dome appears to break into multiple fragments, in a multitude of formations, while at other times it appears to reconfigure itself, becoming partially whole again. This imagery allows one to become aware of the dome structure and materiality while also becoming lost in the meditative ebb and flow of visual imagery.

Figure 20.2

Dome Detail (2010), The Land of Hopeless Utopians, Peats Ridge Festival. Photograph by the author.

The final installation that will be discussed here is *Window Detail* (Figure 20.3), which explores the fragmented spatial perception possible with windows. Our relationship with the window can be thought of as being spatially displaced between interior and exterior. From the interior the window is a filter, a frame through which to view the outside world. Meanwhile, the window also allows the outside to be reflected back into the interior space; that which is present outside affects the occupation of the interior.

In this installation the imagery projected was a slide show of photographs taken of trees from another place and time. These images were set within a claude-glass-like frame, suggesting the distorted view we hold of the other: the exterior. Projected through the window, the image became fragmented. A temporal refraction of the landscape, with an imperceptible delay, reflected onto various layers of the interior—a window, a floating fly screen mesh, a wall beyond the mesh—and reflected back onto a wall behind the projector. This installation highlighted the layered and complex interrelationship between notions of inside and outside, while also blurring and loosening the boundaries and exchanges between them.

Figure 20.3

Window Detail (2010),
Duo-Scope Gaffa Gallery,
Sydney. Photograph by the
author.

Through these creative works, relationships to architecture have been explored as simultaneously distracted and concentrated. The works create a wavering between awareness of the architectural construct and the subconscious absorption in the moving image, while at other times they generate a concentration on the moving image and a distraction from our relationship to the architecture. Therefore, it is not dualistic definitions of distraction and concentration that are important to this series of works. It is precisely through being caught between the states, in fluctuation, that the installation series works. We see concentration and distraction, conscious awareness and subconscious absorption, as ways to experience architecture, highlighted through moving image installations.

References

Benjamin, W. (1936), "The Work of Art in the Age of Mechanical Reproduction," Section XV. Available online: https://www.marxists.org/reference/subject/philosophy/works/ge/benjamin.htm (accessed on January 29, 2016).

Duttlinger, C. (2007), "Between Contemplation and Distraction: Configurations of Attention in Walter Benjamin," *German Studies Review*, 30 (1): 33–54. Available online: http://www.jstor.org/stable/27668212 ?origin=JSTOR-pdf (accessed on January 29, 2016).

4

Part 4
Frames

Dan Graham Waterloo Sunset at the Hayward Gallery
London 2011 Gini Lee

Introduction

Mark Taylor

A key concept of FLOW revolves around notions of the frame or framing and the way it has been used to select or parenthesize various elements in order to divide or separate thoughts, ideas, and territories. The artistic response often partitions space and frames, a field, or territory into a compositional plane concerned with affect, sensation, and intensity. For the artist this can be a deliberate or exclusive act, whereas although doors and windows might be used in a similar manner, they more often frame transitory or accidental scenes in a manner that is not dissimilar to being framed by the edges of a painting.

Architectural openings, including doors and windows, have historically served as isolating or defensive apertures such that the room is presented as a refuge cast against the dangerous outside world. Modernist responses have sought to break this frame and to suggest continuity between the exterior and interior by expanding the size and materiality of these elements. These openings as frames serve architecture by emphasizing the interpenetration of exterior (landscape) and interior (domestic). In this conception, the window is a frame that takes on an ocular metaphor and the "revelatory" aspects of transparency. The question, though, is whether the conspicuous boundaries of the interior suggest that the outside boundaries are similarly restricted, that is, to what extent they disrupt the FLOW between these two states, whether physically, psychically, or emotionally.

Acting as threshold devices, they are points of entry and departure, transitional places that induce moments of pause or hesitation, which in some literature and films are used to extend the present, thus giving both a spatial and temporal dimension to these moments of inflection. Viewed this way, they intensify rather than arrange, enabling the inhabitant to step from one environment to another, or one condition to another. It is this ability that is considered by contributors to this part, in that windows and verandas provide a perspective for both a promissory vision and a continuity of existence. What much of this indicates is that the making of interior is framed through ideas of time and mobility, rather than through the traditional subservient decorative relationship to an architectural context.

In the opening chapter, "Ornamental Transparency in the Modern Kitchen," Sandy Isenstadt, University of Delaware, develops a far-reaching discussion around Julius Shulman's 1954 photograph of the Hutson House kitchen and its seminal place in understanding the modern domestic home. Isenstadt shows that this carefully constructed photographic image contains a number of indicators that capture a feeling of movement, of flow between indoors and outdoors, that was at the heart of Modernism's vision for using new technologies and techniques to remake spatial, material, and social relations. The glass wall not only was a manufacturing feat of industrialization that foregrounded the home within fictions of nature, but also represented a discontinuity between exterior and interior, or nature as existing and nature as represented through artifice. Isenstadt argues that though the glass wall offered a return to nature, it was to a benign landscape, rather than the untamed wilderness, since the Shulman view from the modern kitchen reorientated this room from one of domestic labor to that of domestic leisure.

However, the critical insight is that the image offers three versions of nature, represented by the wider landscape beyond the fence, the conventionally suburban garden, and the vegetable produce of agriculture, or pastoral nature arranged in the kitchen. The suggestion is that there is a seamless transition between nature and food, a condition Isenstadt observes in both period marketing of fresh produce and its home storage. Drawing from Bathes's *Mythologies*, he suggests that raw food is there for visual consumption and an ornamental impulse, not dissimilar to an aspirational window onto plenitude and "an affirmation of modernity's reconfiguration of nature." However, Isenstadt proposes that despite the affirmation of transparency, the Schulman image and other Modernist images were not intended to be emulated or consumed, but were there as a distraction from everyday problems of nutrition and housing, perhaps more as an indicator of what might be idealized living.

The next chapter shifts to the view from a country house verandah. In their "Tracing Events: Material Tales for Country Homes and Gardens, as Found in Rural Australia," Australia-based academics Gini Lee from the University of Melbourne and Mark Taylor from Swinburne University examine domestic histories in a settlement context. They use Yve Lomax's theory of "sounding" to propose the interior exterior as events, relations, and entangled histories that lie outside typological boundaries. Understanding the homestead as an event and relational entity in which there is something going on, such as the goings-on of surrounding homestead events, enables past and future histories to be read together. Lee and Taylor provide a case study of a family homestead that was built in the nineteenth century and is still occupied by family descendants. Engaging with family history, they propose that the flow of events between inside and out is a process that entwines historical fact with stories and remembrances of occupation. Framing the study in this manner enables Lee and Taylor to examine, first, how an artwork overlays narrative settler history with that of women's work and domestic practice, and second, how the house interior overlays formal homestead "history" with that of the individual's history, such as recollections of home and land. The contribution to flow, in an archaeological sense, is that many things and histories are visible but remain as fragments, creating an ambiguity between home and land.

Anca Lasc from Pratt Institute offers a reading of Huysmans's novel *À Rebours* as a prelude to discussing the conspicuous construction of a spatial flow between the interior and an imagined exterior. In "Decorating with a View: The Nineteenth-Century Escapist Window," Lasc draws upon this fictional account of a decadent aesthete's life and home, where in some moments there is a spatial and material continuity between inside and outside. At other times the novel reveals the psychological possibilities of a subjective interior and the physical possibility of the home having an alternate spatial and temporal dimension. She notes how the interior embraces falsity and the ability of mechanized recreations and simulations to affect the senses and create pleasure. This embrace of artifice is brought to bear on the lives of Parisians under Haussmann's urban remodeling, particularly as it affected the view from their windows. Lasc notes that many writers have commented that the increased modernization and urbanisation of Paris caused mental fatigue, leading to the home as refuge from alienating modernity. To offset this effect, decorators provided pattern books with model windows that were illustrated as an elevational composition of artfully arranged curtains, mirrors, flora, and furniture. Critically, Lasc observes that by adding a view from the window into their drawings, these decorators framed the outside world as an alternate reality, artifice, and fantasy. Shifting beyond their normal threshold condition, these windows offered a spatial and temporal flow, in that they completed the illusion of living in a different time or a different place.

In "Curtaining the Curtain Wall: Traversing the Boundaries of the American Postwar Domestic Environment," Margaret Maile Petty, from Queensland University of Technology, examines the thinness of a plate-glass window as a spatial divide that mediated relationships between inside and outside, public and private, architect and decorator. The focus of the chapter is on postwar American suburban homes as they embraced this trope of Modernism. She notes that period architectural magazines framed the expansive window as a means to make the outdoors flow into the indoors through the glass walls, but despite these intentions it tended to frame the garden as scenery rather than as an active space. Working through Rudofsky's analysis of postwar suburban housing, she teases out the contradictory ideological arguments between comfort and aesthetics, particularly as curtains and other window treatments became the primary threat to this indoor/outdoor relationship. Using both design theory and advertising literature, Petty notes that curtain and blind manufactures recognized the problem of the glass wall in that it affected the appearance of the home from the inside as well as from the outside. Popular midcentury shelter magazines offered various means by which interior comfort could be achieved through the use of wall colors and curtains that controlled glare, created atmosphere, softened the view, provided privacy, and balanced a room's focus. These ideas, Petty suggests, enabled homemakers to integrate a personal domestic environment within the dictates of Modernism.

These essays have demonstrated an engagement with the fluidity of space, such that the relationship between interior and exterior is not compartmentalized but exists in a more liquid state. Openings and thresholds are discussed relative to their ability to frame flow between interior and exterior, imperceptibly and critically. However, in the penultimate chapter in this part, Suzie Attiwill from RMIT University (Australia) problematizes the term *interior* when considering the practice of interior design as lying outside a practice defined by an architectural context. Her chapter, titled "Speeds, Slowness, Temporary Consistencies, and Interior Designing," traces theories developed by Deleuze and Grosz to question the notion of interior as architectural confinement, and as a consequence, the possibility of framing "interior" relative to nonstatic spaces. Within this context, Attiwill argues for a theoretical shift in the word *interior* from one confined to a bounded space to one where movements and temporality are foregrounded, from confinement to flow. Through careful observation of a painting, Attiwill suggests that despite the presence of interior soft furnishings and external landscape, the external light and mirrored reflection suggest a "quality of movement and change even though stilled as an image." This observation serves to shift an understanding of the interior as a place for outward view, to one constructed by the folding-in of exterior forces—light, reflection, and so on. It is interior made through relations, and in particular relations with exterior, where exterior is not dependent on an architectural context. Central to this mode of thinking is the notion that interior design can be rethought outside its historical architectural associations, to the process of designing "interior" where interior is not predefined but is in a sense made visible by slowing do wn and partitioning a moment of stability, of occupation.

A visual essay titled "Lines to Make Space," by Sarah Jamieson and Nadia Wagner, is the final chapter in this part. This collaborative work offers a more abstract way to consider creative practice in the built environment. Rather than offering solutions to a fixed problem, this project poses questions around binary structures that are tested through the interchangeability of language across an abstract divide: the horizontal or vertical line. Framed this way, the words slip and move, offering alternate relationships and possibilities for the consideration of spatial structures.

Chapter 21

Ornamental Transparency in the Modern Kitchen

Sandy Isenstadt

The See-Through House

The visual trope of transparency evident in Julius Shulman's 1954 photograph of the Hutson House kitchen, designed by Los Angeles–based Burton Schutt, is by now so familiar that it obscures a fundamental paradox. Human building activity—architecture, in a word—was premised on the separation of inside from outside. When a clutch of savages stepped from the woods to ring a lightning-sparked fire, according to Vitruvius, the darkness at their backs was separated from the light of society on their faces. When some prehistoric clan first drew a circle to stand in to distinguish itself from the larger world, it invented the *domus*, the sphere of human inhabitation. Since that time, separating oneself or one's group from an outside, whether with thick walls or elaborate rituals, has been a mark, perhaps even the start, of civilization. Architecture, in short, has long been centered on the articulation of spatial divisions.

The Hutson House defies this venerable pattern. By suggesting an easy camaraderie between indoors and out, it proposes that one flows effortlessly into the other, that fluid relations between spaces rather than cellular division are the norm. This essay asks how and why it does this, how a still image reads as a snapshot of a flow, what other movements are hinted at, and, conversely, what other currents are blocked by an image of transparency.

Transparency, of course, is a freighted term in architecture, with formal, theoretical, and ideological dimensions that have resonated with new ideas of space such as those of August Schmarzow, new materials like glass, new techniques of representation such as cinema, and new ideas of dwelling that have fascinated architects. Here, *transparency* will refer to the possibility of movement between spaces as well as a visualization of that possibility, in order to argue that, as much as it appears to facilitate movement, transparency also introduces a kind of immobility or cessation of flow by specifying and fixing the character of the relation between spaces. In other words, the visual immediacy of architectural transparency tends to dominate alternative possibilities and new avenues of concourse. In this sense, transparency can be understood as a Modernist and three-dimensional restatement of a representational system such as Renaissance perspective: both are paradigms of perceptual mastery that imaginatively reassert the self and at the same time suggest the limits of subjective possibility. Transparency, I will claim in the end, is akin to plastic in calling attention to itself precisely for its thoroughgoing self-effacement. Moreover, in asserting its invisibility, transparency may be further understood as an ornamental gesture. It directs aesthetic attention toward an ideal of fluid relations between inside and out and away from a situation that is, in fact, considerably more complex.

To review, since the eighteenth century and, to a large degree, up to the present, the Anglo-American detached house type that looms in cultural imagination was understood as a refuge from the larger world, a family-sized inside separate from the society-scaled outside. As the surrounding environment became increasingly mechanized and commercial, the home offered a literal and conceptual distance from the harsh realities of industrializing society. The familiar faces and ordered spaces of the private home annulled the tumult of modernization, which included increasingly frequent encounters with strangers, as Georg Simmel noted in several essays early in the twentieth century. Anxieties regarding the crossing of class boundaries, which in smaller communities would have been all but impossible, and in the city can happen in a moment, let alone in the course of a single generation, were assuaged by carefully chosen decorative objects, rather than random city things, and distinct family roles, often related to specific rooms in the home.

But in responding to and providing sanctuary from society, the private home inevitably, perhaps necessarily, modeled itself on that very society, albeit in negative profile. Tendrils of urban infrastructure such as plumbing and gas piping and, later, electric service, for example, wove through the house's structure, but they were typically hidden in favor of their delivery of commodities such as water, heat, and light. At the same time, all types of objects of industrial origin—decorative objects, furniture, wallpapers and finishes, and so on—came to fill the home, but these, too, often eclipsed the facts of mass production with notions of personal taste or familial representation. References to nature were also common: consider the vegetal motifs common to early electric light fixtures, for instance. Moreover, the private home preserved pervasive social norms, such as gender roles remitted to specific areas, but in terms of the family, a seemingly more natural social unit than, say, the factory. The cellular character of most private homes of sufficient scale likewise rehearsed the social structure of private property. In essence, as the outside world became more and more the product of human making, a set of practical and aesthetic conventions smuggled its core principles into a private sphere imagined as a retreat from that world.

Even the bits of flora that were brought indoors to serve as visual relief and reminders of a nature that was fast disappearing follow the dictates of industrial society. Home conservatories in the nineteenth century, for instance, were modeled on the iron and glass structures being erected in public gardens. The *hortus fenestralis*, or window garden advocated for crowded settings—a remarkable invention that created the sense, if not exactly the illusion, of nature lying just outside the window of the home even if in reality it faced only the windows of neighboring homes—was likewise composed of manufactured goods such as iron or wood framing, glass panels, and even mirrors meant to create a perspective or illusion of depth (Hibberd 1870: 96–7). In other words, nature brought indoors was an aestheticized domestic recapitulation of humankind's industrialized domination of the natural world.

Modernists deplored the self-delusion. They rejected the notion of a home generated by industry but distinct in character from it. The home might well be a place apart for the single family, but modern architects maintained it ought to be the honest product of that society. It should not only function as efficiently as a machine; it ought to look the part, too, to paraphrase Le Corbusier's famous dictum. To that end, modern architects not only utilized new methods of construction and industrially produced materials in factories or places of commerce, where they had been used for many decades, but also began to use them in the most intimate realms of the home. Manufactured building materials such as glass, newly available in large sheets thanks to the recent commercialization of float processing, resonated as both an aesthetic and ideological advance. In many works, a literal transparency between inside and out through entire walls of glass suggested even more: an affinity not just between inside and out but also between the self and the artefactual world, that is, between subject and object of modern life. Modernism in this context was an effort to remake material and social relations in light of new methods of manufacturing and utopian aspirations of egalitarianism.

To dramatize these efforts, many leading architects sited their homes in relatively sylvan settings. The modernism of the house was made visually evident with cubic massing, a taut and planar skin, an emphatic separation of structure from enclosure, and large openings filled with glass. The abstraction was honed to the point that long-standing architectural elements such as window and wall came to be compositionally treated as transparent or opaque phases of a continuous plane, rather than, say, material responses to a human need for light and enclosure. Inevitably, the glass walls overlooked an unpopulated landscape. In some of the best-known Modernist houses— Corbusier's Villa Savoye, Mies van der Rohe's Tugendhat House, Richard Neutra's Lovell House, all from the late 1920s, come to mind—the technically rationalized approach contrasts sharply with the natural setting. Although our representations of such houses were often the result of careful editing, they came to be welded to the image of the modern dwelling. Rather than connote history, function, construction, or language, the modern dwelling refers to the condition architecture had formerly differentiated itself from, even as that condition was, in fact, rapidly receding.

It was the best of both worlds, a machine-for-living-in-the-garden. Glass walls were the product of manufacturing expertise, engineering proficiency, and construction dexterity. They necessitated larger heating plants, and air conditioning once it was available, new insulating systems, temperature controls, and cheap energy to make up for their inefficiencies. Usually, however, such technical developments were concealed in order to heighten the sense of an immediate relation to the outdoors. The somatic experience of manufacturing specialties was presented as the visual experience of nature. Architects routinely discussed the technical advantages of modern construction but foregrounded in their work some conception of nature. Nature was a stage on which technological forms appeared to heightened effect as well as a stunning backdrop for the occupants' daily life. In other words, whereas single-family homes in the nineteenth century tried to counterbalance the social disruptions of urbanization with a well-ordered family group and to mitigate the visual violence of the industrial landscape with fictions of nature, Modernists accentuated the engineered origins of the house's parts and at the same time, by means of new forms of transportation like commuter railroads and automobiles, placed those houses in pristine settings that suggested nature was unchanged.

This was especially the case in the United States as Modernism went mainstream in the 1950s—albeit on terms that were indifferent, at times even hostile, to earlier socialist or utopian visions. There, views of a spreading and unpopulated landscape resonated with a national frontier mythology, recapitulating hazy impressions of American history. As the geographer David Lowenthal wrote, "Our forefathers mastered a continent; today we celebrate the virtues of the vanquished foe: To love nature is regarded as uniquely American" (Lowenthal 1962: 19). A home open to nature could thereby appear to be continuous with a national narrative of spatial and material conquest, as well as its culmination. In this context, a sharp contrast between spare geometric houses and the complex forms of nature was a means to bring together the machined forms of an industrial age with the ageless earth. The more open, the more confident, as a squib regarding Philip Johnson's Glass House reveals:

> A glass house bespeaks more security than a stone house because the owner can afford to dispense with the safety of stone. The liberty to build openly implies trust. . . . By this last magic of a consummate civilization we should be united in freedom with the most primitive hunter for whom all Nature is home. ("Glass House" 1949: 78)

The advance in material culture returned the dweller to a state of nature, as long as that nature was understood as fundamentally benevolent.

The See-Through Kitchen

Kitchens were clearly part of the paradigm. They were the most overtly mechanized room in the home, with an array of large appliances topped by dozens of practical instruments and all guided by a spirit of practicality and everyday usefulness. As such, they were a locus for functionalist planning (Bullock 1988). The best-known example of the kitchen as a kind of factory is Margarete Schütte-Lihotzky's 1926–7 design for the Frankfurt Kitchen, which was installed in thousands of apartments in Frankfurt after World War I. Later, midcentury kitchens likewise considered rational planning—Schütte-Lihotzky espoused the methods of Frederick Winslow Taylor and Christine Frederick—but incorporated electrical appliances such as refrigerators, which the Frankfurt Kitchen lacked. Still, the new kitchen equipment vanished behind flush cabinet doors that presented seamless and smooth surfaces visually and conceptually congruent with building exteriors. As might be expected in borrowing aesthetic cues from larger themes of modern house design, kitchens also featured representations of nature, most dramatically and remarkably frequently in popular period journals, with a wall of glass that oriented the main site of domestic labor to the emblem of domestic leisure, a landscape view.

This much is apparent in Shulman's photograph. Indeed, the photograph suggests three versions of nature, each contextualized by three different spaces—the kitchen, the backyard, and the rising landscape beyond the fence—each demarcated by three distinct planes: the fence, the picture plane of the photograph itself, and, sandwiched between those two, the glass wall. The gentle folds of the rising landscape are conspicuous by the absence of other people, especially since the Los Angeles basin was at the time one of the fastest-growing regions in the nation, and the privacy fencing suggests neighbors nearby. The backyard appears conventionally suburban: a sharp boundary, severe ornamental perimeter planting, a specimen tree, and a somewhat incongruous piece of garden sculpture. The uninhabited backdrop notwithstanding, it is a model of a suburban second nature. Although each space is clearly demarcated, there is a sense of flow: the further landscape is always in view, and the glass wall is open to the garden.

Inside the kitchen is something quite different but no less a representation of nature, a clutch of vegetables resting on a butcher block cutting board: leafy greens, a pepper, an ear of corn, a cucumber, and half a dozen carrots. The vegetables are organized to roughly follow an orthogonal to the vanishing point, hinting that they originated there, outside, in nature. With the vegetables, a version of a pastoralizing prop Shulman employed often and to great effect (Niedenthal 1993), one can read a three-step movement across the three spaces of human-nature relationship depicted in the image: from the rear, nature on its own, untouched by humankind; to a meeting of equals corralled in the yard; to agriculture, nature bent to human will. The addition of the knife, also almost oriented toward the vanishing point, even suggests a fourth stage of the movement: nature ingested. The complete array proposes a functionalist revision of the *hortus fenestralis*. Where that device literally hid an unpleasant view with bits of nature, the evident transparencies in the photograph intimate an untroubled flow between inside and outside, between architecture and landscape, between technology and nature.

The Hutson House is plainly highbrow: it was custom designed, was documented by one of the leading architectural photographers at the time, and, regardless of adjoining properties, faces an appealing view. But, although precisely these themes of transparency are evident in other upscale homes, the house is far from the radical design of, say, the earlier Lovell House kitchen, by Richard Neutra, who likewise hired Shulman—in some sense, discovered him—to document his work. Indeed, with its vinyl asbestos floor tiles, colonial revival styled breakfast table and chairs, electric stovetop, stock metal cabinets, geometric wall finish, fluorescent ceiling panel, and so on, the Hutson House presents itself as a far more middle- or upper-middle-class home than, say, the exclusive retreat of Philip Johnson, where nearly all aspects are custom made, right down to the under-counter refrigerator. In this regard, the Hutson House is representative not so much of actual American postwar homes but of an aspiration about the character of modern living.

However accurately Shulman rendered postwar American dwelling ideals, his portrayal of unfettered movement between indoors and out masks a number of other flows between the private realm of the home and the larger public sphere. Some of these are familiar. The site planning emphasizes landscape, while removed from view are signs of the urban infrastructure that delivers sufficient amenity to locate one's home in a notionally pastoral setting, along with the cars, roads, and filling stations that facilitated daily commutes from remote sites to centers of employment. Indeed, nearly any representation of a residence from this period highlights the view the modern house looks onto rather than what the house looks like from the street. Even a humble backyard view symbolically compensated for modern life by imaginatively reconstructing a landscape that postwar society was fast overrunning (Isenstadt 2005). Advanced mechanical specialties such as radiant heating and residential air-conditioning equipment were likewise pitched as a return to nature. To some extent, this substitution rehearses the "device paradigm," an idea introduced in 1984 by philosopher of technology Albert Borgmann. The term describes a common trait of modern technology, that is, an arrangement of parts that eclipses a productive mechanism in favor of the commodity it delivers. As Borgmann puts it, "The peculiar presence of the end of the device is made possible by means of the device and its concealment" (1984: 48). Surprisingly, some modern architects championed such mystification. Robert Woods Kennedy only slightly overstated the case when he said that in architecture, as in magic itself, "the absolute secrecy of the trick is the essence . . . In architecture, the architect who leaves us mystified, who excites us with an invisible technique, is the most rewarding" (1953: 527). Aesthetic impact flourished, many believed at the time, while rational understanding slept.

Seeing Through the Kitchen

Given the foreground of the photograph, the unmistakable bounty of nature tendering itself for consumption diverts attention from yet another flow, the tsunami of processed foods just then flooding food markets and powerfully reshaping American eating habits. As wartime rations gave way to postwar abundance, the cultural meaning of different foods changed as well. Frozen foods, for example, were seen as an expensive luxury good before the war. But efficiencies introduced by manufacturers as a means to keep the troops well nourished led to wider availability and lower prices for the general postwar population, buoyed by advertising that stressed the suitability of frozen foods for any occasion and all walks of life. Along with canned goods, frozen foods were pitched as a kind of democracy of foodstuffs, a perception not only promulgated in manufacturers' period promotions but also one that seemed self-evident in the national reach of many brands (Neuhaus 1999). In fact, the American government facilitated increased consumption by all social classes as an engine of national economy in the postwar years (Ganksy 2011: 70). In other words, while the subject of diet is foregrounded in Shulman's photograph and its relationship to architecture presented as both utilitarian and symbolic, the great opacity in the midst of all this representational transparency is the changing nature of the American diet.

More to the point, such processed foods were seen as the fruit of modern technologies in particular and a leading attribute of a modern life. Ostensibly, with frozen foods the homemaker was freed from the drudgery of washing, peeling, shelling, seeding, chopping, and, beyond simply applying heat, even cooking food for the family. Slicing and squeezing oranges seemed pointless when easily reconstituted cans of frozen juice were easy to find and cheap to buy. Boil-in bags, an increasingly popular way to prepare vegetables, simplified storage, heating, serving, and cleanup even further. The blessings of advanced material civilization were evident not only in new forms of construction, as exemplified by modern architecture, but also in convenient and economical foods (Hamilton 2003: 43; Gitelson 1992). In a sense, the homemaker's family's freedom to enjoy a lifestyle cradled in a wholesome, natural setting was premised on the time saved due to new conveniences such as frozen foods, along with a host of other amenities. That is to say, to many Americans the modernity of the kitchen had far more to do with new formats for foods than it did with open plans, rationalized layouts, or glass walls.

Nevertheless, the representational registers for such added economy and convenience closely parallel those employed often in modern architecture and in full display in Shulman's image: nearness to nature was the face of both advanced building techniques and advanced food technologies. The maxim takes a number of forms in the context of food and the kitchen. Large appliances, for example, especially the electric refrigerator, were frequently depicted as a return to natural goodness rather than an advance in engineering and were pointedly likened to a view through a glass wall. In 1953 alone one can find Kelvinator's "Foodarama" characterized as a food panorama, a species of view; a Bendix refrigerator "built like a Big Bay Window to put more foods in sight"; and International Harvester's "7-Climate Refrigerator" and its reorganized national food terrain of Florida citrus, Wisconsin cheese, Texas beef, apples from Vermont, and pineapples from Hawaii (Bendix 1953; International Harvester 1953; Kelvinator 1953), Similarly, canned goods were touted for their closeness to harvests. An American Can Company advertisement, for example, overlaps two images—a farm and children enjoying dinner—to suggest the union in the can of wholesome nutrition and modern convenience (Advertisement 1956).

Despite the distant origins of such foods, they all were fresh. Freshness in the postwar era was the consumers'-eye view of the technological slowing of the biological time of decay—things just killed or long dead were equivalent and readily available in the refrigerator's controlled climate. Through the regulation of seasonal fluctuation in food supply, products from different parts of the calendar and from different parts of the countryside could all come together in service to the family dinner. Freshness, of course, is best discerned by smell, taste, or touch, but its mass marketing meant its merit had to be made visually evident, which is where advertisers turned to transparency. Freshness, or rather, the idea of freshness was the nonvisual analog of a landscape view. Du Pont, for example, peddled its Cellophane plastic food wrap in such terms, shielding produce from touch while facilitating visual inspection. A leading theme in the product's advertising from the late 1940s through the mid-1950s maintained: "Cellophane shows what it protects! Protects what it shows!" In other words, the liberation of optic from haptic in pictures of produce was a prelude to the pictorialization of freshness and, more generally, modern life in the modern house (Isenstadt 1998). Shulman, a master of his craft, apparently recognized as much. The vegetables he pictured are practically premodern, so to speak, compared to the average American diet at the time. They are symbolic rather than representative. The leafy greens depicted are defiantly not iceberg lettuce, which by the mid-1950s had become the most common plant appearing in American salads (Petrick 2006). The care taken to include in his photograph a knife, a sign both of tactility and physical labor, aims to restore the sensory matrix that his own photography required be undone.

The double transparency rendered here of architecture and food—outdoors to in; nature to kitchen—and its reliance on a suite of opacities can be understood as the result of an ornamental impulse, following an idea put forward in 1957 by Roland Barthes in regard to baroque concoctions in French cuisine. As Barthes tells it, depicted in the pages of *Elle* magazine is a working- and middle-class hunger for upper-class gentility that reveals itself in foods whose raw form was cleverly disguised, reworked, and then presented for visual consumption. Placing crawfish heads atop their béchamel-bestrewn bodies is one example he gives. The ensuing salmagundi is the product of a two-part movement, not unlike that visible in the Hutson House kitchen. It involves, "on the one hand, fleeing from nature . . . and on the other, trying to reconstitute it" by artificial—one might say, technical—means: distance from nature followed by its contrived pictorialization. An "even sediment of sauces, creams, icing and jellies" guaranteed that underlying foodstuffs would be hidden, not unlike the smooth surfaces overlaying household mechanisms (Barthes 1991a). At the same time, smoothness set off the ornamental gestures reinstating new textures riffing on what lay buried beneath, analogous to modern planes contrasting with complex natural forms (Barthes 1991a). Such ornamental cookery, like the advanced building technologies of modern architecture, was a means to reinstall a relationship to a nature that was well on the wane.

Although Barthes's examples are French ones, many contemporaneous American recipes shared these traits, with Jell-O regnant (Neuhaus 1999: 534–7). Indeed, the defining malleability of Jell-O brings to mind another of Barthes's discussions, on plastic, the key traits of which also characterize transparency: each entails a substance whose reality is, in a sense, its absence, its self-effacing position between two states, a null element that is merely a transit between raw matter and human making, "less a thing than the trace of a movement," as Barthes wrote. Transparency at the Hutson House—in the form of a view and some vegetables—offers a window onto plenitude and an affirmation of modernity's reconfiguration of nature, as well as being a source of great pleasure, akin to plastic, "since the very itinerary of plastic gives [humankind] the euphoria of a prestigious free-wheeling through Nature." Moreover, plastic's ubiquity—"the first magical substance which consents to be prosaic"—displaces the rarity and ideality of nature with a more bountiful artifice (Barthes 1991b).

Transparency at the Hutson House, then, might be described as an ornamental middlebrow Modernism. In diverting our attention from what we know about the infrastructural underpinnings that make life in the modern single-family suburban house feasible, it is a kind of magician's misdirection, an entertaining suspension of disbelief in order to embrace a set of natural values at the scale of the individual family that society itself had already abandoned. Fleeing from nature by technical means only to refashion it anew thus can be understood as the mid-twentieth-century version of humankind's delineation of inside from outside, albeit with the boundaries now transparent. While the return to nature is painstakingly staged, in the end probably no one is fooled. Just as Barthes argued regarding the dishes depicted in *Elle* magazine, readers of shelter magazines in which images very similar to the Hutson House frequently appeared were not expected either to be living in such a setting or even eating fresh vegetables on a regular basis. They were, however, presumed to find in these images of plenty and fluid relations with nature an entertaining distraction from the real problems of housing and assuring adequate nutrition, an aspirational arrow pointing away from the everyday toward an ideal vanishing point of modern life.

References

Advertisement (1956), *Life*, April 23: 60–1.

Barthes, R. (1991a), "Ornamental Cookery," in *Mythologies*, trans. Annette Lavers, 78–80, New York: Noonday Press.

Barthes, R. (1991b), "Plastic," in *Mythologies*, trans. Annette Lavers, 97–9, New York: Noonday Press.

Bendix advertisement (1953), *Better Homes and Gardens*, May.

Borgmann, A. (1984), *Technology and the Character of Contemporary Life*, Chicago: University of Chicago Press.

Bullock, N. (1988), "First the Kitchen: Then the Façade," *Journal of Design History*, 1 (3/4): 177–92.

Ganksy, P. (2011), "Refrigerator Design and Masculinity in Postwar Media, 1946–1960," *Studies in Popular Culture*, 34 (1): 67–85.

Gitelson, J. (1992), "Populox: The Suburban Cuisines of the 1950s," *Journal of American Culture*, 15 (3): 73–8.

"Glass House" (1949), *Architectural Forum*, 91: 78.

Hamilton, S. (2003), "The Economies and Conveniences of Modern-Day Living: Frozen Foods and Mass Marketing, 1945–1965," *The Business History Review*, 77 (1): 33–60.

Hibberd, S. (1870), *Rustic Adornments for Homes of Taste*, London: Groombridge & Sons.

International Harvester (1953), *Better Homes and Gardens*, May.

Isenstadt, S. (1998), "Visions of Plenty: Refrigerator Design in America around 1950," *Journal of Design History*, 11 (4): 311–321.

Isenstadt, S. (2005), "Modern in the Middle," *Perspecta*, 36: 62–72.

Kelvinator advertisement (1953), *Better Homes and Gardens*, August.

Kennedy, R. W. (1953), *The House and the Art of Its Design*, New York: Reinhold.

Lowenthal, D. (1962), "Not Every Prospect Pleases," *Landscape*, 12 (2): 19–23.

Neuhaus, J. (1999), "The Way to a Man's Heart: Gender Roles, Domestic Ideology, and Cookbooks in the 1950s," *Journal of Social History*, 32 (3): 529–55.

Niedenthal, S. (1993), "Glamourized Houses: Neutra, Photography, and the Kaufmann House," *Journal of Architectural Education*, 47 (2): 101–12.

Petrick, G. (2006), "'Like Ribbons of Green and Gold': Industrializing Lettuce and the Quest for Quality in the Salinas Valley, 1920–1965," *Agricultural History*, 80: 269–95.

Chapter 22

Tracing Events: Material Tales for Country Homes and Gardens, as Found in Rural Australia

Gini Lee and Mark Taylor

Tracing Events: An Introduction to an Alternative to Typology

Architectural research about country homes is often focused on the genealogy of their occupants and/or their place in the history of architecture. Much of the latter is based on an examination of the design typologies, development, and alterations to the extant fabric, as well as on discussion of the attributes of artifacts identified with the home. In the rural Australian context, while this adoption of a "style" might have some resonance with geography and climate, it was also informed by imported architectural ideas that took hold during the period of occupation of rural landscapes in the mid- to late nineteenth century. These early squatters and settlers mostly reflected their usual British heritage in the transplantation and overlay of domestic classicism onto the landscape. One issue with this form of architectural classification is that it focuses on the house "type" and creates an object-centered approach to modes of inhabitation, while overlooking the very actions and events that characterize their occupation. The house as an object with utilitarian function repeated across the landscape reinforced the signs of its legality as "an Australian country house for an Australian country gentleman" (Lucas 1987: 88–9). Argued this way, such objects may be considered to conform to a standard model of house (albeit with Australian influences), which nonetheless does little to illuminate the intangible lives of the place and its occupants or the events that contributed to these lives.

This chapter seeks an alternative perspective in order to supplement the architectural record by investigating the material tales of two country homesteads and properties, Purrumbete (c. 1842) and Wiridgil (c. 1885), constructed on the volcanic landscapes of rural western Victoria. When viewed through a microhistorical perspective, the properties, houses, and associated farm buildings (objects) are no longer defined as being fixed to a type, but can be understood as being in a state of constant transformation as homes and compounds for inhabitation (events). That is, by revealing their domestic situations through more abstract means, as found in artifacts

and personal items, including early artists' representations of settlers' lives, it is possible to trace the narratives that persist to contemporary times, offering an insight into the relationship between individuals, home, and society. These early settlers worked the rural landscape, transforming bush frontier into tended agricultural paddocks, while similarly their homes and gardens thrived subject to the economic and social changes that accompanied colonization. The "primitive" developments that informed the early material and spatial arrangements of settler built homes expanded with new wealth and social status. In material form, although some aspects of the original homes might remain today, they have been juxtaposed or "incorporated" into new compositions over time, reflecting the everyday wealth and changing needs of these early families and their descendants.

Figure 22.1

Eugene von Guerard, *From the Verandah of Purrumbete*, 1858, oil on canvas, 51.4 x 86.3 cm, National Gallery of Australia, Canberra, purchased 1978.

The aim of this chapter is to discuss an ecology of home through a recorded and an imagined history of occupation. Ecology in this sense derives from humanist notions of the relational aesthetics arising from human interaction with natural, social, and built environments. As a means of engaging with the genesis and development of the country home, we seek to reveal the transdisciplinary *flow* of events between inside and out, encompassing both house and extant garden, through a process that entwines historical fact with stories and remembrances of occupation. Evoking a contemporary exploratory perspective uncovers tales that reflect the realities of country life over time, expressed in abstract narrative form.

Central to this approach is a repositioning of landscape through domestic practice, and vice versa, in order to demonstrate that interior and landscape are not static elements, but are rather spaces of events. The chapter first examines the representation of the inhabited and increasingly domesticized landscape through artistic and visual imagery that contributes to the representation of settlement and existence in an unfamiliar and undeveloped land, particularly when a feminine presence is applied to the narrative. Second, a brief history of the Manifold settler family and their houses, lands, and agricultural enterprises establishes the means of architectural development and how the fabric of home has reacted to changed circumstances. Enduring familial occupation reveals an ecology of the domestic, albeit interrupted through changed ownership that is revealed in Purrumbete's more recent history in contrast with the continuous family ownership of Wiridgil. A concluding examination of the interior as landscape, and conversely of landscape as interior, draws out the appearance and/or absence of material legacies played out in the contribution of extant ephemera to the backstories and social lives of the people and landscapes that have made and remade these homes and their landscapes over the past 150 or so years.

Living in the Country as Revealed through Artistic Expression

Artist Eugene von Guerard was an early colonial painter who traveled the volcanic country and painted European-influenced, idealized landscapes for the squatters who were developing extensive landholdings in southern Australia in the mid- to late nineteenth century. While on his tour, he painted *From the Verandah of Purrumbete* (1858) (Figure 22.1), described in the painting's citation as a "homestead portrait" (https://artsearch.nga.gov.au/detail.cfm?irn=109026; see also Gray 2002). This work is compositionally unusual in this genre in that the view is framed by the presence of home, including signs of domesticity such as the rug casually airing on the balustrade, transposing the more usual view of the house in the landscape. The landscape is mediated by the perspective and if framed by verandah and garden toward the wilds of the lake and bush beyond.

Von Guerard's sequential paintings of the development of Purrumbete over a number of years represented the transition of the Arcadian landscape from hut to small house to increasingly larger houses with the advent of prosperity. This 1858 rendition reveals the domestic landscape from the verandah, the place of mediation between inner lives and the harsh nature of the climate and the Australian landscape. The rug hanging over the balustrade infers the domestic life and object collection inside, and yet the verandah was also the place of surveillance where activities in the landscape could be apprehended from the shelter and safety of the house.

This compelling mid-nineteenth-century image is the inspiration and provocation for contemporary artist Marion Manifold's series of linocuts made to relate the story of women's lives in this challenging country, remote from the city and the familiar comforts of their former home. Manifold's linocuts appropriate a contained domesticity and invest the lives and hopes of the women and families into landscapes that were more usually described through explorer and land-taming narratives. In *Rosy Dreams from the Verandah of Purrumbete* (2007) (Figure 22.2), the presence of house, garden, and the domestic rituals at play are invested in such things as the teapot, the cup, the Turkish rug, and the roses that reference shards of broken ceramic collected from the old Purrumbete Lake rubbish tip. Manifold's depictions of the women, who typically were thought to spend their days working indoors, instead foreground the nature of women's visibility in the outdoors, working the gardens and enjoying the boating on the lake (M. Manifold 2007).

Figure 22.2

Marion Manifold, *Rosy Dreams from the Verandah of Purrumbete* (2007).

Such generational narratives of settlement, home, work life, and the home-landscape relationship were embedded in the turn-of-the-nineteenth-century renovation of the Purrumbete homestead. Memorialization of the settler family's frontier development at Purrumbete was represented in documentary form by a commissioned mural program to adorn the new great hall. Mr William Thompson Manifold commissioned Walter Withers's six murals (1902) of a narrative of the pioneer history of the site, depicting the pioneering men making their way through the bush to the lakeside, setting up camp, and building the homestead ("The Artists: Walter Withers" n.d.). This later mural program represented a visual record of an Aboriginal attack on white settlers in European terms by depicting an assault on the homestead and family. Although painted at the turn of the twentieth century, the murals are somewhat romanticized narratives of settlement and existence in unfamiliar and undeveloped lands, which as Karen Burns notes are much more complex in their relation to settlement and indigenous history (Burns 2013).

Marion Manifold subsequently created a series of six linocuts, *The Land* (2009), for the Stony Rises Project that "use Walter Withers murals at Purrumbete as a starting point to explore the lives of the Manifold women across 100 years" (Byrne, Edquist, and Vaughan 2010: 44). J. S. Manifold's poem "The Land" (1978) (Manifold 1984) expresses a childhood yearning for the landscapes of home while recalling his envy of the close affinity to land of his Aboriginal friend Pompey Austin. Marion draws upon Manifold's sensibility to the Stony Rises landscapes from a feminine perspective, with each work entitled with the name of the Manifold women; Mary 1831, Alice 1837, Jane 1842, Marion 1871, Hersey 1895, and Beatrice 1928. Of her own linocuts Manifold writes, "The fragmented women and iconography constructed from old photos, wills and letters and the decorative idioms that followed—patterns from blinds, porcelain and china in my home—show the losses and little luxuries that were part of the early women settlers' lives" (Manifold 2009).

These works provide underpinning narratives drawn from oral and written family histories that are also speculations on the ephemeral physical presence of the work of women in their domestic milieu. They bring to the fore often-overlooked aspects that are played out in settler narratives. The narrative depictions seem to move across the landscape without regard to spatial acuity or to linear chronology. They prompt two possible methods for reading and participating in extant interiors and gardens from a contemporary perspective. First, the broader landscape is a palimpsest of physical features, both mapped and physically marked, the grounding wallpaper upon which domestic occupation plays out. Second, personal objects and spatial landscape elements are appropriated to enable everyday lives to be carried out in the middle occupiable ground of "tamed" home and garden.

All three artistic representations, von Guerard, Withers, and Manifold, provide for readings of alternative perspectives. W. J. T. Mitchell suggests that landscape is not an art genre but a medium of exchange between "the human and the natural, the self and the other." It is, he argues, a natural scene mediated by culture, opening a structuralist discourse on the way it is both a representation and a presentation (Mitchell 1994: 5). This idea of exchange embedded in the visual narrative expresses a flow between the tangible traces of everyday life of the country home retold through the juxtaposition of small events in the domestic routines of rural women (and equally rural men) as an expression of the intangible in their everyday life experiences.

Tracing the Historical Record of Two Country Homes

In her "genealogical" history of homestead building in the Western District of Victoria (Australia), Harriet Edquist charted the early "primitive" origins to more "sophisticated" architecture of twentieth-century inhabitation (Edquist 2010). Following an architectural typology classification methodology, Edquist noted that by the 1880s a "regional type" had emerged consisting of a "low, hipped-roof Italianate villa surrounded by a wide veranda." In mid- to late-nineteenth-century Australia, the aforementioned early settler properties, the very culturally significant Purrumbete (c. 1842) and the recorded Wiridgil (c. 1885), were built in this regional style in close proximity to each other in the Western District of Victoria. Although both homesteads were originally built and occupied by the same family, the earlier home, Purrumbete, has had several more recent owners. Moreover, the local architectural record documents important alterations to the building and grounds, including its period of commercial ownership in the late twentieth and early twenty-first century. During this latter period, the architecture and gardens were remade, and thus few material traces of the original ephemera of occupancy remain, apart from the Withers murals in the still extant great hall.

After arriving in Tasmania in 1831, Thomas, John, and Peter Manifold looked for land in the Western districts of Victoria. Traveling through a rugged area known as the Stony Rises, they squatted on 100,000 acres on the edge of Lake Purrumbete in 1839, an area they called "the wished for land" (Manifold 1984). The initial homestead appears to not be particularly elaborate, as noted by James Bonwick, who traveled through the area in 1857, which is when building started on the main core of the house (1857–60). Bonwick, an inspector of schools, described crossing a vast marsh to the edge of Lake Purrumbete, where he found the Manifold's "humble dwelling" on their 4,000-acre homestead, with additional 6,000 leased acres. He noted that "Lake Purrumbete is a charming spot. The water is delicious, abounding with Black fish and Trout . . . the circumference of the lake is six miles, and the average depth is 150 feet" (Bonwick 1858: 25). It was also around this period (mid-1850s) that the squatter settlement was converted to a freehold property.

Following the death of the two brothers, John in 1877 and Peter in 1885, the land was divided between John's sons, with the elder son William gaining the Purrumbete homestead, together with 10,809 acres of farmland. In 1882 the Western District architect Alexander Hamilton made a number of additions that doubled the size of the house. These changes to the bluestone home included bay windows and a generous veranda to all sides. Other alterations included a small cellar and a west-facing conservatory (1884). In 1901 W. T. Manifold commissioned architect Guyon Purchas to extend and modify the house, resulting in the current listed Federation Arts and Crafts building. Purchas's alterations included a new first floor and a large central hall complete with minstrel gallery. This space, together with his modified dining room, reflected an interest in Art Nouveau interiors, a striking feature being the aforementioned commissioned Walter Withers paintings depicting the pioneering settlement and occupation of land by the Manifold family.

Purrumbete has seen a number of owners since the Manifold family divested of it, and a tour of the house in 2008 revealed an intact structure but scant evidence of the original Manifold ephemera collected over time, beyond a single display case of crockery and glassware, perhaps of the type described by Marion Manifold as inspiration for her artworks. Preceding the alterations to the house, the garden had been enlarged in the "Gardenesque" style in the late 1800s and early 1900s, where exotic species were used to structure a more formal garden layout to complement the native flora. Woodland planting to the northeastern edge of the garden captured a wider landscape into the scene. Although the landscape designer William Guilfoyle visited Purrumbete in 1887, "there is no record of him designing a garden plan" (Heritage Victoria 2014).

The bluestone house known as Wiridgil, designed by Alexander Hamilton circa 1885, is still a Manifold property. Although slightly smaller than Purrumbete, the house and land include an elegant carriage stable and other outbuildings that attest to a very prosperous homestead environment. Many remnants and artifacts remain in these buildings, including the carefully set out and poignant pet cemetery adjacent the stables. Architect Guyon Purchas enlarged the original house as the result of the 1907 extensive alterations. This architectural remodeling offers a sense of clarity to the space; from the large entry hall doors lead in all directions to the other wings of the house, and walls are finished with wainscots and picture rails, with the flat-beamed ceiling supported by a shallow timber arch. While the spatial and structural organization is clearly exhibited in the formal areas, the traces of the events that inform and punctuate the narrative history of the home lie in the atmospheric effect of the layers of chattels and artifacts that populate each surface, arranged with evident care. The extensive garden surrounding the home and its curtilage is entered through a gate that punctures the ha-ha wall separating the inner garden from the outer (Figure 22.3). Constructed in Gardenesque style, this outer garden has a wild yet contained exotic beauty, also attributed to influences gained from Guilfoyle through his many visits to the area, although as with Purrumbete, no records of his design exist beyond the telltale design elements and plantings that form the ephemeral lake landscape below the house.

An Ecology of Home: Sounding Country Houses, Domestic Traces

Critical to understanding these homes and their generational development is the expansion of domestic space concepts to embrace home, garden, and the wider landscape, which is so powerfully expressed in the art of von Guerard, Withers, and later Manifold. For the settlers and to the present day, domestic activities contribute as much to the prospering of daily life as do the clearing and working of the land. However, in terms of historical forms of documentation and representation, the celebration of masculinized endeavor in opening up the land and attending to building has been valorized over that of domestic contributions. Not to infer an oppositional gendered approach to developing an expanded mapping of the fabric of rural life, nonetheless these artworks confirm that a rich resource of domestic material is available to enable a complete record of the everyday and temporal existence of the country home and garden.

Figure 22.3

Gini Lee, Looking into the inner garden (2008).

The archive of material traces is not only written, visualized, and recorded but is also present in the aesthetics and events of everyday lives. Markings ever present on the fabric of the building and the garden landscape attest to diverse histories confirmed through tale telling, through stories reread from the material display alongside narratives recorded and spoken by the occupants. This chapter seeks to confirm the nature of the trace, narrative, event, and flow, or rather persistence of material endurance, as important in conveying familial narratives of home life over time. In wondering about what constitutes an event, Yve Lomax proposes *sounding* as a way of engaging events that occur in and around places in relation to material form. She invites us to consider the concept that, say, stone in and of itself constitutes an event, inasmuch as it bears witness to and is often transformed by the events going on around it; "an event is a relational entity; it is a vibration" (Lomax 2005: 84).

Thus soundings measure the depth and duration of an event in time and space to pick up the sounds, whispers, and resonances that reside in the multiple relations and entangled histories and activities of place, in this case applied to concepts of home. Lomax suggests that "for the stone beside me, along with the rosy red apple in the bowl on the kitchen table, as well as the framed photograph on the bedside table, there is no simple location, there is always relata . . . and relata are events" (Lomax 2005: 85). Alongside these materialized events, Lomax suggests we should also include ourselves: in this case, for example, the memory of standing on the veranda, bathed in sunlight and deep in conversation about a moment in time past where a memorable event occurred, the recall spurred by a regard for a treasured object or a climatic event of concern to the safety of the garden. Here self is not an abstract body but rather a perceptive and observational body in time. And time is not a finite entity but rather durational, where "a duration is a passage of events that are . . . passing over each other whilst, as it were, passing, moving on" (Lomax 2005: 87). In the case of the Manifold homesteads, we could say that the house's relations with the goings-on of surrounding homestead events, that is, both things (stone) and bodies (flesh), are in motion, generating a series of relations that result in multiple unique occurrences culminating in the event archive of the country home.

Marion Manifold's artworks act as soundings in the form that Lomax suggests, revealing both the aesthetic qualities of home infused by the politics and domestic concerns of the past. Within the current and past history of the homes in question, a number of overlapping events come together; some are known, whereas others await discovery. In both the Manifold linocuts and the Wiridgil homestead, interior and landscape are brought together not only by the narrative of squatter settlement but also by the inclusion of a gendered and genealogical history composed of various intersections and elements in motion: the dress, teacup, saucer, and so on.

One way to invest these seemingly "haphazard" collections into accounts of domestic events is to evoke American poet and narrator Gustav Sobin's poetic-scholarly writing, which interrogates fragments and traces of a regional past. Sobin's archaeological reading of the landscape furthers material thinking on the nature of seemingly inert material and the event. His archaeological speculations propose that much that is located on the surface (on shelves, walls, gardens, etc.) is fragments that have "suffered displacement (*remaniement*): nothing's where it 'should be'" (Sobin 1999: 104). Inferred in this phrase, and confirmed by Sobin, is the notion that culture, implied by surface finds, can only be examined by "reaching backward, reading downward, searching through the appropriate documentation" (Sobin 1999: 104) in order to understand the mobility of events made present through knowledge of the material traces left behind.

Far from being simple typological objects located in the landscape, the Manifold homesteads and gardens can be framed through "places of identity, of relations and of history" (Augé [1992] 1995: 52–3). Following this conception, and Lomax's notion of "relata," events and activities that occur in the home interior and external landscape are overlaid to become places where "elements are distributed in relationships of coexistence" (de Certeau 1984: 117). Further provocation lies in the ghosting traces that inhabit places where things once were, including the spaces of removal not yet faded, the collections of discarded things awaiting removal, the carcases of senescent trees, and the made-over garden plots now expanded or reduced according to whim or economic constraints. They are the foregrounding elements in the pictorial tableaux that recall material presence imprinted in the domestic fabric and in the oral record.

At Wiridgil a guided tour of the family home and tended garden reveals inner lives mediated through the presence of legacy and ongoing care, where each place is a moment to pause and recall a story, and a collection of experiences and events. Engagement with household articles is through both personal interpretation and related information on what the objects are and how or why they came into the family. Evidently the decorative scheme is not the result of a singular viewpoint, but is the outpouring of accumulated family collection, social activities, and artistic practice, arranged both formally and accidentally. A sounding of this material fabric of home connects the interior fabric to family events in a spatial and temporal sense. To this extent the interior presents a narrative of past and present lives, a living history retold through the descendants.

Figure 22.4

Gini Lee, the Guyon Purchas dining room (2008).

The Guyon Purchas designed dining room (Figure 22.4) is a finely detailed yet extremely formal space with a timber-paneled ceiling supported by double columns at each corner. They frame openings to the inglenook fireplace and bay window with built-in seat, while shallow arches across both openings provide spatial depth. By contrast, the billiard room is a more cluttered working space, offering space for musing about family ephemera. As the evening light gives way, stories of the family ghosts unfold, offering an unnerving narrative. We are reminded of the domestic lives that play out in coexistent space and time. Marion Manifold's poetic, complex, yet confronting linocuts reveal the palimpsest that renders the family tableaux as a sounding space where the objects and their material details hover in the foreground, moving imperceptibly forward and backward in landscape space according to the narrative intent of the author. For a contemporary audience the multiple readings made available through close association with personal histories bring the country home and landscape alive, through juxtaposition of the authentic material collection, the ghosting traces rendered on the building fabric over time, and the re-presentation of the events both real and imagined as captured in the dimension of the artist's work as a necessary extension of the architectural classification of the object fixed in time.

References

"The Artists: Walter Withers," *In the Artist's Footsteps*. Available online: http://www.artistsfootsteps.com /html/Withers_Manifold.htm (accessed January 10, 2017).

Augé, M. ([1992] 1995), *Non-Places: Introduction to an Anthropology of Supermodernity*, trans. John Howe, London: Verso.

Bonwick, J. (1858), *Western Victoria: Its Geography, Geology, and Social Condition: The Narrative of an Educational Tour in 1857*, Geelong: Thomas Brown.

Burns, K. (2013), "Archive Stories/Symptomatic Histories: The Commemoration of Australian Frontier Space at Purrumbete, 1840–1902," *Architectural Theory Review*, 18 (1): 83–104.

Byrne, L., H. Edquist, and L. Vaughan (2010), *Designing Place: An Archaeology of the Western District*, Melbourne: Melbourne Books.

de Certeau, M. (1984), *The Practice of Everyday Life*, Berkeley: University of California Press.

"Early Camperdown History: Recollections of Mr. Walter Lee: Almost a Nonagenarian," (1932), *Camperdown Chronicle*, July 21: 1.

Edquist, H. (2010), "Homesteads of the Western District," in L. Byrne, H. Edquist, and L. Vaughan (eds.), *Designing Place*, Melbourne: Melbourne Books.

Gray, A., ed. (2002), *Australian Art in the National Gallery of Australia*, Canberra: National Gallery of Australia. Purrumbete Amendment." Available online: http://heritagecouncil.vic.gov.au/hearings -appeals/registration-hearings/recent-registration-decisions/ (accessed January 10, 2017).

Heritage Victoria (2014), 'Assessment Of Cultural Heritage Significance To Amend An Existing Registration', heritagecouncil.vic.gov.au/wp-content/uploads/.../H301-Purrumbete-Amendment.doc, p.17.

Lomax, Y. (2005), *Sounding the Event: Escapades in Dialogue and Matters of Art, Nature and Time*, London: I. B. Tauris.

Lucas, C. (1987), *Australian Country Houses: Homesteads, Farmsteads and Rural Retreats*, Sydney: Lansdowne Press.

Manifold, M. (2007), *Colonial Landscapes 2007*. Available online: http://www.marionmanifold. com/?page_id=233 (accessed January 10, 2017).

Manifold, M. (2009), "The Land–The Stony Rises Project, RMIT 2009." Available online: http://www .marionmanifold.com/wp-content/uploads/2014/12/Marion-Manifold_The-Land-The-Stony-Rises -Project-2009-RMIT.pdf (accessed January 10, 2017).

Manifold, W. G. (1984), *The Wished for Land*. Camperdown: Ausbooks.

Mitchell, W. J. T. (1994), *Landscape and Power*, Chicago: University of Chicago Press.

Sobin, G. (1999). *Luminous Debris: Reflecting on Vestige in Provence and Languedoc*, Berkeley: University of California Press.

Chapter 23

Decorating with a View: The Nineteenth-Century Escapist Window

Anca I. Lasc

In May of 1884 Joris-Karl Huysmans published the novel *À Rebours* (*Against the Grain*), a "manual of modern living" for many supporters of the Decadent movement (McGuiness 2003: xiii). The Decadents, a group of artists, writers, and aesthetes, challenged the values of bourgeois domesticity and praised "artifice instead of Nature, contrariness instead of Reason, and degeneracy instead of Progress" (Sowerwine 2009: 92). *À Rebours* tells the story of Jean Des Esseintes, an "anemic" and "frail" thirty-year-old man who spent most of his adult life in search of an ideal décor for his private interior. In his suburban villa near Paris, Des Esseintes engaged with a series of decorating theories that circle around the notion of the "artifice." In order to create his bedroom as a facsimile of a monastery cell, the protagonist proceeded "to reverse the optical illusion of the stage," where "cheap finery" mimicked "rich and costly fabrics" and instead used "magnificent materials" to give the impression of old rags. He hung the walls with saffron silk that imitated the yellow distemper of churches, covered the ceiling with white fabric that created "the appearance of plaster," lined the floor with a red square-patterned carpet reminiscent of a monastery's cold tiles, and used an expensive *prie-dieu* (prayer desk) as a bedside table. Des Esseintes thus "found it easy to imagine that he was living hundreds of miles from Paris, far removed from the world of men, in the depth of some secluded monastery" (Huysmans [1884] 2003: 62–3). The only thing that disturbed this vision was the sight of his female servant walking outside the house to perform her daily chores. To avoid this awakening to reality, he transformed the view beyond his window by arranging that his servant wear a thirteenth-century beguine's attire, with a white cap and a great black hood. Instead of reminding him of the nineteenth-century present, the view of this woman produced for Des Esseintes "an impression of convent life" (Huysmans [1884] 2003: 18–19).

This was not the only time that Huysmans made specific references to a continuation between the interior décor and the exterior world in his novel. When describing Des Esseintes's Paris dwelling, the author recounted a dinner celebration in the guise of a funeral banquet. Everything was modeled on a funeral feast, interior and exterior alike. Dinner was served on a black tablecloth, a hidden orchestra played funeral marches, and the dining room itself was draped in black. For further authenticity, the garden, too, was transformed for the occasion, "the paths being strewn with charcoal, the ornamental pond edged with black basalt and filled with ink, and the shrubberies replanted with cypresses and pines" (Huysmans [1884] 2003: 13). But more interesting than the use of a decorative setting that matched the inside with the outside was the suggestion of a different spatial and temporal dimension that animated the protagonist's daily home life. Des Esseintes's dining room at Fontenay provides another example. Here, the interior décor resembled "a ship's cabin." A small opening, instead of the real world outside, revealed a large aquarium with mechanical fish and artificial seaweed, references to the abundant underwater nature that one might witness from a window submerged under the ocean. To get closer to the experience of dining on a sea vessel, upon refilling the window-aquarium, Des Esseintes would pour in "a few drops of colored essences, thus producing . . . the various tints, green or grey, opaline or silvery, which real rivers take on according to the color of the sky . . . the brilliance of the sun's rays . . . the more or less imminent threat of rain" (Huysmans [1884] 2003: 20). Substituting "the vision of a reality" for reality itself was the very definition of our protagonist's concept of the "artifice." Through the interior décor of his private home and the perfect coordination of the inside and an imaginary outside, Huysmans's character was thus able to experience various temporal realities and multiple spatialities.

This chapter sheds new light on interior decorating practices in the second half of nineteenth-century France. Rather than merely isolating the interior from the outside world and transforming it into a "box in the theater of the world" as critics have argued in the footsteps of Walter Benjamin ([1939] 2002), I argue that decorators strove to unite the inside with an imaginary outside thus complicating the relationship between interiors and exteriors in interesting ways. In order to bend the outdoors to the decorative scheme observed indoors, decorators transformed the outside into a world of "artifice" and fantasy. Interiors offered the upper and middle classes an escape from their daily routine and immediate surroundings by showcasing the view beyond a dwelling's window and framing it as a different space and time from nineteenth-century domesticity. Through the use of window curtains, blinds, and mirrors, decorators achieved a seamless flow between interior and imagined exterior. The exterior thus became a spatial extension of the interior.

Beginning in the second half of the nineteenth century, the views beyond Parisians' windows were affected by Baron Georges-Eugène Haussmann's urban transformations. Up until the 1860s, Paris had largely been a medieval town with a compact center, narrow, dirty streets, and an improper sewage system. Most of the city's populace lived in dark and crowded spaces, while the circulation of people and goods was impeded by the medieval street pattern (Rice 1997). These conditions had allowed for several rebellions to flourish in the first half of the nineteenth century, when the narrow, winding streets facilitated the erection of barricades and impeded easy access of military troops. Attempting to rebuild Paris into the most modern city in the world, Napoléon III and his Préfet de la Seine began to cut through the fabric of the old town, introducing new avenues, parks, and vista points. The grand, flamboyant boulevards came lined with fashionable apartment buildings catering to the middle and the upper-middle classes. The new avenues not only permitted the immediate deployment of military troops to the center of the city, assuaging the fear of revolt and effectively removing the poor from the heart of Paris, but, together with the new parks and gardens, gas-lit sidewalks, clean water, and proper sewage systems, also encouraged the transformation of the city's center into a place of luxury, spectacle, and consumption. The *grand boulevards* of fashionable people, theaters, cafés, restaurants, and new department stores attracted unprecedented attention in the local and international press. When work was finished, everyone wanted to see Paris, learn about Paris, be in Paris, even own a part of Paris. Paris itself became a model for many European capitals at the time (Schorske 1980).

These exceptional developments, however, affected more than the public face of the city. Through large, well-lit windows, the image of Paris reached far into the "cell of privacy" (Clayson 2009) associated with the bourgeois home just as much as the image of private life animated the streets of the city. While poet-*flâneurs* such as Charles Baudelaire sang an ode to interiors seen through closed windows in poems like "Les Fenêtres," artists such as Gustave Caillebotte referenced the *grand boulevards* and their new apartment buildings in paintings featuring Parisians looking outside, including *Young Man at His Window* (1875), *Man on a Balcony, Boulevard Haussmann* (1880), and *Interior, Woman at the Window* (1880).[1] Historian Sharon Marcus has attributed this flow between private and public spaces in the second half of nineteenth-century France to a collapsing of boundaries "between domestic interior and urban exterior" (1999: 152). The private home, Marcus argues, rather than a retreat from the city, became after 1850 a mirror-image of that very city: "Manuals advised women to lure men into the home by making it resemble . . . the very spaces against which they initially defined that home" (1999: 152). If Paris became "interiorized" (Marcus 1999: 139), this was an interiority that referenced the city and its public spaces.

The modern city invaded the private home and the private home mirrored the city. But not everyone liked it. Indeed, the transformation of Paris in the second half of the nineteenth century into the most modern city in the world came with a price. This was the demolition of old houses and the destruction of innumerable old streets, a phenomenon of urban invasiveness that scholars have associated with a negative impact on the psychological well-being of the city's population (Silverman 1989: 17). Coupled with the increasing overstimulation of the senses, the modern metropolis developed by Haussmann led to mental fatigue and physical exhaustion, symptoms that, according to medical practitioners like Jean-Martin Charcot, were main causes of neurasthenia, a disease of the nervous system. The interior became more than a refuge from the external world. As historian Debora Silverman explains, it slowly replaced it (Silverman 1989: 77).

Indeed, the city's interiors, as also presented in books such as Huysmans's *À Rebours*, have been seen as nostalgic alternatives to alienating modernity and a reaction against the commercial spaces promoted by Haussmann. But the more apartment buildings and their interiors seemed to close to external vision, the more they opened up to the world outside and its various landscapes in interior decorating pattern books. Interior decoration designs showcasing the view beyond model windows became a fundamental characteristic of illustrated books in the 1870s and 1880s, when authors often featured imagined rooms with outside views.[2] While no complete "retreat to the interior" (Benjamin [1939] 2002) ever happened, many more interiors similar to Des Esseintes's appeared on paper, where inhabitants of the modern city could leave their present behind as they immersed themselves in a world of fiction and the imaginary. Rather than the modernizing forces at work on the city, their surroundings would reflect their dreams and desires. And their windows could equally challenge the contemporary world, offering representations of alternate realities that extended one's rooms into other times and places.

These developments went hand-in-hand with other escapist tendencies in interior decorating at the time that predated Haussmanization and that had been fueled by an even earlier destruction inflicted upon the urban fabric in the aftermath of the 1789 Revolution (Stammers 2008). Pictures of faraway places that facilitated imaginary travel to a different time and place, often associated with the Orient, had graced, for example, the walls of Romantic artist Camille Rogier's private apartment that he shared with Gérard de Nerval and Arsène Houssaye in the 1830s in the Carousel du Louvre. Rogier's interior was isolated from the modern exterior and "the grimy streets of Paris filled by pragmatic bourgeois" (Knowles 2016: 3). There, through his paintings, the Romantic artist was "free to travel elsewhere in his imagination and his dreams." He "had to go inside in order to go outside," Knowles argues. Collectors, including Alexandre du Sommerard in his private home in the old Hôtel de Cluny, attempted to salvage what was left of the material culture of the *ancien régime*, designing complete interior environments that recreated the impression of life during the Middle Ages (Bann 1984; McClellan 1994; Emery and Morowitz 2003). Du Sommerard and other collectors following in his footsteps mixed old furniture pieces, collectible items, and outright reproductions to create a sense of history as lived reality (Bann 1984). Interior decorating schemes that referenced medieval settings were extended to include themes that referenced Antiquity, the Renaissance, and the eighteenth-century aristocratic past (Silverman 1989; Auslander 1996; Lasc 2013; Martin 2014; McClellan 2014). As history and archeology gained ground and the possibility of travel brought the world closer than ever, exotic decorative schemes also gained support in the second half of the nineteenth century. With Moorish billiard rooms, Egyptian hallways, and Assyrian play-rooms, the escapist approach to interior decorating intensified (Lasc 2013; Hoganson 2002). It thus became commonplace in the second half of the nineteenth century for French private interiors to present alternate realities to the contemporary world.

Yet how could decorators reconcile fantasy spaces evoking distant lands or historic eras with their world outside? They not only refurbished the view beyond a dwelling's window but also framed it as a landscape from a different space and time. The window became more than a threshold that connected the inside to the outside; it was also an extension of the interior space of the room and a gateway into a world made present through imaginative interior décor. Pompeian landscapes, Egyptian scenery, rural settings from the Middle Ages, or aristocratic gardens from the Renaissance thus adorned the topography of late-nineteenth-century French apartments.

Figure 23.1

P. Brunet, "Fantaisie Ecossaise." From *Le Tapissier décorateur de Paris*, plate 38, Paris: Ch. Juliot, 1879. Public domain.

The work of P. Brunet, a "furnishing architect" known for his model interiors, provides an example. Brunet's 1879 pattern book of interior decoration designs, *Le Tapissier décorateur de Paris* (Brunet 1879), stands out through its careful depictions of views beyond model windows. When illustrating a "Scottish Fantasy" drapery scheme with tartan cloth, arrows, a sword and a hunting horn, Brunet included the landscape that he imagined would be seen through a Scottish window, thereby completing the ambience (Figure 23.1). For a more "exotic" arrangement in the Chinese style, the decorator depicted a pagoda beyond the draped window. Placed within a landscaped garden, Brunet's pagoda brought the indoors and the outdoors together under the common theme of exoticism. The nineteenth-century viewer could imagine herself living in a foreign country without ever leaving home. The vicarious pleasure of traveling through one's interior (Rees 1993: 134), fueled by an increasingly more global world due to world's fairs and mechanized travel, demanded a careful coordination between inside décor and outside view.

In other instances, Brunet replaced the theme of living in a foreign or exotic place with that of living in the past, thus offering drapes that would complement the historicizing furniture usually found in nineteenth-century dwellings. A Gothic curtain featuring miniature gargoyles and turrets characteristic of this style was accompanied by a view possibly of Pierrefonds castle. In vogue at the time due to Eugène Emmanuel Viollet-le-Duc's restorations, Pierrefonds was reimagined during the Second Empire as a museum of the Middle

Ages and an imperial residence (Badea-Päun 2009: 80). Its popularity continued during the Third Republic, when it became a popular symbol of the "Dark Ages." Similarly, for a "Louis XIV window," Brunet referenced the seventeenth-century Aubusson Tapestry Manufactory through the use of small tapestry panels attached to the main body of the drapery. He then proceeded to virtually transport his audience to the days of the Sun King through the representation of one of Versailles's landscape gardens, Jules-Hardouin Mansart's 1684 *Bosquet de la Colonnade* (Berger 1991), as the view beyond the window (Figure 23.2). The illusion was supported by architectural details that indicated a balcony or a flight of stairs, both suggesting possible movement between interior and the imagined exterior. Through design, Brunet and other period decorators manipulated time and space. While seemingly letting the outside in, their windows also isolated the inside from the real world by creating imaginary environments of past worlds or distant presents, thus imagining the outdoors as an extension of the indoors.

In the nineteenth century, framing windows with draperies arranged over painted window shades was common practice (Dornsife 1975: 71). While these shades were usually made of linen and were often adorned with painted landscapes, cheaper versions including wallpaper designs pasted onto the linen also existed (Gibbs 1994: 146). A circa 1857 "Dining-Room Window" from Désiré Guilmard's *Garde-meuble* illustrates how shades worked (Guilmard c. 1857) (Figure 23.3). Once pulled down, the blinds not only displayed the decorative pattern in its entirety but also created the illusion of a real landscape beyond the window. Nineteenth-century citizens in search of an escape from their modern surroundings could thus complete their exotic, historic, or entirely imaginary interiors with an equally theatrical window blind that completed the illusion of living in a different time or a different place. *Godey's Lady's Book* mirrored this fashion across the Atlantic, proposing that "a decorated window adds greatly to the beauty of an apartment" and that the issue of the "unsightly inside shutter is a vexed question." As a piece of advice for its readers, the magazine thus recommended that "the amateur artist . . . paint a straggling pattern of vines or flowers across its expanse" or that "India silk . . .

Figure 23.2

P. Brunet, "Croisée Aubusson, Louis XIV." From *Le Tapissier décorateur de Paris*, plate 38, Paris: Ch. Juliot, 1879. Public domain.

LE TAPISSIER DÉCORATEUR DE PARIS PL. 28

CROISÉE AUBUSSON L. XIV

be gathered across it, or small mirrors . . . be inserted in each panel, painted with flowers or a landscape, framed in gilt mouldings" ("The Household" 1895). Diaphanies—colored lithographic prints applied to glass—were also popular, as advertisements in journals like *Leslie's Weekly* made clear. Grimme & Hempel of 310 Broadway, for example, boasted no fewer than six hundred design for such pictures that New Yorkers could use to embellish their door panels, skylights, or regular windows (Grimme & Hempel Advertisement 1893).

Figure 23.3

D. Guilmard, "Croisée de salle à manger." From D. Guilmard, *Le Garde-meuble ancien et moderne: Collection de tentures* 113, no. 329 (c. 1857). Public domain.

In French pattern books, the boundaries between the various media contributing to the interior decoration of a room were so blurred that at times it was difficult to know whether the artist was depicting a painting, a real view outside, a window blind, or a mirror and its reflection. The upholsterer and decorator Jules Verdellet, for example, employed painted blinds as well as mirrored reflections in his work, which further confused and blurred the real and the imaginary. In one 1882 design for an apartment (Figure 23.4), it is difficult to determine whether the landscape behind the mantelpiece is real, painted, or is a mirrored reflection from another window within the room (Verdellet 1882). Given the landscape's position above the fireplace, it is unlikely that it depicts a real exterior, but by placing a half-drawn blind above this image, Verdellet was precisely aiming for this effect.

Figure 23.4

Jules Verdellet, Décoration pour n'importe quelle pièce d'un appartement. From *L'Art Pratique du tapissier* 1, plate 3, Paris, Liège, Berlin: Ch. Claesen, 1882 (reprint of 1871–1874 series). Public domain.

Allowing the viewer's imaginary transposition into a different time or place through the complete coordination of interior and exterior, the view beyond the window became an integral component of interior design in the second half of the nineteenth century, as witnessed by novels and pattern books that emphasized the importance of windows. Isolating the inside from the outside and offering an escape into a different space and time, nineteenth-century interiors and their windows also ensured a flow between the interior and exterior through design, positioning one as an extension of the other. Few Frenchmen could boast large windows, let alone the fabulous landscapes that should have accompanied them, when their view was limited by a set of apartment buildings lined up across the road. The thrill of the famed twentieth-century "picture window," however, was already present in the second half of nineteenth-century France. Preceding modernist architecture was thus more than what scholars have aptly identified as a desire for spaciousness (Isenstadt 2006: 9). It was the dream of experiencing different temporal realities and multiple spatialities that colored the changes and insecurities of nineteenth-century life. Working with space that did not exist, decorators managed to disconnect the inside from the realities of the modern city while successfully avoiding the transformation of this space into a closed-in box isolated from the theater of the world.

Endnotes

1. While part of the Impressionist movement, whose avowed aim was to capture a "snapshot" of daily life, Caillebotte is also well known for having altered his interior views, many of which were posed and made to look differently (Benjamin 2016). More often than not, the artist's private studio morphed into a variety of interiors. The accuracy of the views beyond his painted windows is thus open to debate.

2. To date, I have not been able to identify any view beyond a window illustrated in French pattern books before the 1830s. Claude Aimé Chenavard's *Recueil des dessins de tapis, tapisserie et autres objets d'ameublement* (c. 1830s) includes only one such view.

References

Auslander, L. (1996), *Taste and Power: Furnishing Modern France*, Berkeley: University of California Press.

Badea-Päun, G. (2009), *Le Style Second Empire: Architecture, décors et art de vivre*, Paris: Citadelles et Mazenod.

Bann, S. (1984), *The Clothing of Clio: A Study of the Representation of History in Nineteenth-Century Britain and France*, Cambridge: Cambridge University Press.

Benjamin, E. (2016), "The Modern Interior Stripped Bare: Gustave Caillebotte's *Intérieur Démeublé*," in A. I. Lasc (ed.), *Visualizing the Nineteenth-Century Home: Modern Art and the Decorative Impulse*, London and New York: Routledge.

Benjamin, W. ([1939] 2002), "Paris, Capital of the Nineteenth Century (Exposé of 1939)," in *The Arcades Project*, Cambridge: Harvard University Press.

Berger, R. W. (1991), "Mansart's Colonnade at Versailles: Further Observations," *Journal of the Society of*

Architectural Historians, 50 (2): 189–91.

Brunet, P. (1879), *Le Tapissier décorateur de Paris*, Paris: Librairie artistique, industrielle et littéraire Ch. Juliot.

Chenavard, C. A. (c. 1830s), *Recueil des dessins de tapis, tapisserie et autres objets d'ameublement exécutés dans la manufacture de M.M. Chenavard à Paris*, Paris: E. Leconte.

Clayson, S. H. (2009), "Looking within the Cell of Privacy," in Peter Parshall (ed.), *The Darker Side of Light: Arts of Privacy, 1850–1900*, Washington, DC: National Gallery of Art in association with Lund Humphries.

Dornsife, S. J. (1975), "Design Sources for Nineteenth-Century Window Hangings," *Winterthur Portfolio*, 10: 69–99.

Emery, E., and L. Morowitz (2003), *Consuming the Past: The Medieval Revival in Fin-de-Siècle France*, Aldershot, England: Ashgate.

Gibbs, J. (1994), *Curtains and Draperies: History, Design, Inspiration*, Woodstock, NY: Overlook Press.

Grimme & Hempel Advertisement (1893), *Leslie's Weekly*, December 14: 77.

Guilmard, D. (c. 1857), *Le Garde-meuble ancien et moderne: Collection de tentures* 113, no. 329, Paris: Le Garde-meuble.

Hoganson, K. (2002), "Cosmopolitan Domesticity: Importing the American Dream, 1865–1920," *The American Historical Review*, 107 (1): 55–83.

"The Household: Windows and Cosey Corners" (1895), *Godey's Lady's Book*, December: 786.

Huysmans, J.-K. ([1884] 2003), *Against Nature*, trans. R. Baldick, London: Penguin Books.

Isenstadt, S. (2006), *The Modern American House: Spaciousness and Middle Class Identity*, New York: Cambridge University Press.

Knowles, M. (2016), "The Microcosm as Interior in Théophile Gautier's 'Marilhat,'" in A. I. Lasc (ed.), *Visualizing the Nineteenth-Century Home: Modern Art and the Decorative Impulse*, 3–18, London: Routledge.

Lasc, A. I. (2013), "Interior Decorating in the Age of Historicism: Popular Advice Manuals and the Pattern Books of Édouard Bajot," *Journal of Design History*, 26 (1): 1–24.

Marcus, S. (1999), *Apartment Stories: City and Home in Nineteenth Century Paris and London*, Berkeley: University of California Press.

Martin, M. (2014), "Remembrance of Things Past: Robert de Montesquiou, Emile Gallé and Rococo Revival during the Fin-de-Siècle," in K. Scott and M. Hyde (eds.), *The Rococo Echo: Art, Theory and Historiography from Cochin to Coppola*, Oxford: Voltaire Foundation.

McClellan, A. (1994), *Inventing the Louvre: Art, Politics, and the Origins of the Modern Museum in Eighteenth-Century Paris*, Cambridge: Cambridge University Press.

McClellan, A. (2014), "'Vive l'amateur': The Goncourt House Revisited," in K. Scott and M. Hyde (eds.), *The Rococo Echo: Art, Theory and Historiography from Cochin to Coppola*, 87–107, Oxford: Voltaire Foundation.

McGuiness, P. (2003), "Introduction," in J.-K. Huysmans, *Against Nature*, trans. R. Baldick, London: Penguin Books.

Rees, R. (1993), *Interior Landscapes: Gardens and the Domestic Environment*, Baltimore: Johns Hopkins University Press.

Rice, S. (1997), *Parisian Views*, Cambridge: MIT Press.

Schorske, C. E. (1980), *Fin-de-Siècle Vienna: Politics and Culture*, New York: Vintage.

Silverman, D. (1989), *Art Nouveau in Fin-de-Siècle France: Politics, Psychology, and Style*, Berkeley: University of California Press.

Sowerwine, C. (2009), *France since 1870: Culture, Society and the Making of the Republic*, New York: Palgrave Macmillan.

Stammers, T. (2008), "The Bric-à-Brac of the Old Regime: Collecting and Cultural History in Post-Revolutionary France," *French History*, 22 (3): 295–315.

Verdellet, J. (1882), *L'Art pratique du tapissier*, no. 3 and no. 4, Paris: Charles Claesen.

Chapter 24

Curtaining the Curtain Wall: Traversing the Boundaries of the American Postwar Domestic Environment

Margaret Maile Petty

Punctuated with ever-larger glass windows and walls, the architectural boundaries of the American postwar domestic environment embodied and enabled new concepts of modern living, lessening the visual and physical barriers between inside and outside, and easing movement and lines of sight between spaces and activities. However, such pillars of modern residential architecture contested traditional notions of enclosure, expectations of privacy and hominess, and long-established decorative strategies central to the American domestic environment. Indeed, the large picture windows and window-walls that increasingly characterized American suburban architecture in the postwar era fueled popular and professional debate on the benefits and challenges of an architecturally enabled indoor-outdoor lifestyle. Often these discussions were fraught with the disciplinary tensions that had marked architectural and interior design discourse and practice since at least the turn of the century (Sanders 2002; McNeil 1994; Weinthal 2011; Kleinman, Merwood-Salisbury, and Weinthal 2012). The divergence of disciplinary approaches can be identified in popular and professional trade media from the period. Interior decoration and shelter magazines focused on the integration of the window and the view within the larger decorative scheme of the modern interior, directing their recommendations to professional decorators and suburban homemakers. Architecture journals and trade publications alternatively translated Modernist aesthetics and rhetoric to the suburban context, promoting the lifestyle benefits of modern architecture, emphasizing the potential for bringing the outdoors *inside*, and optimizing the perception of spaciousness through glass apertures (Isenstadt 2006).

This chapter focuses on this narrow domestic boundary, defined by little more than the thickness of a plate glass window, in order to better understand the ways in which it mediated relationships between inside and outside, public and private, and architect and decorator. Looking most closely at a number of key decorative strategies, including the use of curtains, draperies, lighting, and landscaping, this chapter explores the ways in which such traditional domestic and decorative elements served to psychically and visually mitigate the unintended, or at the very least, undesirable effects of modern architecture in a suburban residential context. Comparing the rejection of curtains and other decorative interventions within modern architectural discourse and practice during the postwar period to the ready embrace and situating of such traditional elements of the domestic environment by interior decorators and homemakers, this chapter juxtaposes the recommendations and attitudes advanced by each side of these established disciplinary divides, demonstrating the ways in which both sought to incorporate the glass boundaries of the modern postwar house for the greater benefit of the American family and way of life.

Windows: The Trademark of Modern Architecture

In 1945 architect and designer George Nelson and Managing Editor of *Architectural Forum* Henry Wright coauthored the book *Tomorrow's House: How to Plan Your Postwar Home Now.* This book set out to challenge "all the sweet-scented nostalgia on the domestic scene" and to offer support for "all those who plan to build or buy a postwar home." The list included mortgage bankers, builders, "real estate men," and "every architect" who needed to "stiffen his backbone" when responding to client demands for anything less than modern solutions. Within this practical guide to the "house of tomorrow," the authors promised that readers would not find a "catalogue of 'styles,'" or "orations on good taste," but only "functional" solutions to how a "twentieth-century family lives." They claimed, "There is no other way to get a good house" (Nelson and Wright 1945: foreword).

A "good" modern house, according to Nelson and Wright, was impossible without "big, well designed windows." These glass-walled boundaries, they proposed, brought "together the outdoors and indoors in an integrated visual and functional pattern that makes living in modern houses an exciting new experience." Windows, it would seem, had nearly unlimited potential within the modern residence, as the authors advocated: "In one form or another, they are applicable to every building problem" (Nelson and Wright 1945: 151). However, the authors had little patience for the issues these windows raised for the design and experience of the interior. Nowhere in the book's eighteen chapters is interior design or decoration specifically addressed or advised, while criticism of a variety of traditional decorative strategies appears throughout *Tomorrow's House.* For example, while big windows are presented as a nearly universal solution to architectural challenges, the authors decreed "shades, curtains, and draperies" to be outmoded decorating conventions. According to Nelson and Wright, "modern architecture not only has no sympathy for clutter of this kind—it has no need for it." If modern architecture sought to bring the outdoors and indoors into direct communication as the authors suggested, curtains or other window treatments were the primary threat to this relationship. Well-designed architecture, they suggested, rarely needed such interventions. One of the benefits of unfettered fenestration, Nelson and Wright argued, was the sensation while indoors of being "so much a part of the out-of-doors" (Nelson and Wright 1945: 173).

Despite Nelson and Wright's persuasive text, such visually porous domestic boundaries seemed best suited to carefully directed photo shoots and bespoke Modernists houses set in remote landscapes—like many of those featured in *Tomorrow's House*. In the context of small suburban lots, such virtual indoor experiences of the "out-of-doors" were difficult to come by. However, they argued that with careful planning such views were not impossible. Rather than reducing architectural apertures in close suburban situations, the authors suggested enclosing the boundary of the property, so that one might employ "a continuous glass wall facing a garden enclosed by a high fence." If all else failed, one might make "more than a nominal investment in spiky evergreens" to suggest a private garden beyond which one might imagine expansiveness (Nelson and Wright 1945: 153, 159). In all examples cited by the authors, the architectural composition was preserved along with the transparency of the domestic enclosure.

The Spectator Garden

A decade after *Tomorrow's House*, the well-known, somewhat eccentric, critic Bernard Rudofsky published *Behind the Picture Window*—a scathing account of all he believed wrong with the contemporary American house and lifestyle. Blaming architects, designers, and the general public for uncritically accepting what they were offered by these professionals, Rudofsky suggested that basic human comfort and satisfaction had been sacrificed for the sake of the aesthetic and ideological aims of Modernism. Speaking rhetorically, he argued, "The American's house was never his castle; it does not even afford him privacy. Although one is more or less familiar with his frustrations, nobody ever thought to impute them, at least partly, to his house" (Rudofsky 1955: 68). In particular, he was concerned with the adoption of an architectural model founded on the principle of indoor-outdoor living. He described the living room of the modern American house as "the meanest sort of auditorium, unfit for conviviality" (Rudofsky 1955: 68). Finding fault in the contemporary garden as well, Rudofsky asserted that "no other civilization has produced gardens as melancholy as ours; aesthetics apart, our suburban front lawns and backyards are a gigantic waste of potential outdoor living space" (Rudofsky 1955: 68).

Rudofsky's sardonic analysis of the postwar American domestic environment highlights the often-contradictory attitudes and beliefs regarding the modern house and the postwar American lifestyle. Widespread emphasis on "spaciousness" in popular advice literature addressing the home from the latter nineteenth century onward, combined with growing interest in "indoor-outdoor living" in the twentieth century, contributed to rising demand for transparency in the postwar dwelling (Isenstadt 2006: 239). Numerous articles appearing in architectural journals and shelter magazines in the latter 1940s and early 1950s highlighted the benefits of indoor-outdoor living. In these publications the notion of "good living" was aesthetically and ideologically married to the architectural opening of the inside to the outside. As historian Sandy Isenstadt suggests in his seminal work on spaciousness, "Picture windows became part of the optical infrastructure of a suburban society based on the 'visibility principle'" (2006: 212).

Rather than bringing the outdoors and indoors into better harmony with daily life, the increased size and use of windows in the postwar house, paradoxically, often caused a severing of any real engagement between indoor and outdoor life. When the garden was put on display, framed for the view, this space of potential outdoor living became a spectacle for display rather than ambulatory enjoyment. As Rudofsky had earlier argued, "Like the parlor of our grandmothers, the garden is an object of excessive care. Like the parlor, it is not meant to be lived in" (Rudofsky 1955: 157). Musing over the irony of this situation, Rudofsky wrote, "In an age that puts a premium on usefulness, this is most irregular. The 'picture window,' as the domestic version of the show window is called has contributed to the estrangement between indoors and outdoors; the garden has become the spectator garden" (Rudofsky 1955: 157).

Similarly, Isenstadt has observed that in the modern American house, views were "subsumed within a concept of ornament. Views were not just compared to paintings, photomurals, and scenic wallpaper, they were kin: all were media that organized visible light into a brand of scenery available to enhance a sense of interior space" (Isenstadt 2006: 233). As a spectacle for visual consumption, if not physical interaction, the integration of both the window and the view into the design of the interior was a central concern for decorators and homemakers, as well as the manufacturers who marketed their goods to them. Typical of such commercial advice, the copy of an advertisement for Fortisan curtaining fabrics from 1955 suggested that "new concepts in windows" required "curtaining that looks dramatically lovely from the outside as well as indoors." The more complex design challenge neatly summarized in Fortisan's advertisement was that raised by the increasing domestic apertures introduced by larger expanses of widows. With this architectural opening of the interior to the exterior, suddenly the appearance of the interior was being assessed from the outside as well as the inside. The design of the interior then required consideration of the appearance of the window from the outside looking in, as well as from the indoors looking out. And it was the designer's as well as the homemaker's responsibility to address the dual directionality of the view in the postwar residential context (Figure 24.1).

Flow

NEW 100% FORTISAN* RAYON

FABRICS INSPIRE EXCITING

NEW CONCEPTS IN WINDOWS

Important decorators are building a strong selling Spring around three new curtaining fabrics of Celanese Fortisan.* New drama will focus on windows. New dimensions of beauty and practicality will be demonstrated in window treatments using these latest developments of 100% Fortisan.

Such completely fresh concepts for windows are made practical as well as beautiful by Celanese Fortisan—the super strong rayon yarn that resists sagging, stretching and sunlight deterioration.

Today's increasingly important big windows and window-walls require curtaining that looks dramatically lovely from outside as well as indoors. For achieving such results, the new all-Fortisan fabrics are inspired. Plains and prints are being coordinated in new and extremely interesting effects.

An imaginative national promotion in April will be based on these all-Fortisan fabrics. Don't let your own promotional opportunity fly out the window—plan now. For further details, get in touch with Celanese.

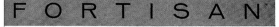

THE SUPER STRONG RAYON YARN

CORPORATION OF AMERICA, NEW YORK 16

JANUARY 1956

37

256

Bringing in the View with Window Dressing

As a counterpoint to the plethora of articles advocating for the larger windows and window walls in residential architecture, by the latter 1940s many shelter magazines, newspapers, and other popular sources of domestic advice regularly described a host of interior design challenges related to the increasing use of glass in the modern house. For example, in "Bringing in the View," *New York Times* columnist Mary Roche consulted with Joseph Mullen, President of the American Institute of Decorators, on matters related to "dealing with various kinds of rooms-with-a-view" (Roche 1947). Using terminology familiar to both the homemaker and the decorator, Mullen shared his "recipes" with readers. When decorating a room with a distant view, Mullen recommended neutral colors throughout the room and soft, neutral draperies hung "well away from the glass area so as not to obstruct the vista." Nearby furnishings, he proposed, should be "covered in one color taken from the distant scene." However, in a room with a near view, Mullen indicated that while the interior color palette should be drawn from the "background of the garden itself," he strongly advised against the use of floral prints that might compete with the living flora beyond. In general, to avoid unforeseen disharmonies between view and interior, Mullen advocated for closer collaboration between interior and landscape designers—however, he never mentioned the architect in this collaborative effort. Curtains, upholstery, carpeting, and other interior fittings, as he described, had to be determined in relation to a view previously established by the (absent) architect. The view determined by the architect, as Roche candidly defined, was "whatever appears at the window."

Dorothy Liebes, a prominent midcentury American weaver and textile designer, similarly endorsed the use of curtains, drapes, and blinds in conjunction with modern architecture's big windows. In an article for the *New York Times* appearing in October of 1948, Liebes offered readers a frank assessment of the rapid transformation of the role of the window in American residential architecture, writing:

> Not so long ago a window was simply a square hole in the wall. It was supposed to serve a number of purposes, but adding grace and beauty to the room was not one of them. Nor was it the focal point, the gathering place for people in the room . . . All this has changed. In the contemporary home, tremendous stress is placed on "fenestration" . . . The window has acquired a new place and purpose in the whole scheme of living. (Liebes 1948)

In response to the newfound and irrefutable presence of windows in the modern home, Liebes outlined the many functions and benefits of curtaining these apertures. Focusing on two principal objectives—to provide comfort first and aesthetics second—Liebes began with the obvious: visual comfort. While curtains were required to control outside light levels, they also had a beneficial impact on perceptions of privacy, a matter more directly impacting psychological comfort. In regards to aesthetics, Liebes raised the issue of the dismal impression of large areas of blacked-out glass at night. The "inky abyss outlined by the window" as Liebes described, did little to "improve the appetite or stimulate the

Figure 24.1a-b

"Fortisan by Celanese," advertisement, *Interiors* (January, 1956).

conversation at dinner." While such considerations were rarely raised in architectural sources, Liebes looked beyond the functional requirements of domestic living spaces to consider the rituals of domestic living, suggesting that in order to avoid such a "depressing sight" curtains be run the full length and height of the wall. Incorporating modern aesthetic objectives as well, she advised that curtains be selected in the same color as the wall and "as nearly as possible in the same texture as the wall, but with lustrous folds, shimmering or not, as taste dictates."

In particular, Liebes identified a real need for the use of curtains as a flexible intervention, addressing the *overuse* of windows in postwar residential architecture. Complaining of architects' "cheerful indifference to the probable use of the room or the placing of furniture," Liebes proposed that curtains be utilized to mask unfortunate windows and to balance off-center fenestration. She also described a host of spatial effects made possible with curtaining—from the impression of added or lowered ceiling height to an increased perception of depth. Aware, on the other hand, that too much curtaining in houses with extensive glazing might prove monotonous, Liebes proposed blinds as an alternative form of curtain that, "with imagination and ingenuity, can be developed as a real structural adjunct to any window" (Figure 24.2). With sensitivity to creating and maintaining atmosphere in the domestic environment, Liebes suggested the possibility of a secondary architecture: an interior surface as fluid as it was solid, offering balance, interest, and enclosure. Only very briefly addressing the view beyond the window, Liebes indicated with economy, "If you have a view, use it. Make it an integral part of the room's ensemble." The view Liebes aimed to help her readers "enhance" was not the view outside so much as visual experience of the spaces within (Liebes 1948).

Figure 24.2

"Aurora Lattiswood," Columbia advertisement, *Interiors* (September, 1955).

Light: An Element of Decor

American lighting designer Richard Kelly was similarly interested in the spatial as well as dramatic potential of window treatments for the modern home when used in combination with a variety of lighting applications as a means of mitigating some of the more challenging implications of glass boundaries in residential architecture. Kelly argued that the increased use of glass in modern architecture had direct implications for interior lighting. Like Liebes, he was concerned about the "unpleasant black mirror" effect of large glass windows at night and suggested that miniature electric lights could be imbedded in draperies to create the impression of many twinkling stars ("Change Proposed in Lighting" 1954). Addressing the distribution of daylight as well, Kelly maintained that the choice of textiles and finishes was an important part of "lighting the modern home" ("Change Proposed in Lighting" 1954). More windows meant fewer available "vertical surfaces to reflect, diffuse, and transmit light," therefore he argued, necessitating new techniques in lighting and greater "dependence on fabrics." Reporting on Kelly's residential lighting strategies in the January 1957 issue of *Vogue* magazine, editor Alison Bisgood described how they provided an "over-all feeling of spaciousness, serenity, well-being" while also conveying a "lightness of curtains and floor" (Bisgood 1957: 137).

Aurora Lattiswood is so modestly priced you can use it "extravagantly."

A WONDERFUL NEW WEAVE IN LATTISWOOD

Aurora by Columbia

Dorothy Liebes designed it . . . took wide and narrow basswood strips (½″ and ¼″) and wove them together in a distinctive new pattern. The result—shades and draperies with unusual freshness and flair. Aurora Lattiswood comes in walnut, natural, cherry, pebble, willow green, lemon peel yellow, gray and white at no extra cost. Special colors to order.

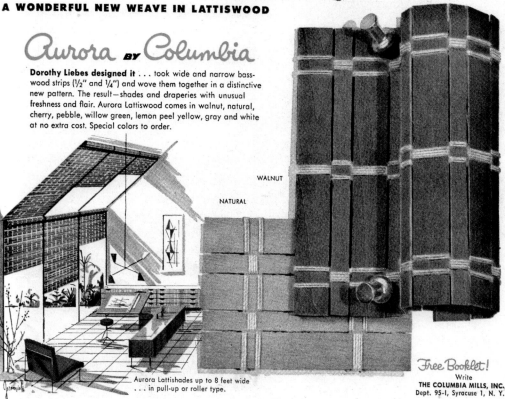

WALNUT

NATURAL

Aurora Lattishades up to 8 feet wide . . . in pull-up or roller type.

Free Booklet!
Write
THE COLUMBIA MILLS, INC.,
Dept. 95-I, Syracuse 1, N. Y.

Collaborating with weaver and textile designer Marie Nichols, Kelly also experimented with textiles woven with metal fibers or wires—something Liebes did as well—in order to create a decorative medium of higher light transmission than glass itself, but without producing glare. Kelly also suggested that "carpets woven to reflect light" would help to further meet modern lighting needs. More than just bringing light deeper and more evenly into the interior, Kelly proposed that such integrated techniques would also have a "psychological effect," creating spaces that would "be reassuring" and more comforting (Bisgood 1957: 138-9). Throughout the article, Bisgood returns to the relationship between the "look" of the domestic interior and how those within it "feel" (Bisgood 1957: 137). Taking somewhat of an unsubstantiated leap, Bisgood suggested that lighting designers, as trained specialists in the composition of light, were "as much authorities on human emotions, reactions, moods, as they are on fluorescent fields . . . as a lighting expert must also, by definition, be a practicing psychologist" (Bisgood 1957: 137).

Conclusion: Conflicting Views into and out of the Postwar American House

The opposing or contradictory forces informing the integration of the view and the lived domestic experience belies any easy reading of the boundaries of the modern American postwar house or lifestyle. Elizabeth Grosz in *Architecture from the Outside* suggests that there is value in approaching such architectural boundaries as "more porous and less fixed and ridged" than has been typically portrayed. She writes, "The boundary between the inside and the outside, just as much as between self and other and subject and object, must not be regarded as a limit to be transgressed, so much as a boundary to be traversed" (Grosz and Eisenman 2001: 65). Grosz proposes that in the movement across such conditions, it is "the process of passage" that "defines and constitutes boundaries" (Grosz and Eisenman 2001: 65).

If we look more closely at the production or negotiation of boundaries within the American postwar domestic environment through such a frame as Grosz proposes, with particular attention given to the cultural and experiential vectors that link inside to outside, indoors to outdoors, we can identity the heavy impact of the vagaries of sight—both real and imagined. In the modern American house, the cultural and lived boundaries between indoors and outdoors were largely dictated by views they enabled, framed, or foiled. As Rudofsky agitated, the increased use of glass walls in the postwar era, rather than bringing the outdoors and indoors into better harmony with daily life, instead questioned culturally conditioned expectations of the engagement between indoor and outdoor life. When the garden was put on display, framed for the view, Rudofsky suggested, the space of outdoor living was little more than a spectacle for conspicuous consumption in the American suburban "visual empire" (Isenstadt 2006: 239).

Returning to *Tomorrow's House*, a more complex and integrated understanding of the dynamic relationship between modern architecture and its large windows, and the notions and needs informing traditional domestic practices and decorative strategies, becomes apparent. While Nelson and Wright were intensely interested in accessing the out-of-doors visually by opening up the domestic enclosure as much as possible, they viewed the use of curtains on a purely "functional basis." However, for contemporary interior designers and decorators, lighting designers, and homemakers, the decorative treatment of windows was an important consideration in controlling glare, creating atmosphere, providing a sense of privacy, and mediating the hard, less-forgiving elements of modern architecture. Seeking new ways to integrate the intimate, personal, and atmospheric requirements of domestic life with the dictates of modern architecture, designers sought inventive uses of curtains, blinds, and other decorative elements—not in opposition to the architectural composition, but complementary to the modern lifestyle and its architecture.

References

Bisgood, A. (1957), "A House Decorated with Light," and "The Light Changes," *Vogue*, 129 (1): 135–7.

"Change Proposed in Lighting" (1954), *New York Times,* October 14: 35.

Grosz, E., and P. Eisenman (2001), *Architecture from the Outside: Essays on Virtual and Real Space.* Cambridge: MIT Press.

Isenstadt, S. (2006), *The Modern American House: Spaciousness and Middle Class Identity,* New York: Cambridge University Press.

Kleinman, K., J. Merwood-Salisbury, and L. Weinthal, eds. (2012), *After Taste: Expanded Practice in Interior Design*. San Francisco: Chronicle Books.

Liebes, D. (1948), "Enhancing the View," *New York Times*, October 3.

McNeil, P. (1994), "Designing Women: Gender, Sexuality, and the Interior Decorator, c. 1890–1940," *Art History*, December: 631–57.

Nelson, G., and H. Wright (1945), *Tomorrow's House*, New York: Simon and Schuster, Inc..

Roche, M. (1947), "Bringing in the View," *New York Times* March 30: SM48.

Rudofsky, B. (1955), *Behind the Picture Window*, New York: Oxford University Press.

Sanders, J. (2002), "Curtain Wars: Architects, Decorators, and the Twentieth-Century Domestic Interior," *Harvard Design Magazine*, Winter/Spring: 14–20.

Weinthal, L. (2011). *Toward a New Interior: An Anthology of Interior Design Theory*, Princeton: Princeton Architectural Press.

Chapter 25

Speeds, Slowness, Temporary Consistencies, and Interior Designing

Suzie Attiwill

Introduction

The orientation of this essay is toward interior design and the practice of interior designing in the production of interior and interiority. Its invitation is to begin with flow, more specifically, begin *in* flow: in a state of constant movement and change as distinct from thinking of flow as a movement between points or things, between insides and outsides. Time as movement and change is foregrounded in the consideration of designing interior, re-posed as a process that involves slowing movement through composing an arrangement that produces a temporary consistency that enables inhabitation, both physically and mentally, as interior and interiority. This essay considers the implications of this repositioning of interior as a temporary consistency to the discipline of interior design and specifically in relation to the topic of "flow." Interior design is re-posed as a practice situated in movement, one that works in the midst of flow where design becomes a practice of arrangement and stabilization.

The conventional idea of interior design as a practice concerned with balance, comfort, and harmony (Kaufmann 1953) continues to resonate; however, the foregrounding of temporality, change, and flow re-functionalizes "interior" from a bounded condition predefined by structure and space to a temporary spatial arrangement of arrested movement that offers balance, comfort, and harmony. "Interior" becomes a relational condition and the practice of interior design a practice situated in relation to an exterior understood as dynamic movement, as flow.

This interest in opening up and posing the question of interior as a contemporary problematic was sparked while reading the writings of the philosopher Gilles Deleuze, where concepts of "interior" and "interiority" are dismissed when conceived of as independent, substantive entities; in particular, Deleuze observes that "we're in the midst of a general breakdown of all sites of confinement—prisons, hospitals, factories, schools, the family. The family is an 'interior' that's breaking down like all other interiors—educational, professional, and so on" (Deleuze 1990: 178). His view challenged me to think about the discipline of interior design and the fact that the

Figure 25.1

Paul Knight, *Sunday 7:27am was in its self as well as me and also the previous Thursday of the pm 11:52*, 2004, 75x65cm, type-c photograph. Courtesy the artist and Neon Parc.

term *interior* is rarely opened to conceptual or theoretical enquiry. Deleuze's writing was an invitation, a provocation, to think differently about the proposition of "interior" and "interiority."

Interior *Designing*

In current practice, "interior" as "enclosed space" inheres in the discipline of interior design as a self-given. This may be as enclosed space conceived of as a void, such as that presented by Shashi Caan, past president of the International Federation of Interior Architects/Designers, in the introduction to her book, *Rethinking Design and Interiors*: "At the core of interiors is an understanding of abstract qualities of shaping this negative space or void" (Caan 2011: 8). Interior design academic John Pile's *The History of Interior Design*, a seminal reference for the discipline, claims that "interiors do not exist in isolation in the way a painting or sculpture does, but within some kind of shell" (Pile 2009: 10), and "interiors are an integral part of the structures that contain them—usually buildings. This means that interior design is inextricably linked to architecture and can only be studied within an architectural context" (Pile 2009: 11). My reason for re-posing interior is not to dismiss or refute these claims so much as open the question of "interior." *Interior design* enables such a questioning. While *interior architecture* and *interior decoration* are other terms that are used interchangeably for *interior design*, the term *interior*, in these conjunctions, is an adjective and hence descriptive of another condition: of architecture and of decoration. While *design* in *interior design* can be read as a noun, *design* is also a verb, and this becomes critical in the re-positioning of interior design as a creative proposition where "interior" is not already defined in advance by a structure and defined as space, but rather one of *designing* interior.

INSIDEOUT

Invited to convene a symposium for the Interior Design/Interior Architecture Educators Association, my colleague Gini Lee and I took this as an opportunity to bring the disciplines of interior design/interior architecture and landscape architecture together in conversation. For my part, I relished the focus on bringing the two disciplines together side by side without including the middle bit, architecture, that usually predefines them as inside and outside. Side by side: in-side-out. Gini and I were interested to see what could be said and be seen in making this conjunction and siding; and I was keen to pose "interior" as a relational condition. *INSIDEOUT* as a siding of the two disciplines enabled thinking of interior and exterior as relations. This could be in a dialectical way as either/or, but it also invited the consideration of other kinds of relations.

During the preparations for the symposium, I encountered a photograph in an exhibition that captured and expressed the ideas I hoped would find articulation in the symposium: *Sunday 7:27am was in its self as well as me and also the previous Thursday of the pm 11:52* (Knight 2004; Figure 25.1). The photograph is taken from the inside of a room, with a window and a landscape. The room is composed of textiles— furnishings, drapes, and carpets—and a glass-top table; the landscape is composed of trees and sky. There is no sense of an intervening structure between inside and outside; to the contrary, there is lack of dimensionality and structure. Outside flows inside, a shift from vertical to horizontal, producing an arrangement of light and color caught and composed in a circle. Movement is held still; the exterior folded in becomes interiorized and produces a condition of interior and interiority.

Philosopher Elizabeth Grosz was invited as a keynote for *INSIDEOUT*. Her writings, including *Architecture from the Outside* (2001) and an earlier lecture she gave (also at the Centre for Contemporary Photography) titled *The Future of Space* (1998)—incited a thinking otherwise in relation to space and time. Asking "how can we understand space differently, in order to organize, inhabit, and structure our living arrangements differently?" (2001: xix), Grosz posed the imperative

> to refuse to conceptualize space as a medium, as a container, a passive receptacle whose form is given by its content, and instead to see it as a moment of becoming, of opening up and proliferation, a passage from one space to another, a space of change, which changes with time. (Grosz 2001: 119)

Her focus on the question of inhabitation and "living arrangements" raised questions for me in relation to the practice of interior design and the fact that then, and still now, interior design is referred to as a spatial design discipline, and the temporal, while acknowledged in terms of the performative and programming, is understood as something that happens in space rather than the other way around—that space happens *in* time. The frame was a key concept that Grosz presented to *INSIDEOUT*:

> The frame is what establishes territory from out of the chaos that is the earth. The frame is thus the first construction, the corners, of the plane of composition . . . the constitution of territory is the fabrication of the space in which sensations may emerge, from which a rhythm, a tone, coloring, weight, texture may be extracted. . . . The frame separates. It cuts into a milieu or space. This cutting links it to the constitution of the plane of composition, to the provisional ordering of chaos through the laying down of a grid or order that entraps chaotic shards, chaoid states, to arrest or slow them into a space and a time, a structure and a form where they can affect bodies. This cutting of the space of the earth through the fabrication of a frame is the very gesture that composes both house and territory, inside and outside, interior and landscape at once, and as the points of maximal variation, the two sides, of the space of the earth. (Grosz 2005: 19)

Grosz elaborated on this concept with reference to Deleuze and Guattari's account of the activity of the *Scenopetes dentirostris*, a bird of the Australian rainforest (Grosz 2005: 27; Deleuze and Guattari [1991] 1994: 184). This bird cuts—separates—leaves from a branch, which fall to the forest floor, where the bird then turns each over "so that the paler internal side contrasts with the earth." After completing the arrangement, the bird returns to an overhead branch and fluffs out its neck feathers, which are pale gold at the roots, to sing "a complex song." This activity made a strong connection for me to interior design as a practice of selection and arrangement: working in an outside, the bird selects, highlights, and rearranges to produce a performance and a territory—a temporary consistency that enables inhabitation: an interior.

Ross Gibson, a writer and researcher who works with film and other media, was invited to present an endnote paper as the closing of the symposium. Gibson addressed framing and insideout/outsidein with reference to the film *The Searchers*. He began by showing the opening sequence: a series of shots of a cabin in the desert, cutting from outside to inside, inside out, outside in, and in between. From outside, looking back to the cabin, the inside was dark and unfathomable, and people emerged and disappeared; from inside, the outside light blasted the threshold, and as it made its way further in, it lightly touched surfaces of textiles and ceramics, making smudges of blue. This resonated with the way the exterior became composed—slowed down—and interiorized as both interior and interiority in *Sunday 7:27am was in its self as well as me and also the previous Thursday of the pm 11:52*. While the film rolled, Gibson directed our attention to the screen as a force field and as energy. Grosz's phrase—"the point of maximal variation" (Grosz 2005: 19)—echoed here. The interior views had an intensity that was suspended; there was a sense of slowing down, an interiorization as a process of domestication, of taming a wild-west exterior to enable inhabitation.

In an issue of the *IDEA Journal* dedicated to a further exploration of the symposium's experiment in bringing interior and landscape together, Gibson contributed a paper titled "Changescapes" that detailed a curatorial system of selection and arrangement as a producing of inside and outside, interior and exterior. For me, this resonated with Grosz's reference to the rainforest bird. Gibson writes of his experience visiting a place in the Pilliga called Muller's Clearing with the intention of meeting Muller. While Muller was nowhere to be seen, Gibson recounts his encounter with the clearing and his search for signs of Muller's presence:

> . . . a clearing bounded on all sides by stacked short bolts of timber that were commercially useless but aesthetically breath-taking, with their knotty convolutions and sappy striations presenting all the colours of blood in sculptural arrays aligned in every which way as if to give shifting volume and spectral tone to the gloaming air. (Gibson 2005: 196)

This was an interiorization in an exterior, a temporary consistency produced through an arrangement as a composing, in both senses of the word. His proposition also engaged with the shift from an emphasis on structure producing interior as enclosed space to one of systems, from space to time: a temporary consistency as a system that finds balance and composition in movement and change in the flow of life.

> A changescaper is more concerned with *systems* than s*tructures*. A structure is founded on permanence and solidity of its constituent parts and joints, whereas a system is a set of contingent relationships evolving, shifting yet persisting through time. A structure is mechanistic, deployed against devolution whereas a system is fluid, in slippery balance with mutability. A system finds this balance when its several simultaneous modes of action, information, remembrance and alteration are moderating each other for the purpose of its survival within the host environment. And a system becomes a changescape when all this complexity is marshalled by human care for aesthetic rather than pragmatic ends. (Gibson 2005: 201)

INSIDEOUT posed the question of interior and inside to exterior and outside as a production of composing forces. At the beginning, I posed interior? in relation to landscape; afterwards, I was left thinking about ?interior, shifting the question mark and hence from a what question to a focus on "interior," where the question mark beforehand produces a pause, a stumbling, and in so doing, opens up interior to the outside. "Interior" becomes a problematic, which requires a re-posing in flow each time anew. Here is the potential of producing "inside and outside at once" and a practice of interiorization as a process of separation that effects a slowing down and enables an arrangement in a generalized exterior.

Inflection

Like the glass tabletop in *Sunday 7:27am was in its self as well as me and also the previous Thursday of the pm 11:52*, an exterior becomes interiorized and movement is arrested and held still, like the leaves turned over by the bird to produce a temporary consistency that effects a cut and creates an arrangement that can be inhabited. A different way of understanding life is presented, not through the lens of bounded form

> but as a complex relation between differential velocities, between deceleration and acceleration of particles . . . So an animal, a thing, is never separable from its relations with the world. The interior is only a selected exterior, and the exterior, a projected interior. (Deleuze [1970] 1992: 626, 628)

Interior design is re-posed as a process of framing situated in the flow of movement where selection and arrangement involve acts of separation as contraction that slow the fugacious exterior down and enable a temporary, provisional consistency—a "fabrication of space," an interiorization in the midst of movement.

This re-posing highlights existing writings on interior design that also approach interior design as a practice defined in relation to exteriors and as a process of interiorization that involves a slowing down to produce a temporary consistency to enable inhabitation. Architectural theorist Hilde Heynen describes the interior as "a static and stable situation" (Heynen 2009: 125). Philosopher Walter Benjamin, often cited for his claim that the collector is the true inhabitant of the interior, wrote of the collector's motivation as a "struggle against dispersion" (Benjamin [1939] 2002: 211);

> to live in these interiors was to have woven a dense fabric about oneself, to have secluded oneself in a spider's web, in whose toils world events hang loosely suspended like so many insect bodies sucked dry. From this cavern one does not like to stir. (Benjamin [1939] 2002: 216)

Interior design is repositioned as a practice situated in flow, an exterior of movement, as a practice of selection, arrangement, and framing that composes, quite literally, through effecting a slowing down that enables an inhabitation. This involves a shift from the current function of arranging materials and objects in relation to a given structure and space to one that addresses relations and forces situated in a fleeting, contingent exterior: interiorizations as arrangements that produce a period of stabilization and balance. Interior design becomes re-posed as a practice working *in* flow—movement and change—to slow down and bring into balance contingent forces to produce temporary consistencies that enable inhabitation and make interiors and interiorities.

References

Benjamin, W. ([1939] 2002), *The Arcades Project,* trans. E. Howard and K. McLaughlin, Cambridge: Harvard University Press.

Caan, S. (2011), *Rethinking Design and Interiors: Human Beings in the Built Environment*, London: Laurence King.

Deleuze, G. (1990), "Postscript on the Societies of Control," trans. M. Joughin, in *Negotiations: 1972–1990*, 177–82, New York: Columbia University Press.

Deleuze, G. ([1970] 1992), "Ethology: Spinoza and Us," trans. R. Hurley, in J. Crary and S. Kwinter (eds.), *Incorporations*, 625–33, New York: Zone Books.

Deleuze, G., and F. Guattari ([1991] 1994), *What Is Philosophy?* trans. G. Burcell and H. Tomlinson, London: Verso.

Gibson, R. (2005), "Changescapes," *IDEA Journal*, 195–206. Available online: http://idea-edu.com/journal_context/2005-idea-journal/ (accessed December 22, 2017).

Grosz, E. (2001), *Architecture from the Outside: Essays on Virtual and Real Space*, Cambridge: MIT Press.

Grosz, E. (2005), "Chaos, Territory, Art: Deleuze and the Framing of the Earth," *IDEA Journal*, 15–28. Available online: http://idea-edu.com/journal_context/2005-idea-journal/ (accessed December 22, 2017)

Heynen, H. (2009), "'Leaving Traces': Anonymity in the Modernist House," in P. Sparke, A. Massey, T. Keeble, and B. Martin (eds.), *Designing the Modern Interior: From the Victorians to Today*, 119–29, Oxford: Berg.

Kaufmann, E., Jr. (1953), *What Is Modern Interior Design?* New York: The Museum of Modern Art.

Knight, P. (2004), *Photographs*, Melbourne: Centre for Contemporary Photography.

Pile, J. (2009), *A History of Interior Design*, 3rd ed., London: Laurence King Publishing.

Chapter 26

Lines to Make Space

Sarah Jamieson and Nadia Wagner

A horizontal line is drawn across a page. This divisive act creates space. Actually, make that two spaces. We call what falls below the line earth and what floats above, sky.

The horizon line indicates the fundamental plane upon which we inhabit the earth. As an indication of the intersection of ground and sky, this single line functions as a universal marker for spatial orientation. The operation of this line suggests that drawing lines is a primordial way to make space.

We initially explored the potential of drawing lines as a spatial design strategy through a series of projects that used thin strips of vinyl, meters of gaffer tape, and a single pencil stroke to separate, divide, and make space. The materiality of the spatial lines drawn in project work may be better described as almost immaterial. These projects informed the development of an animated gif called *Drawing Lines to Make Space*. This visual essay is an adaptation of that animation for print.

A first experiment,
diagramming conceptual
relationships on either
side of a vertical line
(private | public, domestic
| foreign), made visible
their interchangeability;
in language, as concept,
in space, and as diagram
these spatial relationships
are slippery and
negotiable.

down

here

under

domestic

near

mine

earth

up

there

over

foreign

far

yours

sky

there

exterior

foreign

public

outside

yours

here

interior

domestic

private

inside

mine

The horizontal line,
however, possesses a
gravitational force that
holds concepts more
firmly in place. The page's
fold becomes a horizon
line, a set entity made
up of earth and sky
that grounds the binary
opposites.

down

under

near

earth

up

over

far

sky

When language becomes
multidimensional, the
relationships become
more complex. This last
diagram combines the
binary relationships of the
preceding diagrams into a
simple, rhythmic poem. It
plays with the qualities
of slip and pull, which we
discovered in this project.
It highlights how these
binary conditions are
implied and shaped.

　　There is potential here
for spatial designers to
consider the words we use
and to examine how and
where we locate them as
a process of making space.

down

here

under

domestic

near

mine

earth

up

there

over

foreign

far

yours

sky

Index

Index